LESYA UKRAINKA

The Ukrainian national poetess Lesya Ukrainka (1871–1913) has contributed greatly to the development of Ukrainian Modernism and its transition from Ukrainian ethnographic themes to subjects that were universal, historical and psychological. Breaking the thematic conventions of populist literature, she sought difficult and complex motifs and gave them original treatment: themes such as the revolutionary ideological conflicts of the seventeenth and eighteenth centuries, which appear in some of her later poetry, are strengthened, given greater impact by her method of applying the individual and the personal to the more general concepts.

From the beginning of her career her poetry was characterized by the theme of the poet's vocation and by the motifs connected with it—loneliness and alienation from society. Associated motifs deal with her love of freedom (national freedom in particular) and her hatred for anything weak and undecided.

This book, sponsored by the Women's Council of the Ukrainian Canadian Committee, is a discussion of her life and works and includes selected translations: *Robert Bruce* (1903), *Cassandra* (1907), *The Orgy* (1913), *The Stone Host* (1912), and "Contra spem spero." Readers interested in development of poetic style can study the gradual evolution from the lyrical to the precise and analytical manner of the prose-poems of Lesya Ukrainka, and discover the thematic wealth, depth of thought, and emotional power of her poetry.

CONSTANTINE BIDA studied at the Universities of Lviv, Western Ukraine and Vienna before coming to Canada in 1950. He was one of the chief organizers of the Department of Slavic Studies at the University of Ottawa of which he has been head since 1957. In 1965 he was promoted to full professor. Besides his university activities, Professor Bida is the President of the Ukrainian Shakespeare Society, heads the Ukrainian Language Association of Canada and is a member of the Canadian Association of Slavist (president 1960-1961), American Association of Comparative Literature, and the Ukrainian Free Academy of Science-UVAN.

VERA RICH, a translator of Ukrainian works, is the editor of *Manifold*, a quarterly of new verse.

LESYA UKRAINKA

Life and Work

By CONSTANTINE BIDA

University of Ottawa, Canada

Selected Works

Translated by VERA RICH

London, England

Published for the Women's Council of the
Ukrainian Canadian Committee by
University of Toronto Press

Published 1968 by
University of Toronto Press
Reprinted in paperback 2014
ISBN 978-1-4426-5188-3 (paper)

Preface

UKRAINIAN LITERATURE IS, for the most part, not accessible to non-Ukrainian readers since relatively few works have been translated into other languages. Therefore, valuable literary works of Medieval Ukrainian literature, with its numerous genres, remain almost unknown. Unknown to Western readers are the products of Ukraine's national and cultural renaissance in the seventeenth and eighteenth centuries; similarly, the Western reader is familiar with only a few Ukrainian classics of the nineteenth and twentieth centuries. Because of the language barrier, the valuable literary legacy of the Ukraine has found its rightful place in world literature only recently.

Realizing this situation and hoping to improve cultural communication in the Western world, the Women's Council of the Ukrainian Canadian Committee, in this first year of Canada's second century, offers this book as one of its cultural projects to fellow Canadians and to English-language readers in general.

It contains, in English translation, selections of the poems and plays of Lesya Ukrainka; in it as well is information regarding the life and work of this prominent poetess and playwright. Lesya Ukrainka is a great innovator in modern Ukrainian literature and, with rare finesse, combines the most characteristic national Ukrainian features with universal flair in her subject matter, motifs, and optimistic philosophical viewpoint. The young Lesya Ukrainka, her life doomed by an incurable disease, still succeeds, through her fine works, in conveying a healthy hope and inspiration for the emancipation of all oppressed peoples. Her works display an unerring instinct for the future and a prominent independent spirit. For these reasons, Lesya Ukrainka has been chosen as the topic of this publication.

We hope that this book will acquaint the reader with the literary heritage of the great poetess and throw some light on the character of Ukrainian literature.

Ukrainian Canadian Committee
Women's Council

February 1968

Translator's Preface

IT IS THE CUSTOM, in presenting a work of translations to the public, for the translator to acknowledge his or her indebtedness to those many people without whom the said work might never have appeared. In this case, such an acknowledgement is far from being a literary convention, since if, to use an electrical metaphor, the translator is the conductor carrying the current of the literary work from the generator of the original to the glowing lamp it will (it is hoped) kindle in the imagination of its audience, there are, indeed, many who have played the parts of switches, shunts, and condensers, though not (if the pun be permitted) of resistances or impedances.

First and foremost, therefore, may I express my gratitude to the ladies of the Women's Council of the Ukrainian Canadian Committee, who have acted as fairy godmothers to the whole enterprise from a financial point of view;

To Professor W. Shayan, of the Shevchenko Memorial Library in London, who generously made available to me the fruits of some forty years' study of Lesya's works;

To Mr. Volodymyr Bohdaniuk, Editor of *The Ukrainian Review*, for his elucidation of a number of textual obscurities and for numerous and fruitful general discussions, including personal reminiscences of pre-war productions of the plays in L'viv;

To the Spanish Department of King's College, University of London, for their comprehensive assistance in tracing the originals and archetypes of the Don Juan legend, with respect to Lesya's original sources for *The Stone Host* and, in particular, for elucidating, in comparison with *Don Juan de Tenorio* (traditionally staged in Madrid on All Souls' Night), certain theological and psychological complexities in the difficult third act;

To Miss Joan Haldane of University College, Aberystwyth, for some interesting suggestions concerning ancient Greek choric and bacchic dances;

And to the National Library (Inter-Library Loan) Service for tracing a number of rare editions of Lesya's works, so that a comprehensive collation of comparative readings might be made.

My thanks are also due to the illustrious dead—to Lesya Ukrainka herself, for gracing the world with the originals of these works, and to Dorothy L. Sayers, whose ideal of fidelity to form and rhyme, rhythm and alliteration it has been my constant aim to follow. For, if I may interpose a word of comment into this expression of gratitudes, as a poet myself I am only too aware that the form of a poem has a vital part to play in the conveying of the message of that poem: if the meaning is the soul of a poem and the words are its body, then surely the form, in all its ramifications of rhythm, rhyme, and the like, is the skeleton without which the flesh would collapse into an amorphous, amoeboid mass.

Finally, to come to the physical tasks inherent in producing this book, my most personal and grateful thanks are due:

To Elizabeth Anne Harvey and Louise Whitton, who assisted in the typing and checking of what became a very long and unwieldly manuscript, and to Nigel A. L. Brooks who provided a second check on the proofreading;

To the University of Toronto Press for their care in setting and producing the work in book form;

And finally, to those whose professional etiquette demands that they remain anonymous—to Dr. S—— and his colleagues, without whose professional skill and care it is highly likely that this book would have been going to press with another name upon the title page as translator.

To these and to all, my heartfelt and sincerest thanks.

VERA RICH

London, February 24, 1968

Contents

))(⚶)((

Life and Work

By CONSTANTINE BIDA

1. Life

THE TASK of writing an extensive biography of Lesya Ukrainka is made difficult by the fact that her whole life was unusual. Klyment Kvitka, the poetess' husband, describes the circumstances of her life:

Requiring most of her life a much warmer climate than that of Ukraine, Lesya was forced to spend the greater part of her life abroad, at foreign spas, which, however rich in sunshine and warmth, were signally lacking in things artistic and intellectual as well as in interesting people. In fact, Lesya lacked that contact with people which would have provided a background for events and happenings of interest to the general public—the events and happenings which usually fill biographies of famous personalities. Regarding her private life, the publication of any facts which could throw light on her intimate experiences presents problems and requires great tact, especially since in her remarks about biographies of other people, as well as in her published letters, she gave her friends the impression that she was opposed to the publication of facts from private lives and letters of dead people.[1]

Klyment Kvitka was so strongly influenced by this attitude that he refrained from writing those memoirs which could have become the main source for a biography of a great poetess. He imparted to his fellow countrymen only those facts which referred mainly to the genesis or chronology of her works.

The memoirs of her contemporaries throw light only on certain episodes in her life or on some aspects of her intellectual and literary interest. Attempts, such as the work by Dray-Khmara,[2] have been made to collect material about the poetess and put it in order, but, in general, Lesya Ukrainka has not yet received such biographical treatment as has, for example, Charlotte Brontë in English literature.

No extensive biography will be attempted here, but rather an outline of the main phases of her life and some account of her family, the social and cultural environment in which she grew up and developed her talent and point of view, and the external influences which helped to shape her literary attitudes.

[1]Klyment Kvitka, "Na rokovyny smerty Les'i Ukrainky," *Spohady pro Lesyu Ukrainku* (Kyiw: Radyans'kyy Pys'mennyk, 1963), 220.
[2]M. Dray-Khmara, *Lesya Ukrainka* (Derzhavne vydavnytstvo ukrainy, 1926).

LESYA UKRAINKA is the pseudonym used by the poetess whose maiden
name was Laryssa Kosach, and after her marriage, Laryssa Kosach
Kvitka. Lesya's father, Petro Kosach, came from the northern part
of Chernihiv province. After completing his high school studies in
the Chernihiv Gymnasium, where one of his teachers had been the
well-known Ukrainian fabulist, Leonid Hlibiv, Kosach went on to
study mathematics at the University of Petersburg. Two years later, he
moved to Kyiv University and graduated in Law. He then obtained
the position of District Administrative Officer, in Zvyahel, Volhynia,
where in 1868 he married Olha Drahomaniv, the sister of his friend
Mykhaylo Drahomaniv. Laryssa, born on February 13, 1871 (OS),
was their second child; she had an older brother, Mykhaylo, three
younger sisters, Olha, Oksana, and Isydora, and a younger brother,
Mykola.

In Kyiv, Petro Kosach had met and made friends with such distinguished Ukrainian figures as Mykhaylo Drahomaniv, Volodymyr
Antonovych, Kost'Mykhalchuk, Mykola Lysenko, Mykhaylo Staryts'ky,
and others. This *milieu*, which composed the intellectual *élite* of
Ukraine, at that time politically subordinated to the Russian tsarist
regime, made a lasting impression on Lesya's father. The cultural and
social problems of the Ukrainian people became one of his main
concerns. He joined the *Stara Hromada*,[3] the centre of all social and
cultural life of Ukraine, and became a member of the editorial board
of *Kyivs'ka Staryna*.[4] He contributed large sums of money towards
various publications, to funds aiding Ukrainian scholars, and he
financed the publication of both his daughter's and wife's works. Well
educated, highly judicious, and sceptical, "he was a master of irony
and sarcasm, while his phrases, precise characterizations, as well as
separate words, were often repeated in Ukrainian circles."[5] He loved
reading and was versed in world literature as well as Ukrainian
authors. He was also an exceptional *raconteur* and, as he knew countless numbers of people and events, his tales were unusually interesting
and witty.

In her memoirs, Lesya's sister Olha describes the exceptionally
close relationship between Laryssa and her father, noting many characteristics which they had in common:

Of all the six children, Lesya was the most like her father, both phys-

[3]*Stara Hromada* was a secret Ukrainian society which carried on social and cultural
work in the difficult political circumstances existing under the Russian tsarist regime
in the second half of the nineteenth century. From 1876 to the end of the 1890s this
organization was at the head of Ukrainian national movement.
[4]*Kyivs'ka Staryna* was a monthly journal published in Kyiv from 1882 to 1907.
[5]Mykola Zerov, *Do Dzherel* (L'viv: Ukrains'ke vydavnytstvo, 1943), 150.

ically and psychologically. . . . Lesya had inherited her father's features, the colour of his eyes and hair, his medium height, his fragile build. Temperamentally they were both similarly gentle and very kind; but both were capable of great and sudden anger when deeply roused by something particularly annoying. Both were exceptionally controlled, patient, and enduring, with extraordinary will power. Both were highly principled persons: they could be very indulgent to their loved ones or favourite pursuits, but I cannot imagine the person or affair, or anything at all which could force Father or Lesya to do something which they considered not right or dishonourable. . . . Both had a wonderful memory. . . . Both father and Lesya were similarly delicate in their relationships with people, always trying not to be burdensome to anyone, troublesome, or too demanding. When suffering pain, sorrow, or misfortune, they tried not to worry or burden others with their feelings, but instead overcame them within themselves by superhuman effort. . . . Father and Lesya had one more especially precious characteristic in common: they placed a very high value on human dignity in every person, even the smallest child and always behaved in such a way, so as not to offend or disregard this dignity.[6]

In spite of all these physical and spiritual traits which both shared, there was one respect in which they differed. Lesya's father had a gift for mathematics but no gift for languages. Lesya, on the other hand, completely lacked any aptitude for mathematics but had an extraordinary talent for languages. In her sister's opinion, this talent, which was characteristic of the entire Drahomaniv family, was inherited by Lesya from her mother.

Ólha Drahomaniv was one of the most notable women in Ukrainian social and cultural life of the pre-war period. Better known under her pseudonym, Olena Pchilka, she was active both as a leader in public life and as an author who had found a distinguished place among Ukrainian women writers. To her was due the literary atmosphere in which her daughter Lesya was brought up.

She was always assiduously engaged in the matter of bringing up her children. Concerned about their education, she tried to obtain the best textbooks and reading materials for them. For this purpose, she began translating foreign authors into Ukrainian.

By her own work on translations, Olena Pchilka inspired her children to similar attempts. Thus, both Lesya and her older brother, Mykhaylo, very early began translating certain tales by Gogol, which their mother prepared for publication.[7] At the same time she was also

[6]Olha Kosach-Kryvynyuk, "Z Moyikh Spomyniv," *Spohady pro Lesyu Ukrainku* (Kyiv: Radyans'kyy Pys'mennyk, 1963), 52–4.
[7]The book, *Vechornytsi* (Tales by M. Gogol), was translated by Mykhaylo Obachnyy and Lesya Ukrainka. Mychaylo Obachnyy was the literary pseudonym adopted by Lesya's older brother, Mykhaylo Kosach.

bent on directing her children's attention to the riches of Ukrainian folklore. Lesya, the future author of *Lisowa Pisnya* (Song of the Forest), was the most avid listener to the countless Volhynian folksongs which her mother sang to the children. Olena Pchilka encouraged her children to read the works of such Ukrainian authors as Panteleymon Kulish and Marko Vovchok, and Serbian folksongs translated by Mykhaylo Staryts'ky. The ballad "Tvardovs'ky" by Petro Hulak-Artemovs'ky Lesya knew by heart, and like other generations of Ukrainian children, she and Mykhaylo grew up on the works of Taras Schevchenko. Mme Kosach did everything she could to teach her children correct Ukrainian. Often she took them to the country so that they could hear the pure language of the people as well as the many folksongs of the region. Lesya learned the Volhynian dialect in great detail and later used it very successfully in her works.

Lesya's friend, Lyudmyla Staryts'ka-Chernyakhivs'ka, reveals that, as "an intelligent mother of deep convictions, she [Mme Kosach] knew how to influence the intellects of her children; she supervised their education and did not allow it to stray far from its national basis. In those times this was difficult. . . ."[8]

Olena Pchilka herself admitted that she had done her best to educate her children in a Ukrainian spirit. In a letter to a Ukrainian literary historian, O. Ohonovs'ky, she wrote:

I wanted to transfuse my spirit and thoughts into my children—I can say with certainty that I was successful. I don't know if Lesya and Mykhaylo would have become Ukrainian writers if it had not been for me. . . . It was I who directed them and always provided them with an environment where the Ukrainian language was closest to them so that they learned it from childhood. Life with me and among the Volhynian people favoured this.[9]

In 1878 the Kosach family moved from Zvyahel to Luts'k, and then to Kovel'. Petro Kosach bought an estate in the village of Kolodyazhne, near Kovel', where they settled and where Lesya spent the rest of her childhood. The Kosach children found playmates among the peasant children and grew up in the clean, healthy atmosphere of Ukrainian life, in direct contact with Ukrainian folk culture.

In Kolodyazhne, Lesya's mother began writing the poems that were later published in Kyiv in 1886 in the collection *Dumky-*

[8]Lyudmyla Staryts'ka-Chernyakhivs'ka, "Khvylyny Zhyttya Les'i Ukrainky," *Literaturno-Naukovyy Vistnyk*, X (1913), 14.
[9]O. Ohonovs'ky, *Istoriya Literatury Rus'koyi*, III, 1127.

Merezhanky (Embroidered Songs). She increased her over-all literary activity at this time and began publishing poems in *Zorya* (Star) and other Ukrainian literary magazines.

When the time came in 1882 to give the children a more systematic education, Olha Kosach took them for the winter to Kyiv. There Lesya and Mykhaylo began taking music lessons and a regular secondary school course under private tutors. And there Lesya started Latin and Greek studies. In 1884, when Mykhaylo went to study permanently in the Kholm Gymnasium, Lesya and her mother returned to Kolodyazhne where they remained almost continuously until their final move to Kyiv in the 1890s.

Her long residence in Kolodyazhne brought Lesya even closer to her native soil. These years, passed in such close association with the people, gave her a deep, organic understanding of the language and life of the people and filled her poetry with the native mythology which she so successfully brought to life in *Lisowa Pisnya*.

Lesya was never registered at a secondary school; she was ill with tuberculosis of the bones and was forced to spend whole months in bed. Her younger sister writes about the beginning of the illness which would plague Lesya all her life:

On January 6, 1881 while still at Luts'k, Lesya went to the river to take part in the religious ceremony of the blessing of the water and got her feet very cold. Soon after this she fell ill; the pain in her right foot was so great that it made her cry. The doctors diagnosed a severe case of rheumatism. She was treated with baths and ointments, and after some time the pain disappeared and the foot did not hurt for a few years. But this was the beginning of Lesya's "thirty years' war" against tuberculosis as she herself jokingly called it. For in fact this was not a severe case of rheumatism but the beginning of tuberculosis of the leg-bone which seemed cured for a time only to recur.

In the meantime, while her foot was well, tuberculosis attacked the bones in the palm of her left hand. This was cured by an operation in the fall of 1883.[10]

But soon the pain returned to her foot, and an operation was performed in 1889. The disease soon attacked her lungs and could only be arrested by prolonged sojourns at Italian spas and in the Carpathian mountains. But her struggle against illness was resumed when tuberculosis attacked her kidneys.

Staryts'ka-Chernyakhivs'ka recalls Lesya in these early years:

[10]Olha Kosach-Kryvynyuk, "Z Dytyachykh Rokiv Les'i Ukrainky," *Spohady pro Lesyu Ukrainku*, 71–2.

"When I remember my childhood years I always see a spring day and lots of gold and glitter—everything around sparkles and laughs—and amid this laughter and sparkle, I see the figure of a pale girl with deep intelligent eyes and a gentle smile on her lips. . . . Even then Lesya had a delicate look, was quiet and shy. . . ."[11]

While other children were playing together Lesya for the most part lived alone. This solitary existence developed in her profound insight and a lively imagination. She loved to look at pictures in large books and to reconstruct in her imagination the whole story of which the particular picture was but an illustration. Like most other children, she was fascinated by romantic, chivalrous heroes. It was not, however, the proud and fortunate conquerer who defeated his enemy and thrust a spear in his heart that Lesya favoured. Instead, she was captivated by the vanquished knight who, even as he felt the sharp spear of the victor in his heart, refused to give in but proudly cried: "Kill me; I will not surrender!"[12] In the poem "Mriyi" this attitude is clearly evident and was to be developed later in her dramatic works.

In another of her early poems, an elegy entitled "Do Moho Fortepyano" (To my Piano), she paints a scene from her childhood: In the midst of the singing and laughter of carefree company someone plays a gay dance on her piano, while she, still a little girl, fights to control the tears brought to her eyes by the ominous feeling that her future life is to be a thorny path of continual physical suffering. In a later verse, the poetess who loves music so despairingly remembers the prophetic scene as she bids farewell to her piano—the friend and confidant of her troubles and the witness of all her thoughts—happy as well as sad, because the operation on her left hand made it impossible for her to play ever again.[13]

The condition of her health and her seclusion from the outside world during her prolonged confinement not only greatly extended the world of her imagination, but also gave rise to much reflection on the ideals of truth, heroism, and beauty. When these absolutes came up against reality, a deep and insoluble conflict was created, which became a dominant element in all her dramatic works.

Her childhood and early youth, however, were not devoid of many happy moments. From an early age, Lesya and her brother Mykhaylo were closely linked by their deep affection for each other, and until

[11]Staryts'ka-Chernyakhivs'ka, 14.
[12]*Tvory Lesi Ukrainky* (New York: Tyshchenko-Bilous), II, 15.
[13]In her letter to Drahomaniv (December 6, 1890) she wrote: "It seems to me that I would be a much better musician than a poet."

she was thirteen Lesya was almost never parted from him. They
played, read, and studied together. They staged dramatic scenes from
Greek mythology in which Mykhaylo always assumed the role of the
hero, while Lesya was the virtuous maiden or wife. In their repertoire
they also included scenes of fantastic voyages to unknown lands and
primitive peoples. In these plays, Mykhaylo was usually a typical
Robinson Crusoe and Lesya his faithful follower and friend. Often
Lesya was so fascinated with playing the role of heroine that she was
capable of completely forgetting reality.[14]

Even though the games they played were of such serious and pre-
cocious content, and even though she read a great deal (Lesya read
well by the age of four), she was, nevertheless, very gay and loved to
dance and sing. But, as in all other things, she danced mainly with
Mykhaylo. She never played with dolls as did her younger sisters
because she was always with him, who, as Lesya's younger sister
writes, was very despicable and tortured his younger sisters' dolls.
Then to soothe her sisters Lesya would fashion "nymphs" of grass,
dressing the younger girls in robes of leaves and flower petals. She
also skilfully embroidered shirts, stiched pretty dresses, made wreaths
of tiny flowers, and strung beads of various seeds for the wounded
dolls.[15]

In later years the close relationship between Lesya and her brother
was never strained. When Mykhaylo entered the University of Kyiv
they corresponded very often and in their letters exchanged thoughts
and ideas about their personal lives and their literary endeavours. She
wrote some of these letters in poetry conveying tones of sincerity and
intimacy: we find her grieving one day that her Muse is "dumb as a
doornail," her imagination like herself incapacitated, or she tells her
brother that she intends to translate Musset, or again she confesses
how difficult it is to write when suffering from pain.

Lesya began writing poetry very early. Her first poem "Nadiya"
(Hope) was written towards the end of 1879 or at the beginning
of 1880. The arrest of her aunt, Olena Kosach, who had won the
affection of both Lesya and Mykhaylo during her stay with them in
Zvyahel in 1879, provided the occasion.[16] The wave of arrests of
political leaders in 1879 took along with it Olena Kosach who was at
the time living in Petersburg; she was deported to Siberia in 1881 for
a five-year sentence. This shocking event deeply affected nine-year-old

[14]Staryts'ka-Chernyakhivs'ka, 15.
[15]Olha Kosach-Kryvynyuk, 65.
[16]*Ibid.*, 71.

Lesya. The short poem in which she expresses her sorrow may be child-like in its simplicity, but it is genuine in its expression of longing and pain.

This poem was her literary *début*. Others were to follow soon, and some were to be included in her first collection, *Na Krylakh Pisen'* (On Wings of Song), which was published in 1892 in Lviv. These poems are full of obvious childish impressionism, simple verse construction, and unsophisticated rhyme. Lesya's mother carefully supervised her daughter's first attempts; she corrected her rhythms, rhymes, and language and sent her poems to literary journals under the pseudonym "Lesya Ukrainka," which her daughter continued to use. Poems such as "Konvaliya" (Lily of the Valley) and "Sapho" (Sappho) appeared in *Zorya* in 1884.

From her early youth, Lesya paid attention to foreign authors also. She read Heine, Musset, Hugo, Byron, and later Shakespeare, Maeterlinck, Hauptmann, Mickiewicz, and Ibsen. To the latter she gave more and more attention. Her studies of Latin and Greek, begun in 1882, made it possible for her to know at first hand Ovid, the great tragedians, and Homer. While still in Kolodyazhne, she translated into Ukrainian three songs from the *Odyssey* and was trying her hand at translating Ovid.

From Heine, the German lyricist, she learned new poetic forms, and his influence on her is evident in her prosody and versification, but most of all in the typically Heine-esque tone of light irony introduced into some of her poems. Together with M. Slavyns'ky she worked for several years on a translation of Heine's works. These were published in a separate volume in 1892. Later, in 1903, the two translators published a second volume of translations from Heine. In her introduction to the first volume, Olena Pchilka emphasized the value of translating foreign literary works into Ukrainian as a means of developing a suitable lexicon and style for the Ukrainian language. This was a task which her daughter so brilliantly realized in her works.

The environment in which the young poetess grew up was one in which ideas of cultural development and the idea of the freedom of the individual and of a nation were prevalent, and one which was favourable to spiritual and intellectual development.

THE INFLUENCES of her own family on the development of the young Lesya's talent and *Weltanschauung* were supplemented by two Kyiv families, Starysts'ky and Lysenko, even before the Kosachs moved there permanently in the 1890s. Like the Kosachs both families were active in the literary, artistic, and social fields Lyudmyla Staryts'ka-Chernyakhivs'ka writes that, "In . . . our families, there reigned a special literary spirit; therefore anyone who had even a spark of talent found it impossible not to write. Here everyone wrote, analysed works, read them, published collections, and generally lived in the midst of social and literary interests. Both Olha Petrivna [Lesya's mother] and my father encouraged anyone who showed the least desire to write—fanned the smallest spark of talent."[17] Mykhaylo Staryts'ky was a noted dramatist, an excellent director and a poet. His poems are infused with that romantic, social lyricism which is so strongly marked in Lesya's early poems. He, as well as his entire family, regarded Lesya with sincere affection.

It was in this atmosphere that Lesya's first collection of poetry *Na Krylakh Pisen'*, and her translations of Heine, *Knyha Pisen'* (Book of Songs), made their appearance in Kyiv. Lyudmyla recollects the moment when Lesya appeared with the two small volumes at the Staryts'ky home:

I remember, as if now, that day when Lesya, at that time a very young girl, slender and tall, in Ukrainian attire, came to see us with these two books. This was a general celebration. My father put on his pince-nez, picked up the paper knife, gently patted the greyish-blue volume as if it were a child, and began to cut the pages carefully. This was not the feeling with which we now pick up a new Ukrainian book—this was a feeling of special joy: this book which had travelled from abroad in such great danger—either in an envelope or deep in someone's pocket—lay now in front of us—new and fresh, like a message about the possible fate of the Ukrainian language, about some far away future life. All of us, together with the young author, sat around—my father recited beautifully and so everyone loved to listen when he read aloud. He read all of Lesya's poems —some of them several times. Father was very excited. . . . But the matter did not end in praise alone. Immediately there followed criticism also—but this was friendly criticism, the kind that sees the weaknesses of a work and seeing them, does not try to decry or deride the writer, but draws his attention to them; so that he himself may see and understand them. This type of criticism was always present in our circle: old and young authors alike read their works to their friends and welcomed advice.[18]

Lesya's books had indeed been smuggled into Kyiv. The growth of the Ukrainian national movement had resulted in the Ukase of Ems of 1876 which made it illegal to print anything in the Ukrainian

[17]Staryts'ka-Chernyakhivs'ka, 15.
[18]*Ibid.*, 16.

language except historical documents.[19] Cultural and political life was regimented by the tsarist government which forbade the importation of Ukrainian publications. Ukrainian theatrical and musical performances were also banned. On the surface it appeared that police tyranny had almost suppressed Ukrainian culture but, in fact, it was not dormant. Poets, writers, and intellectuals strove spontaneously towards the works which they loved and almost deified. Groups were formed and their members, unified by common ideals and interests, continued their activities.

One of the most active groups centred around Mykola Lysenko, a noted composer, and his family. Although none of its members wrote they were still keenly alive to even the weakest pulse of Ukrainian life. They valued every young intellect. Every Saturday older writers and beginners alike met at the Lysenko home. The leaders of this group were also the leaders of contemporary cultural life. Among them were Olena Pchilka and Mykhaylo Staryts'ky. The older generation was represented by Oleksander Konys'ky, Kost' Mykhalchuk, and the younger generation, in addition to Lesya and Mykhaylo, by M. Slavyns'ky, V. Samiylenko, M. Hrushevs'ky, E. Tymchenko, I. Steshenko, O. Chernyakhivs'ky, O. Lotots'ky, and many others.

The group's aim was primarily literary; their job, as they saw it, was to enrich Ukrainian literature with translations of foreign (mainly Western European) authors: Lesya Ukrainka was translating Heine, Slavyns'ky worked on the poetry of Heine and Goethe, Steshenko on the works of Beranger and Schiller's *Maid of Orleans*, Chernyakhivs'ky on Schiller's *The Robbers* and Heine's works, and Tymchenko on the Finnish folk epic *Kalevala*.

At their meetings they read not only translations, but also their own works.

This was a meeting of friends, who loved not only . . . those or other personal interests, but cared for writing and the spirit of Ukrainian life. One and all felt a great solidarity of interests and social responsibility. They read their works, discussed both content and form, and when the matter was closed, they dreamed about a Ukrainian press, a Ukrainian language, schools, Ukrainian life. They drew up programmes for new literary ventures. But the dreams always seemed so elusive. . . . Yet, one wanted to realize them, if only in the smallest detail.[20]

---

[19]On June 18, 1876, in Ems, Germany (where he was taking a cure), tsar Alexander II signed a ukase by which he forbade the printing in Ukrainian language of anything except historical documents.

[20]Staryts'ka-Chernyakhivs'ka, 17.

Such meetings took place by turns in the Kosach home and in the Staryts'ky home; but in the Lysenko home they took on a particularly warm, intimate, and artistic character. Here the cult of literature was united with the cult of music. Everyone loved music, especially young Lesya who felt and understood it.

The exceptional fascination which music held for her was obvious from childhood. Lesya had to spend months at a time in bed with both her arms and one foot in casts. Yevhen Krotevych describes how once Lesya's aunt, Oleksandra Kosach, noticed that the little girl, while lying in bed, was beating out time with her one free foot. In answer to her aunt's question about what she was doing, Lesya softly answered, "I am playing the piano."[21] Her soul was full of sounds, and often she thought in musical terms. This is most obvious in her poetry—for example, "The clouds glided and glided across the moon, one after another *pizzicato*," and "In the orchard there was such a singing silence, as if she played the gentlest *adagio, pianissimo*." In one of her letters from Italy, she wrote, "Yesterday there was a truly Wagnerian storm, the thunder rose in a crescendo, and sometimes I had the strange impression that the sky was falling somewhere aside into nothingness." The forms and tone of her poetry are also musical. "Our famous poetess was very close in this to the great bard, Taras Shevchenko, who in his journal called Beethoven and Mozart the representatives of sensitive harmony, and described one enchanting sunset as a "magnificent mysterious oratorio without sound."[22]

It was because of her appreciation of music that she respected, and almost worshipped, the famous composer in whose home she spent so many memorable hours. Her spiritual union with Lysenko and Staryts'ky was strengthened by feelings of mutual respect and friendship, cultivated and constantly refreshed by common creative interests.

After their deaths, the poetess wrote a letter to Staryts'ka-Chernyakhivs'ka in which a clear light is thrown on her relationship with both men: "With Mykola Vitaliyevych [Lysenko]—are connected my most precious memories of youth; I lived through so many memorable events in his home. Staryts'ky, Lysenko—for others, these names belong merely to literature and art, but for me they will ever recall live portraits, as names of close and beloved people, who actually never die, as long as our consciousness lives."[23]

[21]Yevhen Krotevych, "Lesya Ukrainka za Zhyttya," *Spohady pro Lesyu Ukrainku,* 271.
[22]*Ibid.,* 272.
[23]Dray-Khmara, 23.

Lesya's friendship with the Lysenko and Staryts'ky families became even closer after she moved permanently to Kyiv in 1894. Soon after this, her father got a new job in the capital and both parents came to live in Kyiv. The planning and realization of many literary and artistic projects were taken up with renewed enthusiasm. This had an obvious influence on the poetess' world of idea, stimulating her to even greater literary activity. The contemporary cultural and political problems, which were discussed in the salons of all the leading families of the capital, helped her to form opinions on important matters concerning the life of her nation. These same problems were echoed strongly in her works.

IN ADDITION to all the other influences which had so strongly marked the development of her talent and the formation of her mind, there was another person who played a major role in Lesya's life. While still a child, and then again in the last months before his death, Lesya met her uncle, Mykhaylo Drahomaniv. Although he lived almost continuously abroad, he nevertheless had a great influence on the development of Lesya's individuality. They exchanged letters regularly, and when Lesya learned that he was about to die, she went to live with him for the last months of his life.

When Lesya was five years old, Drahomaniv was forced to leave the country for good. Accused of lack of loyalty to the tsarist regime, he lost his professorship at Kyiv University. As a result of this, a Ukrainian underground organization, *Hromada* (Community), sent him abroad to defend the Ukrainian cause. In 1876, Mykhaylo Drahomaniv went to Vienna and from there moved to Geneva, where he carried on his scholarly research and published a magazine, *Hromada*. In 1889, the Bulgarian Government invited Drahomaniv to take the Chair of History at the University of Sofia, and until his death, he lectured there on pre-Hellenic civilization. Throughout this period, and even earlier, he devoted a great deal of time to research in Ukrainian and other Slavic literature and folklore.

The correspondence between Lesya and her uncle throws a great deal of light on the influence that Drahomaniv had on the young poetess.[24] A keen intellect, freshness of thought, search for truth and justice, and lack of compromise in defending higher principles were all characteristic traits of the Drahomaniv family. Lesya's mother and her brother were typical exponents of these qualities. Although Lesya

[24]Petro Odarchenko, "Lesya Ukrainka i M.P. Drahomaniv," *Tvory Les'i Ukrainky*, III.

did not see her uncle for eighteen years, the spiritual contact between them, which was fostered by their correspondence, never weakened. From the beginning of 1888 their letters were very much to the point. She consulted her uncle on many of her literary undertakings. He supervised her reading, recommended the appropriate scientific or literary works of Western European writers, and sent her many of his own works. He tried to develop in his niece the ability to think independently and clearly; he sought to widen her literary horizons and to develop a fresh attitude towards social and political problems. Matters of Ukrainian literature and culture, as well as those of the political and social order, were very tightly interwoven in his scholarly and publishing activities. In his mind, all these matters had a common source; they all mirrored the Ukrainian mentality, which he wanted to see healthy and strong, capable of waging successful battle against historic and political cataclysms. Typical Drahomaniv freshness, health, and fighting spirit come through in Lesya's attitude to national problems.

Between 1890 and 1891, Lesya compiled a handbook for her younger sister, entitled *Starodavnya istoriya skhidnykh narodiv* (Ancient History of Eastern Peoples), later published by her sister in Katerynoslav in 1918. At the outset of this undertaking, Lesya turned to Drahomaniv for advice on sources which she had to consult for this course in history. Drahomaniv took this request very seriously and sent her German and French works, along with his own methodological suggestions regarding the compilation of the handbook.

In one of her letters of 1890, she asked her uncle to advise her about adapting folklore material to music. Drahomaniv recommended appropriate English and French works on the subject and especially the magazine *Meluzine*. In a letter of 1891, Lesya writes about her research: "Generally, I have luck with ethnography . . . in four months I have collected 150 ritualistic songs. . . . Now having worked hard in writing down the music, this activity does not seem so difficult to me. There is only one problem and that is that I cannot write down the music directly from hearing it sung without the help of an instrument. But collections of songs without music, I no longer acknowledge. . . ."[25] She sent her uncle several of the recorded songs along with her comments. She was fascinated, in the first place, by the straightforwardness, sincerity, and highly developed poetry of lyrical songs. She wrote to Drahomaniv: "It always seems to me that if it is ever possible to see the nature of the people, then it is more

[25]*Ibid.*

so in lyrical songs and in 'kolomyyka' [a lively dance song] . . . than in ballads and historical songs."[26] When Drahomaniv asked Lesya to send him the necessary materials for his research on folk demonology, Lesya very willingly collected the various folk beliefs.

At a later date, taking advantage of Lesya's knowledge of Ukrainian folklore, her husband, Klyment Kvitka, recorded from her singing many Ukrainian folksongs, which he later published in two separate volumes.[27]

In his letters, Drahomaniv encouraged Lesya to use themes from other literature in her works. It was he who inspired her to study English, which she learned to speak fluently, along with German, French, and Italian. Knowing Greek and Latin, as well as Polish, Russian, and Bulgarian, the poetess could read and appreciate almost the entire wealth of European literature and acquire the wide knowledge of European science and culture that awed her contempories. Her mental horizon was greatly broadened, and she was capable of reaching a degree of vision in which was near-at-hand and familiar could never obscure her view of that which lay beyond—a vision in which one could see problems of nationality with the same clarity as those of humanity in general. There can be no doubt that the saturation of all her lyrical and dramatic works with non-Ukrainian subjects is the result of the wide Western European education that she acquired in her youth under the direction of her uncle.

Occasionally Drahomaniv asked Lesya to paraphrase into verse form various excerpts from the Bible, which he later used in his research. She did this willingly and sent him versified translations from the books of Isaiah and Ezekiel and suggested translations for him of excerpts from Jeremiah as well. Asking his niece for this favour Drahomaniv had no intention of exploiting her as his helper; he wanted to turn her attention to reading the most valuable books and to interest her in the eternal and profound sources of all poetry. Already, under the influence of her mother, Lesya had used biblical themes in her early poems and was fascinated by the Bible as a source of great ideas and great poetry. She prepared herself carefully for her biblical subjects and in this area Drahomaniv also recommended appropriate references. He advised her to read Verne's *Précis d'histoire juive*. The magnificence of the biblical images appealed to her throughout her entire career and were an important source of her

---

[26]*Ibid.*

[27]Narodni Melodiyi, Z Holosu Lesi Ukrainky zapysav i uporyadkuvav Klyment Kvitka, I, II (Kyiv, 1917).

poetic inspiration. The misfortunes of the Israelites reminded her constantly of the fate of her own politically subjugated nation, and this led her to search for biblical themes in which to express her profound national sentiments.

In June 1894, Lesya went to visit her uncle in Sofia. In his vast library, under his direction, she avidly read and studied many historical sources and learned the Bulgarian language. Here she witnessed his death in June 1894. Lesya remained in Bulgaria with her uncle's family until the end of July and then returned to Ukraine, taking with her a handful of soil from Drahomaniv's grave.

HER VISIT to Bulgaria, the long discussions with Drahomaniv, and the intense course of study in his library brought about the final crystallization of her attitude towards political and cultural matters. It was there that the twenty-four-year-old poetess ultimately developed her uncompromising nature and strengthened her resolve to proclaim to her people the idea of struggle which from then on saturated her works. After the death of Drahomaniv she began to turn from personal lyricism and poetry on social themes, which as yet lacked clear ideological aims, towards verse ringing with manly, fighting tones. Almost invariably, her theme is the heroic deed; she sings of the "brave descendents of Prometheus." Herself so frail of body, she sounds the battle cry for the rights and freedom of her people. It was at this time that she wrote the cycle of poems known as *Nevilnychi poeziyi* (Poems of Slaves), which is imbued with strong and courageous tones.

Svitozor Drahomaniv remarks on his father's teaching:

The strength and depth of her uncle's ideological influence I have personally heard on many occasions from Lesya. She emphasized the methods of this influence. Uncle, in Lesya's own words, skilfully and somehow unnoticeably planted the seeds of creative truth in her soul, the beginnings of thought, and then allowed them freedom to develop under the influence of Lesya's own creative energy. . . . This lack of any kind of forcible pressure from her uncle, was probably the strongest and most characteristic sign of his influence.[28]

Yet Lesya Ukrainka was not completely captive to the brilliant individuality of her uncle. She accepted all his positive ideas but developed them in a peculiarly personal manner. Herself a thinker of great creative power, she developed her themes in her own original

[28]Svitozor Drahomaniv, "Vplyv Mykhayla Drahomanova na Lesyu Ukrainku," *Nashe Zhyttya*, no. 13 (1946), 5.

way: "Beholden to her uncle for many attitudes, many intellectual interests, always maintaining in herself the cult of his ideas, she nevertheless achieved an intellectual independence and herself came to all the necessary conclusions based on his knowledge."[29] She did adopt Drahomaniv's motto, which underlined the kinship between Ukrainian aims and those of other European nations: "There are no other aims than those of all Europe; there are no other means."

After spending a year with Drahomaniv's family in Sofia, Lesya rejoined the activities of the literary and cultural life of Kyiv, which centred mainly round the Literary-Artistic Society. Here she maintained a close link with the younger generation; she read papers at the Society's meetings and completely immersed herself in intensive literary work. Gradually she was becoming well known. In 1898, during the centennial celebration of modern Ukrainian literature, when Mykhaylo Staryts'ky recited her poems the public greeted them with loud applause. And when Staryts'ky brought the young poetess on to the stage the ovation seemed to be unending.

RENEWED BOUTS of illness often interrupted Lesya's work. She had to spend weeks and sometimes months at a time in forced idleness. Despite the constant hope that she might be cured, the illness progressed. The pain was so severe that at times she lost consciousness; injections proved unsuccessful. No matter how much she loved Kolodyazhne in Volhynia, her visits there were for short periods only at widely spaced intervals. The dampness of the Volhynian forests was bad for her health. Consequently, she spent most of her time in Kyiv. In summers she stayed at her mother's summer home, Zelenyy Hay (Green Glade), near Hadyach. For some time between 1897 and 1898 she lived in Chukurlar, near Yalta, and then in Yalta itself. Then in the winter of 1899 she lay ill in Dr. Bergman's clinic in Berlin where she underwent an operation which improved her health somewhat. On her return from Berlin, Lesya immersed herself again in literary activity, writing a whole series of critical essays. She had begun these essays in 1895, and in the years that followed she added many new works.

Between 1897 and 1903 she wrote a number of articles and essays on socio-cultural and literary subjects. In an article entitled "Kupala na Volyni" (The Festival of Kupalo in Volhynia), she gave a vivid description of an ancient Ukrainian ritualistic festival. In another essay, she analysed "Utopiya v literaturi" (Utopia in Literature), and

[29]Zerov, 29.

in "Dva napryamky v novitniy literaturi" (Two Tendencies in Modern Literature) she discussed the works of Gabriel D'Annunzio and Ada Negri, two of whose poems she had translated. In a paper entitled "Ukrains'ki pys'mennyky na Bukovyni" (Ukrainian Writers of Bukovina), she considered the works of three noted Ukrainian writers: Yuriy Fed'kovych, Olha Kobvlyans'ka, and Vasyl Stefanyk. The emancipation of women is the subject of her article "Novi perspectyvy i stari t'in'i" (New Perspectives and Old Shadows). In "Uvahy pro novu pol's'ku literaturu" (Observations on the New Polish Literature) she gave original analyses of such Polish writers as Orzeszko, Sienkiewicz, Prus, Zeromski, Sieroszewski, and others. In a study, "Evropeys'ka sotsiyalna drama kintsya XIX stol'ittya" (European Social Drama at the End of the Nineteenth Century), she dealt with the more important characteristics of German, French, and Scandinavian dramatic literature, with special attention to the works of Hauptmann. In each essay her approach to the question is highly original and based on aesthetic as well as on ideological principles.

LESYA's improved health lasted only a short time. By 1900 it had deteriorated to such a degree that the poetess could spend only very short periods of time in Kyiv; the rest of her life she had to spend in warmer and drier climates, mostly in clinics and at foreign spas. The summer of 1901 she passed in Bukovyna, and for two winters, those of 1901–2 and 1902–3, she was in San Remo in Italy. These prolonged sojourns in foreign countries gave rise to reflections on her native land, which are mirrored in her poems and dramas. A close friend of hers writes: "She often said that she no longer had the strength to live this life of a hot-house plant, torn away from her native soil, and yet she had to live, and living so far from her native country, in her thoughts she remained in it."[30] And yet disease never weakened her spirit but strengthened her will to battle against death. During her struggle for life, her talent crystallized and grew, her literary output was doubled, her mastery over language became progressively more powerful, and the beauty of form became more distinct. A second collection of her poems, *Dumy i Mriyi* (Thoughts and Dreams) appeared in 1899 in Lviv. The third collection, *Vidhuky* (Echoes), published in 1902 in Chernivts'i, represents the best of her lyrical form.

At this time another characteristic began to develop in her works. More and more often she began to adopt the dramatic genre. "While,

[30]Staryts'ka-Cheryakhivs'ka, 26.

earlier, the drama was no more than implicit in the conventional forms of her early lyrics, now it took a chief role in her works and became the main-spring of her creative process."[31]

Her first drama, *Blakytna Troyanda* (The Azure Rose) appeared in 1896. Between 1896 and 1904 she wrote three dramatic poems: *Oderzhyma* (Obsessed) in 1901, *Vavylons'kyy Polon* (The Babylonian Captivity) in 1903, and *Na Ruyinach* (In the Ruins) and two dramatic sketches *Praschannya* (Farewell) and *Iphigenia v Tavrydi* (Iphigenia in Taurus). She also began working on two other poems: *Cassandra* and *U Puschi* (In the Wilderness).

She continued to live the life of a "hot-house plant." After the winters spent in San Remo, she spent the winters of 1903–4 and 1904–5 in the Caucasus in Tiflis, visiting her mother's estate only during the summers. The winters of 1905–6 and 1906–7 she spent in Kyiv, devoting a great deal of her time and enthusiasm to work in the cutural-educational society, *Prosvita* (Enlightenment), where she collected books and reorganized the library. The spring of 1907 was spent in Crimea. On her return to Kyiv that summer, she married the ethnographer and musicologist, Klyment Kvitka, and went to spend the winter of 1907–8 in Yalta.

Lesya Ukrainka wrote many of her dramatic works during these years of continual travel to various spas. After concluding *Na Ruyinach* in Tiflis, she began work on *Osinnya Kazka* (Autumn Tale), a drama based on a fairytale motif. During a visit to her mother's estate, she wrote the dramatic dialogue, *Try Khvylyny* (Three Moments). In the fall of the next year she finished her dramatic poem, *V Katacombakh* (In the Catacombs), and the dramatic dialogue, *V domu roboty, v krayini nevoli* (In the House of Work, in the Land of Slavery). In 1907, Lesya finished *Cassandra*, one of her best dramatic poems. The spring of 1907 saw the completion of *Aysha and Mohammed*. Then followed her drama *Rufin i Pristsilla*, completed in 1909, and such dramatic poems as *Na poli krovy* (On the Field of Blood, 1909), *Johanna, Zhinka Khusova* (Johanna, the Wife of Khus, 1909), *U Puschi* (In the Wilderness, completed 1909) and *Boyarynya* (The Boyar's Wife, 1910).

Revolutionary feeling began to spread throughout Russia in the first years of the twentieth century, reaching a climax in the 1905 Revolution. During these memorable times, the long-nourished hopes of the Ukrainians for political independence from the Russian regime

[31]Dray-Khmara, 39.

seemed closer to realization. The powerful wave of ideological and national feelings of the uprising engulfed the poetess during this period. National problems of the Ukrainian people, their political independence, cultural autonomy, and the improvement of the lot of all impoverished classes of Ukrainians captivated Lesya's intellect and her heart and found a powerful echo in all her works—especially in the dramas.

BUT WHILE national events captured her attention and directed her thought to things of a higher order, her frail body dictated her way of life. Her health worsened to such a degree that by the spring of 1908 she went to Berlin again, hoping to undergo another operation. But the doctors refused to operate. The only thing they could do to help her condition was to prescribe the warm climate of Egypt. They did not expect her to live longer than two more years. Lesya then returned from Berlin to the Crimea, living first in Evpatoria and later in Yalta. In the winter she moved to the Caucasus, settling in Telavi. In the fall of 1909 she went to Egypt with her husband to escape the harsh winter of her native land. While there Lesya visited the famous Egyptian museum at Cairo, drove out to Giza to see the pyramids and the Sphinx, and studied Egypt's history. By May 1910, when the poetess found it necessary to return to the Caucasus, the general state of her health had improved, if only slightly.

Her new trip to the Caucasus brought the poetess no rest. After settling in Telavi for the summer, Lesya found it necessary to journey in the autumn to Kutaisi, where her husband had been transferred. The journey over bumpy mountainous roads, the adjustment to a new life, and the absence of experienced doctors in these out-of-the-way places did little for her except bring about further deterioration in her state of health.

In January 1911, in an attempt to have her exhausted body strengthened by the southern climate, she left again for Egypt. It was indeed a painful journey for the already feeble woman. She had to travel in a small Italian steamer wholly unsuited to passenger transport and weather a great snowstorm. Upon her arrival in Egypt Lesya was at a very low ebb.

Her two last journeys to Egypt, which she accomplished alone, testify to her spiritual strength and unfailing courage. These virtues she demonstrated at a time when strength was forsaking her pain-wracked body. One of Lesya's friends, in her recollections writes:

"The journeys to Egypt were a miracle of Lesya's spiritual strength. Ill, feverish, weakened, prepared for death at any moment, she set out alone for the long journey, across a stormy sea. On her departure she had calm words of reassurance for everybody."[32]

After a short stay in Egypt, Lesya decided to return, stopping at Kyiv in order to see her family and friends. At Kutaisi, gazing at the deep azure mountains and the superb landscape which rose from the drab little Caucasian town, she was always transported in thought to her native Volhynia and Polissya, there to relive happy moments of her youth. At this time, when her life's pathway was nearing an end, scenes of the Ukrainian landscape rose before her in all their beauty and vitality and inspired thoughts on the essence of human life, on immortality, and the eternal human spirit. It was this that inspired her fairytale *Lisowa Pisnya*, which she wrote in the summer of 1911 and which remains her best work, her greatest legacy to Ukrainian literature.

Having spent the summer of 1911 in Kutaisi, in the autumn Lesya and Kvitka departed for Khoni, where she wrote her celebrated dramatic poem *Advokat Martiyan* (The Lawyer Martian). Her stay in Khoni was brief, for she soon returned to Kutaisi, where she lived for almost the entire year of 1912.

The autumn of 1911 yielded dry warm weather in the Georgian mountains, and the poetess decided against journeying to Egypt for the winter. By December, though, she was so weakened by her illness that she was confined to bed until May 1912. Although these were months of unbearable suffering, they also witnessed the birth of the idea for her drama, *Kaminnyy Hospodar* (The Stone Host). When Lesya arose from her bed she wrote six acts of *Kaminnyy Hospodar* in which she elaborated upon the subject of Don Juan.

The more severe Lesya Ukrainka's lot became and the greater her malady weakened her body, the more she drew upon her spiritual and creative strength. The result was that during the years of her most grievous physical pain, she wrote such masterpieces as *Lisowa Pisnya* and *Advokat Martian*. Her final great dramatic poem, *Orgiya* (Orgy), written shortly before her death in 1913, overflows with strength and faith in the high ideals of national life.

Some of her works were written in a mood of extraordinary creative exaltation. While writing, she was at times stirred to the point of

[32]Staryts'ka-Chernyakhivs'ka, 27.

passion, and consequently some of those creations were written spontaneously and completed in a few days. It exhausted Lesya's strength to such an extent that in a letter to her mother, she wrote:

After the completion of Lisova Pisnya I was so afraid of a recurrence of my last winter's illness. (Other works were painful but less costly) but none was in vain. Now let no one say, that I "neither having burned with desire, nor having suffered" procured for myself "laurels," because in a literal sense I burn and suffer pain each time. And yet, when I intentionally force myself to a certain peaceful type of work, some kind of invincible, despotic illusion "assails" me, torments me during the nights and simply, drinks my blood, by God!"[33]

In spite of the speed with which Lesya could write, her creative process was not always so spontaneous. Although the idea for literary work frequently came to her instinctively, the conception and the meditation were developed over a period of years. Dray-Khmara writes:

. . . what unexpectedly burst forth in Lesya in the course of several days or hours, had been germinating for years. Thus for instance, the character of Mavka, who appears as the central figure in Lisova Pisnya, was conceived by Lesya in her childhood. She "kept in her mind" the image of Mavka all her life, until before her death when she was homesick for the Volhynian forests.[34]

Other literary works were written more slowly. Having begun to write the drama U Puschi in 1898, she returned to it many years later and finished it in 1909.

In the latter years of her life, her inspiration and creative genius helped her to endure all her sufferings courageously:

I am able to struggle only (or more quickly to forget about this struggle) with my enfeeblement by a high fever and other symptoms which overpower the intellect, when simply a certain idée fixe or a certain invincible power stimulates me. During the night, the throng of images does not let me sleep but torments me like a new illness. Then a demon appears, crueller than all my maladies, and commands me to write. . . .[35]

WITH THE ARRIVAL of the cold autumn of 1912, Lesya's journey to her winter retreat in Egypt was once again undertaken. Upon the

[33]Dray-Khmara, 54.
[34]Ibid., 55.
[35]Ibid., 56.

entreaties of her husband and her family she prepared for her voyage to the south. Although the outbreak of war between Turkey and the Balkan Entente made sailing through the Black Sea and the Dardanelles dangerous, Lesya prepared to travel by sea and not by land. Leaving Kutaisi, she sailed for Odessa where she was met by her sisters Olha and Isydora, and friends. The poetess arrived safely in ancient Alexandria in the middle of November after a most dangerous and stormy crossing during which the steamer could have struck a mine at any moment. From Alexandria she journeyed to Helwan. After the dense fogs and cold weather experienced during her voyage, she was able to enjoy sunny, tranquil weather and breathe mild, dry air. However, by this time Mediterranean warmth could scarcely have helped her sick body. In a letter to a friend, she wrote: "I was so thoroughly exhausted by my illness and my tedious journey that only now am I recovering my senses. The condition of my kidneys has improved somewhat, but the general state of my health grows no better. . . . I have even grown thinner in spite of all the treatment."[36]

In May 1913 Lesya left Egypt for the last time. By then her health had deteriorated so severely that the doctor who treated her in Egypt told her jestingly 'Madame, vous devenez tout ésprit." A close associate, meeting Lesya, wrote of this occasion: "The last time in May, when I saw Lesya, I could not help recalling the doctor's words. Her appearance astounded me. She was completely pellucid; only her large eyes gazed so assiduously and in the depth of their dark pupils, one could see something deeper and wiser, gazing beyond life."[37] The poetess returned home in a critical condition. Neither medical treatment, nor the life-giving sun of the south could preserve her departing life.

Arriving at Odessa at the beginning of May, she rested at the home of her close friends for several days. She then travelled to Kyiv to visit her family and consult the doctors. Ill, and for the most part confined to bed, Lesya still took a most active interest in literary affairs and spoke about her projects. Her one remaining ambition was to write a story about the lot of an Arab woman. She set about accomplishing this task shortly before her death.

Taking advantage of Lesya's visit to Kyiv, her friends organized a ceremonial gathering in her honour. As Dray-Khmara mentions in her recollections "there was something inexpressibly sad [in the ceremony] that stirred and pulled the heart apart. Lesya's pale and transluscent

[36]Ibid.
[37]Ibid.

figure with arms full of flowers, with words full of energy, love and faith and with death in her eyes."[88]

On the day of her departure from Kyiv for the Caucasus, she left her home unnoticed and drove to Volodymyrs'ka Hirka (Volodymyr Hillock), from which she gazed attentively at the wide, overflowing Dnipro River and at Kyiv's extensive panorama. For the last time she bade farewell to the Dnipro, to Kyiv, and to her people's historical monuments.

At the beginning of June 1913, upon her return to Kutaisi to join her husband, Lesya's final agony began. Her diseased kidneys began to cause her unbearable pain and her fever failed to abate. It was in these circumstances that she tried to write her pensive story of Arabic life, *Ekbal'-hanem*. Moreover, lying in bed grievously ill, she dictated to her husband texts of folksongs she remembered from her childhood days in her native Volhynia.

Learning of the hopeless state of Lesya's health, her mother, Olena Pchilka, with her youngest daughter, Isydora, arrived in Kutaisi in the middle of July. Although the illness had so changed the poetess that it was indeed difficult for Olena Pchilka to recognize her, Lesya yet retained her old spirit and was completely lucid. She began to dictate to her mother the plan for a dramatic poem, dealing with life in ancient Egypt.

On the advice of her doctors, Lesya was sent to Surami. Surami, lying between Kutaisi and Tbilisi, was at a higher altitude and thus during the summer it was drier and cooler. The change helped the poetess very slightly. Perhaps because of the foreboding of her impending death, Lesya requested that a letter be written to her beloved sister, Olha who lived in Ukraine, asking her to come. The sisters, however, were not destined to meet again. At daybreak on the first of August 1913 (OS), just as Olha arrived in the outskirts of Surami, Lesya Ukrainka died in the arms of her mother and husband. A large funeral was held on August 8, 1913, in Kyiv and she was buried in the Baykove cemetery, in a tomb beside those of her father and brother whom she had dearly loved.

A friend, very deeply moved, wrote on the occasion of her death: "Life continues to sparkle as if it does not comprehend what is lost. I live, gaze all around and stand on guard over the precious graves. As the fog rises over the autumnal forest, so from the depths of my soul there arises indignation at this loss."[89]

[88]*Ibid.*, 57.
[89]*Ibid.*, 58.

2. Poetry

LESYA UKRAINKA's first literary efforts were lyrical poems. Although it was in the dramatic genre that her talent was to achieve its finest and most profound expression, her lyrics represent not only a valuable contribution, but also a bold and important step forward in the evolution of Ukrainian poetry. She entered the literary arena in the 1880s, a time when Ukrainian poetry was still bound by tradition. Writing had stagnated, awaiting new indigenous trends which would enable it to flourish.

The impact of Shevchenko's genius had profoundly stirred the weary soul of his countrymen. His role was thus historical and unique, as Olexander Bilets'kyy wrote in his *Twenty Years of New Ukrainian Lyric Poetry*:

For long afterwards, the emotions and ideas of the reading public were nourished by his works, for their whole outlook was shaped by them. The voice of the great Kobzar (Bard) has not died yet, even in our own day it can still be heard, angry and anguished, calling us to battle against injustice. But, nevertheless, it is already a distant sound which reminds us of the past that must not be forgotten while the future is being built.[40]

Shevchenko was far ahead of his time: his poetry possessed a characteristic national spirit which fertilized the hearts and minds of future generations. But almost simultaneously with the powerful influence exerted by Shevchenko on Ukrainian writers and poets, there appeared an unoriginal and imitative trend. Works were produced by poets and writers of the post-Shevchenko literary school, some of them undoubtedly original and outstanding talents, but who were unable to achieve Shevchenko's original mode of expression. A discussion of the development of Ukrainian poetry in the last half of the nineteenth century is, therefore, in order.

PANAS MYRNYY (1849–1920), for example, the author of the Ukrainian social and psychological novel, began with weak copies of Shevchenko's poetry. In Myrnyy's verses, written in the sixties, Shevchenko's themes; subjects, style, and basic tone constantly recur, but the over-all quality is much below the level of Shevchenko's

---

40O. Bilets'kyy, "Dvadts'at' rokiv ukrains'koyi l'iryky," *Pershyy Zbirnyk "Pluha"* (1924)

poetry. Myrnyy was later to find an original mode of expression in prose.

The late-Romantic poet Yakiv Shchoholiv (1824–98), who was only ten years Shevchenko's junior and who made his debut in the forties, became silent for almost two decades, re-entering the literary field only after Shevchenko's death. The peak of his creative output was not reached until the eighties and nineties, when he was an old man, with the publication of two collections of his poems: *Vorsklo* in 1883 and *Slobozhanshchyna* in 1898. Shchoholiv was undoubtedly an original talent; his great merit lies in the fact that he gave beautiful examples of Ukrainian poetical language, delved deeply into the treasures of Ukrainian popular song tradition, and enriched the lexical sources of the contemporary literary language with living national vernacular elements. His poetic language is endowed with such rhythmical qualities that much of it has been set to music. In Shchoholiv we already find new traits: a lighter humorous trend, a noticeable irony, and jocular notes.

Shchoholiv was nurtured by the Romantic tradition and served as a link between two literary epochs—Shevchenko's and Lesya Ukrainka's. The peak of his literary fame coincided with the period when Lesya began to write her first poems; he died as the young poetess was concluding the first stage in her literary development and was making her transition to the dramatic genre. While contributing to the enrichment of the Ukrainian poetic language, he still adhered to the traditional stylization of folksongs. His poetry is permeated with the social motifs of the old literary school. This is because his aesthetic views had been formed as far back as the early 1840s, the period in which the young Shevchenko had gained his poetic fame. They had, moreover, been formed under the influence of the ideological and literary principles of his teachers at the University of Kharkiw, Sreznevs'ky and Kostomariv, who were both Romanticists. Shchoholiv's poetry also bears the imprint of his contemporaries, the early Romanticists such as Metlyns'ky and Korsun. His historical poems, included in the collection *Vorsklo*, display the same concern with his people's past that is so pronounced in Shevchenko.

A similar part was played by another Romantic poet and associate of Shevchenko's, Panteleymon Kulish (1819–97). He began writing in the 1840s but could not muster enough courage to publish his poems during the lifetime of his great contemporary. However, after Shevchenko's death in 1861, Kulish, who was endowed with a most remarkable and versatile talent, became the leader in Ukrainian literary circles. As a writer, critic, novelist, publisher, translator of foreign classics, an outstanding ethnographer, and a student of folklore, Kulish was relentless in his search for new ways and new values. In 1862 he published a collection of poems, *Dosvidky* (Dawns), in 1882 the collection *Khutorna Poeziya* (Village Poetry), and in 1893 another entitled *Dzvin* (The Bell). Kulish was essentially a poet of the old literary tradition. His Romantic philosophy of history and the nation was coloured by certain social and patriotic overtones. Kulish's poetry did not achieve prominence, having been overshadowed by his other talents. He carried the tradition of the old school into the age of Lesya Ukrainka, contributing only such original formal features as stanzaic verse composition and his specific metre.

Mykhaylo Staryts'ky (1840–1904) was a brilliant theatrical producer and talented playwright, in whose home Lesya Ukrainka found a warm and artistic atmosphere. His poetry was representative of the social lyric, which was to gain prominence, slightly tempered by a specific contemplative mood. His poetry of the seventies, eighties, and nineties possesses a typically social-patriotic character.

Finally, during the 1880s Olena Pchilka appeared with her poetry, which was also of a social and contemplative character. She was extraordinarily active in the social and cultural field and was the author of a number of ethnographic works, a translator, a publisher of almanacs, and an editor of the periodical *Ridnyy Kray* (Native Land). She did not bring into Ukrainian poetry anything remarkable enough to lift it to greater heights and give it a new shape; all this fate held in store for her daughter.

Among Lesya Ukrainka's contemporaries, Ivan Franko, the representative of Western Ukraine, was one poet who ranks among the greatest figures in Ukrainian literature. In the 1880s Franko, author of "Kamenyari" (Stone-Hewers), had not yet reached his maturity as a poet. This period in his literary career is characterized by social lyrics such as are found in his collection *Z Vershyn i Nyzyn* (From the Summits and the Foothills). Only in the nineties and in the following decade did Franko achieve the height of his literary creation. In his deeply lyrical and philosophical poetry and in his poems, "Ivan Vyshens'ky" (1900) and particularly in "Moysey" (Moses, 1905), the real gems of Ukrainian literature are found.

Franko was a man of exquisite literary taste and had an intimate knowledge of world literature. He was always ready to assist the younger generation with his advice and was deeply interested in Lesya Ukrainka's literary output. He described the early poetical experiments of the young poetess as "distant echoes of Shevchenko's ballads without the sound basis of real life experience and without social contrasts."[41] In Lesya's early verses he also noticed her lyrical and dramatic talent, which he believed would assure her a prominent place in modern Ukrainian literature.

She in turn respected Franko and his advice, always addressing him in her letters as *cher Maître*, although he was only her senior by fifteen years. Before sending the manuscript of the first volume of her poetry to the editor, she asked him to read and comment on it, and in 1891 she dedicated to him the cycle of her lyrical verses, *Sl'ozy—Perly* (Tears—Pearls). In the years to come she was to follow Franko's footsteps by exercising constant concern for poetical form and by using a variety of highly artistic stanzas.

LESYA UKRAINKA'S three collections of poems—*Na krylakh pisen'* (1892), *Dumy i Mriyi* (1899), and *Vidhuky* (1902)—to a great extent, reflect consecutive stages of her poetic development.

Her first collection contains some of her poems which are still, as far as subject and style is concerned, largely based on her childhood impressions and on the literary works of other Ukrainian and foreign authors. A certain timidity of expression and a limited range of subject are apparent in them, and, true to the tradition of the Romantic school, the tone of her early poetry is rather melancholy and pessimistic.

When the young poetess made her literary *début*, she was still visibly influenced by the patterns of preceding decades. Mykola Zerov rightly notes that, "having arrived on the scene of her first works in the early spring of youth, she did, for a time, keep to the conventions and restraints of the post-Shevchenko literary school, in the old Romantic pattern."[42]

Her first poem was prompted by the arrest and exile to Siberia of her father's sister, Kosacheva. It reveals "childish impressions clad in primitive verse," as do most of her other poems written before 1887. They represent, therefore, the literary creation of a teenage girl. Nevertheless, Franko, a poet whose own talent had been developing stage by stage, recognized that hers was "one of those talents which takes shape gradually and achieves mastery over form, the contents, and over the language and ideas, through a great deal of painstaking work."[43]

---

[41]*Literaturno-Naukovyy Vistnyk*, VII (1998), 6–28.
[42]Zerov, 160.   [43]*Ibid.*

This early poetry is marked by restraint of expression, modesty of style, and a limited choice of subjects—the legacy of Romanticism. "Rusalka" (Water-nymph), first published in the women's journal *Pershyy Vinok* (The First Wreath), is rather a weak imitation of a Shevchenko ballad, without his melodiousness and his depth of poetic tone, although, as Franko noted, "this poetry is already characterized by what one may describe as new, unconventional, if only tentative notes."[44]

The lexical and syntactical aspects of Lesya Ukrainka's early poems did not differ in any special way from those of the post-Shevchenko poets. Since she had been practically brought up on their works, it is not surprising that she would have introduced some of their characteristic features into her own poetry. She inherited the use of many of the diminutives which were typical of the Romantic Ukrainian poets, for example, *Kvitochku zivyalu, ruta zelenen'ka, ne zhurysya divchynon'ko, shche zh ty moloden'ka, pryymy moye znebuleye serden'ko.* Her early poems also show a characteristically high proportion of the double synonyms, nouns, and other forms derived directly from folklore, such as, *naturo mat'inko, mene zhal'-tuka obiyma, bez shchastya-dol'i.*

To master the difficulties of literary expression, Lesya had to work hard to clothe the tenderness of her feelings and depths of her being in a suitable attire of language, and then to combine new and original elements in her versification with the syntactical and lexical elements of contemporary Ukrainian. The stylistic and linguistic values of her later dialogues demonstrate the great progress she made by her determination to improve her language and style.

Some of her poems—"Konvaliya" (Lily of the Valley), "Safo" (Sappho), "Nadiya" (Hope), "Zav'itannya" (Visit), "Vyazen'" (Prisoner), and a series of others—are imbued with sadness and despair, and they greatly resemble in their motifs the early Romantic poets, Mykola Kostomariv and Ambroziy Metlyns'ky. Still in the Romantic spirit she tended to glorify the happy past while looking at the present as a source of sorrow and grief. In fact, this poetic mood was generated more by her mode of living than by deeper spiritual stimuli: ailing, and therefore isolated from the outer world, she spent long hours reading the books which evoked her dreamy and sentimental images.

An early cycle, *Zoryane Nebo* (Star-lit Sky), and verses such as "Na davn'iy motyv" (On the Old Theme) are permeated with the senti-

[44]*Ibid.*

ment of a sensitive girl who is escaping reality. Her spirit is still overshadowed by a tone of youthful sentiment and nostalgic meditation.

But almost alongside these elegiac verses, she writes "Contra Spem
Spero," in which she exposes her inner self. The impasse seems to be
over; her melancholic conception of life seems to lose ground. Unexpectedly, her real character, her zest for life, and her conception
of passionate struggle find strong expression. Emphatic tones, bold
words, the stubbornly repeated phrase, "I will live," now disclose her
deeply hidden determination to face life in its complexity and reality.
This unusual outburst of energy now appears to pervade her whole
conception of life:

> No, I want to smile through tears and weeping,
> Sing my songs where evil holds its sway,
> Hopeless, a steadfast hope forever keeping,
> I want to live! You, thoughts of grief, away![45]

The usual sad overtone is still heard in her lines, but her indomitable
will to live—to struggle against all odds and to create—dominates each
word of her poem:

> Up the flinty, steep and craggy mountain
> A weighty ponderous boulder I shall raise,
> And bearing this dread burden, a resounding
> Song I'll sing, a song of joyous praise.

"Contra Spem Spero" became, in a sense, Lesya Ukrainka's motto for
both her life and work. More and more frequently the notes of optimism and of acceptance of life break through the veneer of her
timidity. Her appreciation of life with its contradictions and perplexity
deepens, prompting Franko to comment that "the songs of the nightingale, the flowers of spring," lose their enchantment for her. As she
turned from dreamy images to clear notions and energetic tones she
began to demonstrate her exquisite taste for poetic form and artistic
device.

In 1890 she wrote the cycle *S'im Strun* (Seven Strings), which
she dedicated to Mykhaylo Drahomaniv. Each of the seven poems of
the cycle bears the name of one note in the musical scale: *Doh, Re,
Mi, Fah, Sol, Lah, Si.* As indicated by the subtitles, the poem *Doh* is
written in a manner of a hymn, *Re* is a kind of folksong, *Mi* is a
lullaby, *Fah* is a sonnet, *Sol* a rondeau, *Lah* a nocturne, while the

---

[45]Lesya Ukrainka's poems quoted in this chapter have been translated by Vera
Rich except for the last four lines on p. 36.

author has called *Si* a "settina." The cycle shows a variety of stanzas, and tasteful harmony between the thoughtful and the musical and between the theme on one hand and its metric and stanzaic forms on the other.

The hymnal character of the verse *Doh* is strongly reinforced by solemn amphibrachic metre. This poem, whose serious tone resembles that of an epos, contrasts with the verse *Re*, composed in the pattern of a folksong. The lullaby, *Mi*, is charged with affectionate and lyrical pensiveness. The sonnet, *Fah*, distinguishes itself with elegant phrasing combined with Ovidian laconism. The scarcity of rhymes in the rondeau, *Sol*, emphasizes the acoustic effectiveness of this verse. The poem, *Lah*, resembles, by the image of enchanting night, a musical nocturne. The concluding verse, *Si*, both thematically and structurally, harmonizes with the whole cycle. In *Si*, Lesya refers to her own poetic work, in the imagery of music as "seven strings I pluck." The cycle is excellent documentation of Lesya Ukrainka's developing poetic talent.

Between 1890–92 Lesya Ukrainka wrote a series of poems in which her skill began to shine brilliantly. She produced her cycle *Kryms'ky Spohady* (Crimean Recollections) which is comprised of "Zas'piw" (Introductory Song) and twelve poems. They were inspired by the beautiful and unforgettable scenes of the Crimean countryside which the young poetess was for the first time enjoying. This series is marked by the enrichment of poetic technique, profound meditative tone, and a dramatic conflict of feelings. The artistic landscape in it stimulates thought and sustains the theme. Lesya Ukrainka equals in these poems the great Slavic Romantic poets, who have paid their tribute to the beauty of the Crimean land.

Another cycle of her poems, *Sl'ozy Perly*, written in the years 1891–93, merits mention as well as the *Crimean Recollections*. The high poetic value of this cycle rests in its deep ideological overtones and its artistic recapturing of feelings, in its vivid expressions and elegant phraseology.

In addition to the lyrics, which reveal strong social overtones, Lesya wrote a number of poems which have a deeply intimate character. Such personal tones already permeate her early poems: for instance, the sonnet "Natura hyne vsya v ozdobi, v zloti" (Nature perishes—all adorned in gold), or in such poems as "Os'in" (Autumn). Other remarkable poems of this type are those in the cycle *Melodiyi* (Melodies). Indeed, they are pearls of Ukrainian lyric poetry. One may sense in them the complete association of nature with the human soul and an emotional intensity which, however, never trespasses the author's sense of modesty and tactfulness. Some of her emotional verses, such as "Pytannya" (Question), "Vidpovid'" (Answer), and "Na motyv z Mitskevycha" (From the Motif of Mickiewicz), in accordance with the wish of Lesya Ukrainka, were not published during her lifetime, since they reveal the outburst of her great love and her sorrowful intimate experience.

Her poem "Romans" (Romance), written in 1897, is a classical example of the love lyric. Though it consists of only two anapest stanzas of fourteen lines, it creates a deep impression through its intensity of emotion, laconic expression, effective acoustics, fortified by alternating feminine and masculine rhymes, and inter-stanza anaphora. Her portrayal of the various facets of her emotions, and the delicate utterance of her soul do not obscure the lucidity of thought and image. Absence of any affectation makes her verses sincere and deeply persuasive.

In 1893, at the same time as her significant lyrical cycle *Melodiyi* was being written, Lesya wrote two longer poems, "Davnya Kazka" (The Ancient Tale) and "Robert Bryus, Korol' Shotlands'kyy" (Robert Bruce, King of Scotland). In the former, which represents a perfected variation of the somewhat weaker poem "Misyachna Legenda" (The Legend of the Moon), in a style typical of Heine, she tells a story which enables her to discuss the role of a poet in society.

"Robert Bruce, King of Scotland" is an excellent indication of her new concern for serious social themes. Robert Bruce, the only Scottish lord who remained faithful to his people in their struggle against the invading English army, scores a great victory over the King of England and saves the independence of Scotland. Although still hampered by some stylistic difficulties (she applies, in places, the stylistic devices of Ukrainian *duma*), Lesya begins to demonstrate the ideological pathos which was to saturate both her lyric and dramatic works. Her interest in Robert Bruce's struggle for Scottish independence no doubt was inspired by the struggle of her compatriots for their own national cause.

A VISIT made by the poetess to her uncle Mykhaylo Drahomaniv in Bulgaria during 1894–95 greatly influenced her works. At that time she was writing little, as she was engaged in reading a great number of volumes from his library. Lengthy discourses with her uncle, a man of great erudition and broad world views, crystallized her own outlook on the problems of the political, social, and cultural life of her nation and contributed to her spiritual enrichment and virility. Soon the newly engendered ideas found expression in her poems.

Following her sojourn in Bulgaria appeared the cycle *Nevilnychi Pisni* (The Songs of the Slaves). The main theme of the poems was the political subjugation of her fatherland. The struggle for political independence and the dynamic and heroic tones permeating the poems of this cycle are echoes of the classical poems by Franko and Shevchenko. Franko was led by heartening temper of these poems and their ideological overtones to comment on Lesya's place in Ukrainian literary circles in *Literaturno Naukovyy Vistnyk* in 1902:

> Reading the light and disjointed or cold moralistic writings of our contemporary Ukrainian writers, and comparing them with those cheerful, vigorous, and courageous writings of Lesya Ukrainka in which ideas are couched in such simple and sincere phrases, one cannot help reflecting that this sick weak girl is more of a man than anyone else in the whole Ukraine of today. . . . Ukraine cannot, in our opinion, boast today of a poet who can compare with Lesya Ukrainka as far as the force and versatility of her talent are concerned.[46]

Dynamism, energy, and action are typical of the entire spectrum of her works. It is easy to agree with Donstov, in his study *Poetka Ukrains'koho Risordzhimenta* (The Poet of the Ukrainian Risorgimento), when he writes:

> Not a hedonistic, but simply a forceful motivation of the will is the springboard of her philosophy, since her tragic writings could not have originated in her passive suffering, but only in a source which shows nostalgic longing for action and enobles her mind and soul. Such a purpose could not have sprung from the morality of relativism, but only from a conflict between the *Vis-major* and a strong will which prefers sacrifice and death to the betrayal of principles.[47]

Notes of deep anxiety and concern over the fate of the Ukrainian nation are audible in her poetry. Her soul, kindled with protest against the ravishing of her people, bids her to speak candidly about national problems. She composes such poems as "Pivnichni Dumy" (Thoughts of the North, 1895), in which she bids farewell to her "castles in the air" and greets "new dreams" of "new radiant light" leading her through "thorny paths" to the battlefield of a great national cause.

Her poem, "Do Tovaryshiv" (To Colleagues, 1895), is the echo of

[46]*Literaturno-Naukovyy Vistnyk*, 24.

[47]D. Dontsov, "Poetka Ukrains'koho Risordzhimenta," *Literaturno-Naukovyy Vistnyk*, LXXVI–LXXVIII (1922), 39.

her discourses on ideological themes in Sofia. In it she condemns the
delusions, silence, and passivity of the young generation, who being
overwhelmed by the national subjugation, are unaware of the fact
that they have the great mission of accomplishing the national renaissance. In "Hrishnytsia" (The Sinner, 1895), she introduces a form
of dialogue to deal with an episode of heroic struggle. In it an anonymous girl sacrifices her life in accordance with the precept: "No man
has more love than he who gives his life for his fellowman."

The motives of her "new dream" of freedom and heroic struggle
are stressed even more in the poems written in 1896. The five-stanza
poem "Khvylyna Rozpachu" (The Moment of Despair), embellished
with the beautiful inter-stanza anaphora, is a great hymn of freedom,
a curse on subjugation and captivity. In the poem "O Znayu Ya"
(Oh, Yes, I Know) the poetess dreams of the birth of a "new
individual tempered as steel."

Soon to follow is "Fiat Nox." Not one of her poems of that time
was infused with so much dynamism, spontaneity, and longing for
"light" and heroic deeds. The energy of the iambic line beautifully
harmonizes with the mighty heroic spirit. The use of such antitheses
as the light, the Promethean might, on the one hand, and bondage
and darkness, on the other, and the burning intensity of her bitter
apostrophe to her fellow countrymen who though "the descendents
of Prometheus" are yet "not bound . . . to Mt. Caucasus," make this
work a masterpiece of Ukrainian lyric poetry. The echo of Shevchenko, of his "Kavkaz" (Caucasus) in particular, is evident in "Fiat
Nox."

The ideological pathos in which the poetess lived at that time stimulated her, upon the completion of "Fiat Nox," to compose on the very
same day (November 25) the poem "Slovo, chomu ty ne tverdaya
krytsya?" (Word, Why art Thou not of Tempered Steel?). Lesya
masterfully created an association of the poetic work with the sword
of steel, reflecting her progressively intensified wish for the effectiveness of her poetic words in the regeneration of her country.

This pathos, intensified in her later poetry, is accentuated in the
cycle Krymsky Vidhuky (Crimean Echoes), written in the years 1897
and 1898, and especially in the autobiographical poetry her Mriyi
(Dreams) cycle. In it, Lesya discloses the basis of her idealistic world
view. As a very young girl she kept dreaming about the gallant and
the great; she envisioned a vanquished knight's heroic struggle for
freedom. Even then she was dreaming of a bloody sacrifice: "Cursed
be the wasted blood/ Left unshed for home land." She envisioned

the freedom fighters, including those who were awakened for battle by the clattering of the shackles ("Porvalas' Neskinchena Rozmova" / Ending an Unfinished Discourse, 1898). Using the wandering of the Israelites as her motif, she preached to coming generations "bitter suffering leading towards a clear and certain goal" ("U Pustyni" / In the Desert, 1898). The theme of bondage constantly recurs in her cycle *Yevreyski Melodiyi* (Hebrew Melodies, 1899), in the poems "De Tiyi Struny?" (Where are Those Chords? 1902), "Izrayil v Yehypti" (Israel in Egypt, 1904), and several others.

Lesya's philosophy of a vigorous and active soul, a person of great deeds and endeavour is reflected in a passage in "Epiloh" (Epilogue), written not long before her death:

> He who dwelt not among tempests
> Cannot strength's true valour savour
> Cannot realize how sweet to
> Men are struggle, toil and labour.

The contrast between her strong will and brave tones, on one hand, and the fragility of her health, on the other, is underlined with poise in numerous poems. "Who said to you that I am frail, that I submit to fate?" she asks in one of her last poems. Her query sounds like a rebellion against her physical infirmity, and she exclaims, with deep sincerity:

> Fighters, if you could but know it,
> What it is when hands are feeble!
> What it is to be unmoving,
> Like one shipwrecked by fate's danger. . . .

The conflict between strength and weakness, will and helplessness, is undoubtedly one of the sources of the tragedy which permeates her poetry and which finds its strongest expression in her dramatic works.

With great clarity there began to crystallize her idealistic world outlook, which was deepened and broadened by her suffering and which is typically her own: a view of life as a struggle for higher ideals. In this struggle, action leads to heroic deeds; in it lies the true purpose of life. This lofty idealism constitutes the framework of all Lesya Ukrainka's works both lyric and dramatic. In her collection *Vidhuky* we find fully developed the concept of a "thorny path":

> The thorny wreath shall always be more beautiful
>   Than the King's crown,
> And the path to Golgotha is more dignified
>   Than the triumphal march.

This outlook on the world manifests itself as well in her private life. As Staryts'ka-Chernyakhivs'ka writes: ". . . in 1913, a short time before the poet's death, when Kyiv society graciously expressed its gratitude for her literary work, she answered: 'Why complain of various injustices and wrongs inflicted by others? It would be difficult to live without struggle or without suffering.' "[48]

However, the elements of strength, the urge to action and heroism did not deprive Lesya Ukrainka of the underlying tenderness which is reflected particularly in cycles such as *Melodiyi* (Melodies, 1893–94), *Rytmy* (Rhythms, 1900–01), *Khvylyny* (Moments, 1900), and *Osinni Spivy* (Autumn Songs, 1902). In her writings all these elements are organically homogenized:

With all her heroic feelings, intensity of will, cult of superhuman strength and manly virtues, Lesya Ukrainka remains always and in every respect a woman in all her poetry. She is an "Ukrainian Sybil" who, in her prophetic imagination, sees "only blood and more blood" on her native steppes (as Donstov characterizes her). She is Miriyam, "the sinner, whom Love has taught the love of hatred." Lastly, she is simply a most attractive female character who, once she has been inflamed by the sacred fire of imagination, will remain so all her life. It is because of these qualities that she personifies strength and occupies an enviable position in the history of Ukrainian literature as a writer, who, in her writings, maintained a fusion of passion, impulses permeated by a Promethean spirit and fervour, combined with the tenderness and praise of a woman's heroism, suffering and self-sacrifice.[49]

THE GLORIFICATION of poetry as a dominant creative power appeared in her early collections and continued without interruption to her death. Lesya also sought solace in her poetry and found therein inspiration and strength, both for living and for creative work. This theme is not new in Ukrainian lyric poetry: it was thoroughly developed by Taras Shevchenko in the Romantic style and was continued by Kulish, Staryts'ky, and Franko. None of these writers, however, gave it so much attention or brought it to such a degree of refinement as did Lesya Ukrainka.

In "Pivnichni Dumy" (Midnight Reflections), in beautiful metaphor, Lesya unites the power of poetry with the idea of the national rebirth of her nation. In her poems "Buty Chy Ne Buty" (To Be or Not to Be) and "Anhel Pomsty" (The Angel of Revenge), the realization of the writer's role and her poetic destiny is expressed clearly,

[48]Staryts'ka-Chernyakhivs'ka, 14.
[49]Zerov, 164.

powerfully, and profoundly. The continuous dialogue of the Muse with the genius of creativity is a constant and powerful theme in Lesya Ukrainka's works, which reflects her search for poetic significance and a clear awareness of her destiny.

We again find an apostrophic reference to the Muse as the ruler of the soul and heart of the poetess in her poem "Ave Regina." "Zymova Nich Na Chuzhyni" (A Winter Night in a Foreign Land) continues the dialogue with the Muse and unfolds Lesya's own idea of art and poetry. In 1898 Lesya Ukrainka wrote her improvisation, "Zorya Poeziyi" (The Star of Poetry) in which she clearly defined the role of poetry in her life and glorified it as a divine gift. Here she was also prophetically aware of her future role in Ukrainian literature.

The poetic device most frequently resorted to by Lesya Ukrainka is personification: through the person of the Muse, she is able artistically to express and convey her veiled objectives and messages. The Muse appears at times as a counsellor, a teacher full of sisterly love, and then as an alluring figure inviting the poet to take wing with her to the stars. Sometimes her Muse is a merciless sovereign who "blinds her with her deceitful rays"; who "deceives her heart with an alluring mirage of happiness"; who "steals her words that should have died together with her"; who is consoled by the song of the poet as if by the song of her captive; who rules the poet, bringing tears and grief upon her, until she exclaims: "Rejoice, gracious monarch, the captive welcomes you." Thus the idea of poetry, symbolized by the figures of Genius, Fantasy, the Star, and the Muse in the lyric poems of Lesya Ukrainka, is developed in minute detail and in a great variety of forms. There are these "evil and ominous clouds," and "unbearable sorrow" from which the "star of poetry" leads her to a "bright path illuminating it with midnight fires, leading her through the dark and stormy sea, and fascinating her weary eyes with the rays and splendour of a new hope."

In a Promethean impulse the poet is compelled to drown the clanging of chains and fetters with a song destined to become a mighty weapon in the struggle with evil. As one critic states, in her poetry "living creativity becomes an instrument in her struggle: a mighty weapon in defence of all that man holds sacred. It becomes a social force."[50]

Poetry, as Lesya Ukrainka sees it, is a formidable force indeed. In the many and varied themes of poetic creation in which she develops and conducts the deeply intimate dialogue with her Muse, she em-

[50]Mybola Yevshan, "Fiat ars!" *Ukrains'ka Khata*, X (1913), 611.

phasizes the role of the poet and the function of poetry in the social and national spheres. In her early poem "Davnya Kazka," she develops, in a series of vignettes, the idea of art and poetry and of their far-reaching significance in the life of an individual and of a nation, equating art with beauty and with the highest human ideals: truth and freedom.

Some months before her death she wrote, in Egypt, her cycle *Tryptykh*, a collection of three poems, of which one "Orfeyeve Chudo" (Miracle of Orpheus), written in dramatic style, deals with the role of poetry. Poetry is an indomitable force. It inspires and animates the human spirit and summons people to heroic deeds and sacrifice. Never before in Ukrainian literature had the purpose of poetry, with its lofty ideals and the concept of its artistic value to the individuals and the nation, been developed in so fundamental a manner. This motif of the essential function of poetry, which in somewhat different fashion, has a long-standing tradition established by such Romantic poets as Wordsworth, Coleridge, Keats, Shelley, and Novalis, found powerful expression in the lyrics of Lesya Ukrainka. With the Ukrainian literature standing on the threshold of a new literary epoch, she gave this motif still greater profoundity of expression in her dramatic works.

EVEN HER early poems are marked by considerable originality in the use of various metres and verse structures. A sonnet, "Ostannya Pisna Mariyi Styuart" (The Last Song of Mary Stuart), published in 1888 when the poetess was seventeen, reveals the hand of the young master. The rigid form of sonnet demands great skill if harmony is to be maintained between the words and the flow of thought, as well as a feeling for rhyme and rhythm. The poetess succeeded remarkably well in this difficult lyrical genre.

Already, in her first poetic experiments, she is clearly searching for new stanzaic forms peculiar to herself.[51] She applied a variety of forms to her four-line stanzas—*aa bb cc ab ab aa bb ab ba*—and she used an interesting hexametric form with the rhythm of the folk dance *kolomyyka*.

In the field of metre and verse structure Lesya Ukrainka had few predecessors. Shchoholiv had brought in certain innovations and Pantelymon Kulish, who was thoroughly familiar with Western European literature, had introduced some variations in versification and metre into his poetry. Klyment Kvitka notes that Lesya considered

---

[51]B. Yakubs'ky, "Liryka Les'i Ukrainky na tl'i evolutsiyi form ukrains'koyi poeziyi," *Tvory Lesi Ukrainky* II, viii.

Kulish "a true writer and her teacher"; she used to say that in her childhood no one had as great an influence on her as Kulish and often mentioned his translations which had been her early reading. Although in later years she sometimes criticized Kulish, as in the case of his translation of *Macbeth* and other Shakespearean tragedies, she availed herself, with success, of Kulish's poetic innovations.

Western European literature had an important effect on the poetry of Lesya Ukrainka. Her wide knowledge of that literature as well as her work on the translations of Heine were important sources of the innovations in the themes and in the formal aspect she introduced into her verse. She introduced into Ukrainian poetry a wealth of stanzaic forms: in her first collection there are six sonnets, several tercets, royal stanzas, and the highly original octaves. There are at least twenty different verse forms in her complete works, and the variety and precision of her versification are certainly striking.

As in the sphere of versification, so also in the metrics her many innovations became apparent already in her early works. There are many trochaic metres in her early poems: tetrameter and trimeter, hexameter and trimeter, and pentameter. She also used iambic hexameters, pentameters, and tetrameters. In her early poems she used mostly three-syllable feet (anapaestic and dactylic), known as "song metre," as contrasted with the two-syllable iambs and trochees characteristic of the so-called "conversational metres." She liked the liveliness of the anapaest; fifteen poems out of fifty-seven published in her early collection are written in this metre. Fourteen of the poems *Na Krylakh Pisen'* are written in amphibrachic and seven in dactylic metres.

It has been noted by critics that in her youth Lesya Ukrainka devoted only a small part of her attention to Shevchenko's metrics and rhythm (his most characteristic metre is iambic tetrameter and the folk, especially *kolomyyka* rhythms). In this sphere Lesya Ukrainka went her own way, introducing into her works a large degree of metrical diversity.[52]

As in her first collection *Na Krylakh Pisen'*, there is a great metrical diversity in all her lyrics, but trimeters predominate. Among these an honoured position goes to the anapaest, which gives a particular melodiousness and lilt to her poems. Out of one hundred and ninety-two poems only sixty-five are written in iambic metre. In her later work, Lesya used the iambic metre when dealing with social themes to give her a serious and purposeful tone. For her more intimate lyrics

[52]*Ibid.*, VIII.

she used melodious three-foot lines. Students of Lesya Ukrainka's
lyrics point out that while toying, as it were, with various structures,
she is constantly on the lookout for the most interesting and for the
most exquisite. Lesya Ukrainka uses 1,592 rhymes; 628 of these are
perfect rhymes and 964 are imperfect.

Lesya Ukrainka adapted many of the genres to her purpose,
although she failed to introduce many new ones. Shevchenko used
mainly the elegy, *duma* (either in lyrical or folklore form), the poem
(of elegiac nature), the satire, and the ballad. Kulish, strongly
influenced as he was by Western European literature, tried almost all
of its forms: *duma*, poem, ballad, ode, elegy, song; typical of his poems
were *duma* and elegy. Lesya further developed the epic poem, a genre
which had flourished in Shevchenko's poetry but which had become
an empty form in the period that followed, endowing it with deep
psychological tones.[53] It can be said that the essence of her contribution to the evaluation of genres was this accent on psychology. In her
elegies we find a more intimate tone, more intimate subjects, in a
highly stylized formalistic framework. The *duma* in Lesya Ukrainka's
work is completely lyrical; she used no oratorical formula of the kind
often found in Staryts'ky. She introduced the romance, which was so
popular in Western European literature, into Ukrainian poetry. She
frequently used the legend, the epistle, and improvisation.

In her poetry she attempted to unite poetic and musical elements,
which is evident even in the titles of some of her works, for example,
Sim Strun, Melodiyi, Yevreyski Melodiyi, Osinni Spivy, and *Rytmy*.
Lesya's poetry comes very close to music by her use of rhythms and
tonality as well as in her choice of theme.

THE BEST lyrical works of Lesya Ukrainka appeared in the 1890s and
early 1900s. After her return to the dramatic genres, she continued to
write poetry until 1908. After that she produced only a few poems:
"Khto Vam Skazav, Shcho Ya Slaba?" (Who Said to You that I Was
Frail?), "Na Narodyny" (On the Birthday), and the poetry which is
included in the two smaller cycles *Vesna v Yehypti* (Spring in Egypt,
1910) and *Z Podorozhnyoyi Knyzhky* (From an Itinerary, 1911).

It was during these last years of her life that she produced her
greatest dramatic works. Her lyrics are permeated by pathetic, tender,
and intimate feeling, as well as by a true and unpretentious heroism.
Some of her poems reflect unusual virility and zeal bordering on
asceticism, self-renunciation coupled with the highest possible degree

[53]*Ibid.*, XXIV.

of self-sacrifice. They reached aesthetic fulfilment in the harmonious fusion of form and idea, in clarity of thought, in classical language. In them we find the fusion of several constituent elements: the qualities of intellect, poetic intuition, the profound tenderness peculiar to the female psyche, creative strength, as well as a high level of imagination.

From the point of view of form, subject matter, and basic tone, the lyrics of Lesya Ukrainka constitute a significant mile-stone in the history of Ukrainian poetry. The wealth and variety of her prosody and her talent for modern versification greatly enriched Ukrainian lyrics. By introducing new subject matter and jettisoning the older stereotyped social lyrics, she rejuvenated Ukrainian poetry and imbued it with a new vigour. Thus she laid the foundation for a new era in Ukrainian literature—the age of Modernism.

3. Drama

WHATEVER HEIGHTS Lesya Ukrainka achieved in her poetry, she surpassed in her dramatic works to which she turned her attention in the early 1900s. The transition from the lyric to the dramatic genre was not, however, entirely sudden and unexpected; certain dramatic elements are apparent in all her lyrics, although partly obscured by the natural form of the lyric genre itself.

One can find well-developed dialogue in almost all her poems. Such works as "Samson," "Hrishnytsia" (The Sinner), "Davnya Kazka" (An Ancient Tale), and "Robert Bruce" are all dialogue in pattern. The collection of poems, *Vidhuky* (Echoes), contains numerous dialogues and monologues, and one of her most fascinating dialogues is found in "Yeremiye, Zlovisnyy Proroche" (Jeremiah, an Ominous Prophet), in the *Yevreyski melodiyi* (The Jewish Melodies).

Indeed, the natural propensity to dramatize became apparent even in her early years. While still a young girl in Zvyahel in Volhynia, she staged Homer's *Iliad* and *Odyssey* along with other young girls. During her prolonged sickness and subsequent solitary convalescence, her lively imagination gave rise to tales of derring-do and of brave knights whose conflicts, battles, and clashes of ideas eventually found portrayal on the canvas of her dramatic works. All she read enriched her creative power, while the new scenes that passed through her mind in the course of her long sickness acquired concrete form with the passage of time. Her early dramatic motifs, subject matter, and plots underwent considerable modification before they finally achieved perfect artistic form.

It is interesting to note that these motifs are not confined to one genre only. They appear in the early lyrics and then reappear in later works, especially in the dramatic narratives and plays. The elements of conflict, of relentless struggle for justice, and of higher human ideals already exist in her lyrics, but this general mood finds its elaboration and complete realization primarily in the dramas and dramatic poems.

While still a child, she dreamt of the heroism of a wronged knight, whom she portrayed much later in a verse "Mriyi" (A Dream, 1897). The wronged knight reappears in more vivid colours in the poem

"Trahediya" (Tragedy) in the cycle *Legendy* (Legends), written in 1900. It is even more fully developed in the dramatic form, where each scene acquires new dimensions, and the conflict becomes more acute, whereas, in the lyrics, the motif of the wronged knight had been limited to brief fragmentary episodes. The once feeble and mal-treated knight now appears as an artist and sculptor, who devotes himself to art and truth, enduring dishonour and injustice in a narrow-minded, puritanical society. The drama, *U Puschi* (In the Wilderness), maintains the continuity of former themes, which had sprung up so abundantly in her lyrics. Idea and tone remain basically the same, but the form and the setting are changed. The knight now appears as a brave, uncompromising champion who bows in homage only to truth and beauty. In drama, Lesya was able to bring her earlier fancies to fruition in a fashion typical of her creative and artistic energy.

Mykola Zerov states that, "the keen and extraordinary reaction to auditory impressions, coupled with an imagination which itself de-pended largely upon auditory sensations, explains why pure descrip-tion and narrative emerge less successfully from the pen of Lesya Ukrainka than her monologues and dialogues about the favourite heroes of her childhood."[54] He also notes that the poem "Robert Bruce," in which dialogue plays a secondary role, is a much weaker work than "Davnya Kazka" (An Ancient Tale), although they were written at the same time. In the latter, more space and time is allotted to conflict and dialogue, and the celebrated exchanges between Bartold and the minstrel seem to clash like hostile spears in a battle.

Klyment Kvitka, in his memoirs, recalled that the poetess did not possess the gift of narrating a plot in an interesting manner and that, when undertaking a new work, Lesya often liked to consult her friends on the choice of plot. She usually narrated her ideas in so uninteresting a manner that she often sensed a cold reception on the part of her listeners and, as a result, frequently abandoned her plans. But whenever a plot was realized in a dramatic form "the finished product was, unexpectedly, refined and exquisite, unlike the previously related plot."[55]

While she lacked the gift of narrative, she often showed unusual talent in creating the dialogues that are so characteristic of her dramas. As Zerov observes, "the play of images in Lesya Ukrainka's writings often resembles a tournament of words, a persistent struggle between

[54]Zerov, 172.
[55]Kvitka, 250.

two antagonists, each defending his thesis to the end with all the means at his command."[56] Indeed, her heated exchanges are often, as in Greek drama, replete with masterful aphorisms, elicited by the dramatic situations and crystallized by the swift "give and take" of statement and retort. These "rhetorical duels" remind one of the Greek tragedians—Aeschylus, Sophocles, and Euripides. Solely out of her love for the classical style, she introduced ancient Greek tragic motifs and such characters as Cassandra and Iphigenia into her own works. She was especially moved by Sophocle's *Antigone*.

THE STYLE of the ancient Greek tragedies, while strongly affecting her dramatic writing, did not lessen her interest in the Western European theatre. Even in her adolescence she enjoyed reading Shakespeare's tragedies. While studying the English language, she dreamt of the time when she would be able to read *Hamlet* and other works in the original. To the Kyiv literary circle, she recommended that *Othello, Hamlet, King Lear, Richard III*, and *Coriolanus* be translated into Ukrainian. Greatly impressed by the English dramatist's creative genius, she herself began to translate *Macbeth*.

Another of her favourite dramatists was Schiller, whom she describes as the embodiment of true artistry. As an eighteen-year-old girl, she had prepared a list of literary works, in which were included Schiller's *Maid of Orleans, The Robbers, Don Carlos*, and *Mary Stuart*.

Although not entirely uncritical of Western European folk theatre, she valued highly the Austrian playwright, Anzengruber, in whom she observed the subtle, quick-witted elements of folk theatre. And she considered Hauptmann's *Die Weber* (The Weavers) as a significant work in world drama and an excellent model for social drama.

Ibsen, immensely popular as he was in Ukrainian theatrical and literary circles at the turn of the century, did not have as much influence on Lesya Ukrainka as some critics assert. Both in her philosophy and in her style she stands apart from Ibsen. The unequivocal attitude to life, and the penetrating philosophy of her protagonists who are always face to face with reality and with circumstances outside themselves have little in common with Ibsen's solitary heroes who are constantly involved in the thicket of their own private lives. Nevertheless, the great Norwegian artist had some influence on her work, especially in details of dramatic technique and in certain motifs.

Although in the dramatic poem and the versified drama Lesya

[56]Zerov, 172.

Ukrainka had such predecessors as Yuriy Fed'kovych, Ivan Franko, Volodymyr Samiylenko, and Mykhaylo Staryts'ky, she should be considered an entirely original playwright who opened the way for new subject-matter rich in philosophical overtones.

Like Shakespeare, Lesya Ukrainka turned to antiquity for the majority of her themes: motifs already hallowed by mythology and popularized by literary tradition and history. She depicts the acute social problems of contemporary life by means of familiar historical or legendary figures. There is no doubt that if these problems had been presented by her in strictly contemporary garb they would have lost much of their depth and symbolism.

Although her heroes have their origins in the ancient history of Babylon, Egypt, Greece and Rome, or in the medieval Roman world, as well as in the period of American colonization and the French Revolution, she never wrote a genuine historical drama. Her heroes are not representatives of historical events or historical epochs but merely the incarnation of her own ethical and philosophical concepts. Her manner of expression was similar to that of Goethe who expressed his most important philosophical problems in *Faust*. Such was the case with two other Ukrainian classic writers—Taras Shevchenko and Ivan Franko. However remote and alien their subject-matter, in essence both dealt with the same everyday problems of Ukrainian life, the former, particularly in his famous poems: "Neofity" (Neophyte) and "Mariya" (Virgin Mary); and the latter in the poems "Moysey" (Moses), "Ivan Vyshensky" and "Smert' Kayina" (Cain's Death). As one critic of Lesya Ukrainka writes: "As a poetess-philosopher, [she] chose as her subject matter themes which would give her wide scope for the development of ideas and for their verification and vindication in the action of her characters. The same characters, while remaining real, became figures—symbols of great ideals."[57]

It is solely for this reason that her plays show a clear association of the past and the present. The ancient serfdom of the Hebrews reflects the condition of her subjugated native Ukrainian people. The resplendent and subtle portraits of such outstanding protagonists as Mariyam, Antey, Ricard, Rufin, and Cassandra reflect the ideas of her own world. In Lesya Ukrainka's plays two aspects seem to blend: the personal and national on the one hand, and the universal on the other. In her dramas there is nothing so deeply personal that it does

[57]Oleh Babyshkin, *Dramaturhiya Les'i Ukrainky* (Kyiv: Derzhavne Vydavnytstvo Obrazotvorchoho Mystetstva i Muzychnoyi Literatury, 1963), 363.

not have a universal significance; and the most intimate national problems always find close parallels in the history of other nations. It is not only because of her subject-matter, but also because of her intuition and her innate poetical and dramatic power, that she can be considered an artist of universal stature. She viewed the world in broad perspective and, at the same time, she was able to perceive and discern many problems besetting the Ukrainian people, which found powerful expression in her dramatic works.

LESYA UKRAINKA's first plays were not written in a style typical of her later period. The artistically sharp dialogue, the profound philosophic grasp of a problem tinged with aphoristic wisdom, are absent from *Blakytna Troyanda* (The Azure Rose), written in prose in 1896. This drama, her first important attempt in a dramatic genre reflecting her search for a dramatic style, was written at a time when the Ukrainian theatre was undergoing profound changes.

During the 1890s the realistic drama of Kropyvnyts'ky and Tobilevych began to lose its popularity. The younger generation was turning with enthusiasm to the dramatic plays of Hauptmann, Sudermann, Ibsen, and Chekhov. Following this new trend, Staryts'ky wrote his play *Talan* (Talent, 1894), which was the first attempt at psychological drama. Such writers as Staryts'ka-Chernyakhivs'ka, Samiylenko, Steshenko, and others who belonged to Lesya's literary circle, translated the new works of Western European playwrights. Influenced by this trend, Lesya's *Blakytna Troyanda*, introduced a number of psychological traits.

The drama is about the love of a girl who cannot find happiness because of an hereditary illness. The heroine, Lyubov, having fallen in love with a young literary man, Orest, suffers intensely because of this tragic situation. Having a presentiment of her impending insanity, a sickness which had afflicted her mother, she concludes that she must renounce her undying love for Orest, in order to save him from unbearable suffering.

Orest's eventual illness, caused by this tragic situation as well as by his mother's negative attitude to his beloved, deepens the tragedy and causes Lyubov's death at a time when the exalted sentiment, "to be happy only to give happiness to another," becomes impossible to realize. The central conflict revolves around the problem of the impossibility for the heroine of attaining personal happiness.

The action takes place amongst the Ukrainian intelligentsia, and provides a sample of Lesya's daily life in the 1890s. For the most part, the action is not concentrated upon external events but on the inner workings of the human soul. In fact, the action is built on purely psychological motifs, and it is the sentiments and convictions of the characters that produce the dramatic conflict. Doubtless, Lesya's own chronic illness gave rise to thoughts about the conflicts in her own personal fate. Consequently, *Blakytna Troyanda* could have been an inspired episode from her own life in Kyiv society and environment. Hereditary disease as a motif bringing about a hopelessly tragic situation and hovering as an iniquitous threat over life and human happiness reminds one of the influence of Ibsen's *Ghosts* on her first drama. One may also conclude that the poetess was well aware of Zola's concepts of heredity as stressed in the *Rougon-Macquart* cycle.

The external events and the development of the action in the drama proceeds according to the laws of growth in a psychological tragedy. Some of the details bring to mind the plays of Ibsen and Hauptmann, but as yet the young dramatist in no way compares with these European masters. Her dialogue is not yet fully developed, and she is unable to handle it sparingly. The motivation of the hero is incomplete, while the action does not move forward smoothly and steadily. Moreover, the conflict in the dialogue does not develop *pari passu* with the action. Lesya herself was critical of her play as she indicates in a letter to her mother: "At times I am very sceptical and critical of my drama and then it seems to me that it contains more faults than merits. This thought is indeed bitter, but it occurs to me more and more often."[58]

Certain elements of the future artist are perceptible in this first drama. At times, her stage directions more than make up for the imperfections of the dialogue; extraordinarily colourful, they intensify the drama. Moreover, Lesya handles the device of contrast dextrously, and the tendency towards aphorism is already apparent.

These same attributes are evident in her short dialogue sketch *Praschannya* (Farewell), written in prose, probably in 1896 (the manuscript is undated). The love motif is well worked out, and lengthy stage directions are also found. The terse expression and indirect suggestion add a specific tone to her style. Behind the tranquil world of the drama there is a hint of a profound spiritualism, which leads certain critics to suggest that the heroine of this brief sketch is already the prototype of the future Mavka, in *Lisowa Pisnya*, and Cassandra.

[58]P. Rulin, "Persha Drama Les'i Ukrainky," *Tvory Les'i Ukrainky*, V, 28.

IN THE YEARS that followed *Blakytna Troyanda* and *Proschannya* she introduced into her dramatic writing biblical and ancient Christian themes. In them she found appropriate motifs and atmosphere for the expression of the ideas and feelings which then preoccupied her.

She began this group of works with her dramatic poem *Oderzhyma* (The Obsessed). This genre, which she introduced into Ukrainian literature, perhaps owes something to her favourite poet, Alfred de Musset, who, in 1832, used the name *poème dramatique* for some of his dramatized poems.

From 1901 until her death she wrote no less than ten dramatic poems. *Oderzhyma* was written in the course of one night, at the beginning of 1901, in Minsk. The poem consists of four scenes in which monologues and dialogues predominate, and it is only in the fourth scene that elements of dramatic action are noticeable.

The theme of *Oderzhyma* is the boundless love of Miriyam for the Messiah. This love forces her to follow Him, whom she recognizes from afar in the desert, and at the sight of whom she begins her monologue. His loneliness, exhaustion, and the foreboding of His approaching bitter lot rend her heart. As the Messiah imperceptibly approaches Miriyam, there begins between them a dialogue which betrays the deep conflict that characterizes their differing outlooks. Although Miriyam idolizes the Messiah, she is not disposed to accept His teaching of love towards one's enemies. Her infinite love for Him excludes love towards His enemies. For her this is a logical course of action; she is not in a position to love the enemies of the Son of God, and yet she is aware that she will eventually suffer for this.

The scene in the Garden of Gethsemane deepens the tragedy. The sight of His disciples sleeping during the hours of His great suffering evokes in Miriyam a feeling of hatred towards them. After the crucifixion Miriyam stands alone under His cross, immersed in her reflections on the paradox of the idea of love. The Messiah has forgiven His enemies and those who were indifferent to Him, but Miriyam remains unforgiven simply because, as a result of her love for Him, she has come to hate His enemies, those who cried "Crucify Him, Crucify Him!" The inability of Miriyam to follow the teachings of Christ in the absolute sense, and at the same time her love towards Him as a Messiah, provide the source of her tragedy, and finally her martyrdom on the square in Jerusalem when she curses everybody who is responsible for Christ's death.

Klyment Kvitka mentions in his memoirs that Lesya Ukrainka

considered *Oderzhyma* one of her best works. Ivan Franko, who at first regarded the poetess as a purely lyric talent, began to consider her as a talented dramatist after its appearance.

Oderzhyma was written as her close friend Serhiy Merzhynsky was dying, and the poem, therefore, affords a revelation of the soul of the poetess herself. In a letter to Ivan Franko, Lesya spoke of these circumstances: "I confess to you that I wrote it during such a night after which I shall certainly live long, if I still remained alive at that time. I wrote without even digesting my sorrow, in its very climax. If anyone would ask me how I emerged from all this, then I would also be able to answer: *J'en ai fait un drame. . . .*"[59]

The tragic events of real life stimulated her literary work, acting upon the unusually creative intensity of her genius. Her profound suffering found creative expression in *Oderzhyma*. The first dramatic poem, however, does not occupy an isolated place in her works. Later dramas, such as *Na Ruyinach*, *Cassandra*, *Rufin i Priscilla*, and *Lisowa Pisnya*, also reflect the strength of conviction, the readiness for self-sacrifice and courage of their heroines; but none of these expressed all these qualities with such *élan* and spontaneity of feeling as Miriyam.

THE THEME of poetry and song as a constructive and decisive factor in the struggle of a nation for its freedom occurs very frequently in the works of Lesya Ukrainka. *Vavylonskyy Polon*, dated February 15, 1903, describes one of the most tragic periods of the Hebrew nation's history, the Babylonian Captivity. Near the waters of the Euphrates and the Tigris, a sad picture of the misery experienced by the Jewish prisoners is presented. Famine, harsh treatment, and death are decimating their ranks. At the time of this historic cataclysm the Judaean prophets are conducting a bitter dispute with the Samaritan prophets in an attempt to prove the superiority of their tribe. The young prophet-bard, Eleazar of Babylon, pleads with the two factions for unity in the face of their common slavery and captivity, which are the punishments for their discord, and indicates to them one common goal—return from captivity to Jerusalem.

The dialogue of Eleazar and the Hebrews is maintained throughout the poem, constituting its core. Eleazar defends himself before the Jews against the charge that he is singing his songs for the Babylonians and thus bringing shame upon his people, and ends by challenging them to find a way to Jerusalem. As long as the nation is

[59]Babyshkin, 54.

still spiritually alive, and as long as the people are ready to struggle for their survival, he says, it is premature to speak of defeat, for the road to Jerusalem is still open.

The period of the Babylonian Captivity, with the accompanying problems portrayed in this poem, is clearly associated with the condition of the Ukrainian people when Lesya Ukrainka was writing. The discord and fruitless quarrels which undermine the unity of the captive Hebrew nation are a clear parallel with the case of the Ukraine. In making a plea for his imprisoned brethren in the struggle for survival, and uttering a cry of confidence and faith in the future, Eleazar is the personification of the poetess' own preoccupation with the bitter lot of her countrymen.

However, some of Lesya's contemporaries, failing to read between the lines in *The Babylonian Captivity*, expressed surprise that she should deal with such distant and alien themes. However, in September 1904, while at her mother's cottage, she wrote her second dramatic poem, *Na Ruyinach* (On the Ruins). In this poem she brought out the plight of the captive Hebrew nation even more clearly and underlined the similarity between the yoke of the Hebrew and that of her own nation.

From the point of view of formal structure and main idea, the two are twin sisters. *Na Ruyinach* is only a companion-piece to the *Vavylons'kyy Polon*. In both of these poems the action develops around one central character; in both works the conflict is based on the radically differing views of the main hero and the Hebrew population; in both works, especially in the closing sections, there is a long monologue by the main character, forming the climax of the dramatic action.

Whereas the action of *The Babylonian Captivity* takes place on the plain where the Tigris and the Euphrates meet, against the radiant background of the setting sun, the action of *On the Ruins* takes place on a bright, moonlit night on the plain of Jordan, against the background of the ruined cities and villages of Israel, and far away from the barely visible peak of Mount Sinai. In the first poem, night pacifies the Babylonian prisoners and brings the action to its conclusion, while in the second poem, the night serves as the initiator of action. As a result, *On the Ruins* appears as the chronological continuation of *The Babylonian Captivity*.

The role of idealistic teacher of a captured and disunited people is taken in *On the Ruins* by the prophetess Tirtsa, who appears among her subjugated countrymen scattered about the ruins of their settlements and tries to rouse them from their torpor to a new life, to extricate them from despair and despondency.

And just as in *The Babylonian Captivity*, one basic thought is stressed; that the subjugation of any nation by a foreign power in no way decides its future. The strength of a nation resides within the nation itself, in its vitality, in its faith in itself, in its labours, which must guarantee its existence, and in its optimism, which should inspire the young generation whose task it is to regain freedom for their nation. One should not poison the soul of this new generation with sorrowful lamentation. When there comes a period of ruin and destruction after the lost battle, the sword should be forged into a plowshare. Similarly, the hearts of the subjugated people should be forged by "fire and water." "A slave is not a person who has been subjugated," cries Tirtsa to the Jews lamenting over the ruins of Israel by night, he is "only a person who, of his own free will, carries the yoke of slavery." "The heavy sleep of an indifferent slave is more burdensome a yoke than the iron chains and fetters which the prophet Jeremiah was once forced to carry," says Tirtsa of one of the sleeping Jews.

When the bard tries to reproduce the lament of Jeremiah, and to play the harp which Jeremiah himself once played, Tirtsa seizes the harp from him and hurls it into the River Jordan. Jeremiah's harp represents lament and ruin, and this symbolizes the pitiful and disgraceful past. The prophetess calls out to the Jewish bard that the subjugated nation needs new bards who will sing new songs and "invent new words, fashion new strings."

Enraged at Tirtsa's contempt for the Holy of Holies, the Jews want to drown her and the Samaritans try to liberate her and win her over to their side against the Judaeans, but the prophetess rises above the internecine strife and misunderstanding. "Blind and unfortunate ones!" she exclaims, "do you not know that the time has come to realize the word of the prophet Isaiah? It is time for the lion to lie down with the lamb."

Tirtsa presents a new and constructive ideology for the subjugated nation with even greater force and precision than did Eleazar. Her discourse on life, embodying new principles able to restore the strength and vitality of the captured nation, is permeated with aphorisms which convey wisdom in her every thought. In certain instances, particularly in the abstract, the words of Tirtsa later find their echo in the words of Moses in the famous poem by Ivan Franko. Furthermore, her optimism—"the years will pass, the prisoner will return, and the song of Sinai will again come to its own. . . . And the prisoner will embrace his brother, and both, side by side, will rebuild the walls"—vividly recalls the prophetic vein of Taras Shevchenko, as expressed in his epistle *I Mertvym I Zhyvym I Nenarodzhenym . . . (To the Living, Dead and Unborn)*. Every word of the prophetess. Tirtsa applies most concretely to the Ukrainian nation subjugated by Russian imperialism. Through the words of the prophetess Tirtsa, Lesya Ukrainka presents the ideology of a new life for her nation, an ideology which should awaken the nation spiritually, and restore its power and faith in the future.

If she clad typically national problems in biblical subject matter, it was not only because she found ideal historical parallels in the Bible, but also because she admired biblical heroes as well as the restless and passionate elements of biblical themes. Her heroes, the solitary spokesmen of great ideas, come into conflict with reality. They are uncompromising thinkers who judge life from their own point of view and according to their own principles for which they prepared to sacrifice their lives.

THE FERMENT which culminated in the Russian Revolution of 1905 is visible in many of the works of Lesya Ukrainka. *Vavylons'kyy Polon* and *Na Ruyinach*, eloquent as they are of the problems of her native land, already show that, in accordance with her principle, she was dedicating her Muse to the national cause so much in the Ukrainian mind at that time. After long political servitude, the Ukrainians were awakening to a clear consciousness of their political rights and aspirations. And during the years 1905–6 she wrote four short pieces which occupy a rather insignificant place in her literary heritage but which show, nevertheless, her determination to find answers to the problems confronting her nation.

The first work of this series, *Osinnya Kazka* (Autumn Tale), which the poetess called "a fantastic drama," was written in January 1905 in Tiflis and was published for the first time in 1929. She did not finish this work, nor did she prepare the manuscript for publication. Perhaps her husband's criticism discouraged her from finishing the job and she gave it up. The piece was to be a drama, but it has all the elements typical of a fairytale. The knights who are trying to reach the princess imprisoned by a tyrant king in a glass mountain all perish in their vain attempts. One knight who is liberated from prison by a servant also fails to reach her. The princess throws herself down the mountain in an attempt to escape her lot and, although she is injured, she regains her freedom. Then a builder and his workers appear and they also begin struggling to capture the mountain in the hope that their efforts will eventually be crowned with success. The liberated princess joins them in their task.

The idea of *Osinnya Kazka* was prompted by political reality. The Revolution of 1905 now seemed to present fresh hope for the over-throw of Russian absolutism and the liberation of the subjugated nations. Simultaneously, the idea of freedom and hope for the destruc-tion of the old political order dawned in the minds of patriots.

During those days Lesya became more and more concerned with the problem of the role of poetry and art in the national struggle, a problem which she stressed so emphatically in both her lyrics and drama. The princess symbolizes poetry and art and, once liberated from servitude, is to play an important role in the national rebirth.

In August 1905 the poetess completed the dialogue, *Try Khvylyny* (Three Moments). Certain problems of the Revolution in Russia suggested the use of a theme from the French Revolution, and in this dialogue, consisting of three scenes, there are two characters—the Jacobin and the Girondist—who represent two diametrically opposed views on the problems raised by the Revolution. The first scene depicts the Jacobin's hatred of the Girondist, which is typical of that stratum of society which utilizes revolution for personal gain and advance-ment. The second scene takes place in prison, where the Jacobin stands guard over the Girondist. In a dialogue, they discuss the problem of the struggle for ideals. For the Girondist, the ideal is eternal and does not die with the protagonist; for the Jacobin, the ideal dies with the person. He persuades the Girondist to escape from the Conciergerie just before his execution, convincing him that his death would in no way benefit either his friends or the idea of the Revolution. With the Jacobin's help, the Girondist does indeed escape.

The third scene takes place in Switzerland where for the past three years the Girondist has been living as an *émigré*. Wholly immersed in his thoughts, he lives high in the mountains from where he can see Lake Constance. Enjoying liberty, he yet longs "for the walls of the Conciergerie . . . the sad and dismal witness of heroism." The favour shown by the Jacobin and the advice he acted upon have become a bitter punishment for him. Freedom and the beauty of the mountains have lost their charm. In France there was real life, a life of trial, struggle, and outbursts of joy. There, in the whirl of Revolu-tion, he trembled for his life, but still he lived a full life. Finally, he comes to the conclusion that everyone is predestined to be either an avenger and a fighter, or nothing, because on earth one can only live or die. The scene ends with the Girondist preparing to return to France.

In spite of its historical subject-matter, *Try Khvylyny* is in reality a work with pronounced philosophical tendencies. Neither the Jacobin nor the Girondist is a spokesman for the ideas of their respective parties. By means of the dialogue which develops between them, and the Girondist's monologue in the last scene, Lesya Ukrainka presents a series of problems which were becoming urgent during the Russian Revolution. One of the questions raises the point that the death of an adversary, at the behest of his enemy, makes him a hero. She criticizes terror as a weapon in political struggle. In one of her articles on the Jacobin and the Girondist revolutions in 1793 and 1794 she states that "both revolutions . . . were predestined to failure because both degenerated into terror."[60] An ideal cannot be destroyed by terror. The struggle for the common good, "the urge to action, the great joy of happiness while sacrificing oneself for the idea, the torture of doubts, the joy of a dream and death of the inevitable tragedy," all make life worth living. The quiet, passive, and carefree life, enjoyed by the Girondist amid the beauties of Switzerland at a time when his followers are ready to sacrifice themselves for the common weal, turns into a source of anguish for him and as a result he begins to long for the dismal walls of the Conciergerie. Thoughts of the awakening of the political consciousness of the Ukrainian people surged in the mind of Lesya Ukrainka, forced as she was to lead a sheltered life.

After *Osinnya Kazka* and *Try Khvylyny*, Lesya turned again to her favourite ancient Christian subject-matter. In October of 1905, she completed her short dramatic poem *V Katakombakh*, the action of which takes place in the catacombs near Rome amidst the Christian people who gather there for prayers. The poetess discusses the problem of the absolute physical and spiritual freedom of man. By a pointed representation of a slave neophyte, who is searching for truth among the Christians and seeking protection against subjugation, the poetess also poses the problem of freedom and human dignity, *V Katakombakh* is devoid of psychological background and dramatic action, and as Gudzy aptly described the poem: "In it there is little internal action and the portraits are not typified by psychological complexity. The play is regarded as a rather abstract dispute between the two

[60]*Ibid.*, 117.

antagonists, who appear not only as living individuals but as exponents of two mutually opposed ideas."[61]

In her early dramatic poems, Lesya Ukrainka presented characters who were primarily the spokesmen of certain definite philosophical ideas: they were abstractions rather than living people. Her dramatic technique was subjected to the philosophical duel which was to lead to the discovery of truth, rather than to actual conflict in life. But, as a Babyshkin has noted

... she felt that in spite of the masterly dialogue and the logical development of thought, her characters lacked the complexity of feeling, were deprived of the many-sidedness and versatility of the human soul, and that her heroes were always exponents of certain ideas, even obsessed by them. They were always passionate, ready for sacrifice and, for the most part, endowed with identical feelings and one *idée fixe*. ... She saw that such a one-sided portrayal does not help one to comprehend or grasp the idea in a literary work and seldom makes it sufficiently convincing.[62]

She knew that what renders dramatic writing alive and convincing is the incarnation of the complex human character in the literary work. In her later works this way of representing an idea, coloured by a didactic tone which made her dramatic poems more like poems than dramas, has almost disappeared. Now she clothes her characters in flesh and blood and penetrates to the depths of their spiritual and psychological life. Their conflict is engendered already in complex life situations.

A HINT of this change in her dramatic style is already noticeable in her short dialogue *V Domu Roboty, v Krayini Nevol'i* (In a House of Labour, in a Country of Servitude), written in Kyiv in October 1906. Here Lesya does not abandon her stock themes: the action takes place during the Babylonian Captivity in Egypt; the basis of the dramatic action is provided by two slaves—one an Egyptian and the other a Jew—differing considerably in external appearance and in outlook. The Jewish slave presents a pitiful figure, being thin, emaciated, and covered with mud. The Egyptian slave is broad shouldered and appears as a strong and vigorous man. He looks with scorn and derision on the Jewish slave. Their external appearances reflect their diametrically opposed mode of life: their views on slavery are different, if not contradictory. The Jew hates Egypt, the country of his servitude. If only he could, he would destroy all the Egyptian temples, their pyramids, and "he would build a dam on the Nile and thus inundate

[61]*Ibid.*, 131.   [62]*Ibid.*, 132-3.

and submerge the entire country of his enslavement." To the Egyptian
slave Egypt is a country of famous temples, where Ra and Osiris are
praised and worshipped. He works as do other Egyptians "not only as
a slave, but from his own volition." In all probability, he would work
even better, if he were free, but in his work as a slave he sees sense
and benefit. When the Jewish slave curses the Egyptian Holy of
Holies, the Egyptian slave strikes him. When the guard beats both
of them and chases them out to work, the Egyptian tries to justify his
rough expression of anger, but the Jew, turning away from him, says:
"So, thus it should be, I ought to know that I am a slave and nothing
else, that this country of enslavement is foreign to me and that I have
no friends here."

The slaves unmistakably symbolize the two social strata, represented
in Russia by the Russian Social Democratic Party and in the Ukraine,
subjugated by Russia, by the Ukrainian Social Democratic Party. The
events of the Revolution showed that unity and close co-operation
based solely on common social interests was an impossibility. Only
national interests, the community of interests of one culture and one
fatherland, could unite a society. The Jew arrives at the conclusion
that he is not only a slave of Egypt but also of the Egyptian slave for
whom Egypt is a native land. In the social sphere, the Ukrainian
could find no common language with the Russian, since for the latter
Russia is "as a kingdom, in which the temples are built for the gods,
while for the former it is a 'country of enslavement.'"

Although the characters in this dialogue are merely the spokesmen
of two contradictory views, as is the case with other early dramatic
works of Lesya Ukrainka, we now notice a greater complexity of
situation, greater intensity of contradiction, and a weaving of several
themes—an evolution in Lesya Ukrainka's dramatic style.

WHILE STAYING in Kyiv in the fall of 1906, the poetess began to write
her most ambitious five-act play, *Rufin i Pristsilla* (Rufinus and Priscilla). She prepared herself very thoroughly for the task and, although
she spent a long time completing it, she wrote the first two and a half
acts fairly rapidly. At the third act she stopped and began a meti-
culous study of the historical sources of the early Christian era, which
were abundantly supplied to her by Ahatantel Krymsky, a well-known
Ukrainian poet and scholar. In the fall of 1907, in Yalta, she resumed
her work on the play, finishing the remaining acts in 1907 and 1908.
Aware of the recurrent symptoms of her terrible disease, she exerted
herself to the utmost to finish the play. In one of her letters she

expressed the fear that she would not finish it, that she would die without being able to put into words what she wanted to say most of all.[63] But, in April 1910, in Telavi, she at last completed the final editing of the play.

The assiduous preparation that went into it shows how highly Lesya Ukrainka valued this work. Unfortunately, however, the play did not reward her great effort. Mykola Yevshan makes a typical critical observation:

> ... At all events, we must say that the work is worthy of the author's name, although we cannot include it among her best works. She concentrated her attention on the revelation of the conflict between two viewpoints or worlds—the old Roman and the new Christian—and, as a result, overlooked, or rather allotted a secondary position to the psychology of the main characters. In the end, the work emerged much more interesting in its ideological than in its artistic aspect, and, therefore, may be considered as one of the most literary plays of Lesya Ukrainka; only here and there does the action come to life and then we have scenes of full dramatic power. ...[64]

She concentrated on the conflict of ideas, the conflict between the new world of Christianity and the old world of the Roman empire. On this antithesis rests the central subject of the play.

In Rufinus we see a young Roman of noble birth and of great intelligence, who is a staunch supporter of the Republic and who does not recognize the authority of Caesar. Loving his wife Priscilla above everything else, he reconciles himself to the fact that she is an active Christian, although the Christian ideal is foreign to him. Priscilla, on the other hand, values the Christian faith above everything else, even above her own personal happiness and above her love for her husband. It is clear to Rufinus that Priscilla's devotion to the Christian faith has disrupted his marital happiness. When he learns, however, that the secret meeting place of the Christians has been discovered and that imprisonment threatens the Christians as well as Priscilla, he immediately warns his wife of the danger. To save the Christians Rufinus offers them his home for the meeting. The patrician Crusta arrives by chance at Rufinus' home while the meeting is in progress and proceeds to inform the Roman authorities. As a result of Crusta's denunciation, Priscilla and Rufinus are arrested along with the Christians. Whereupon the Christians begin to suspect that the pagan

---

[63]*Literaturno-Naukovyy Vistnyk*, X (1913), 30.

[64]Mykola Yevshan, "Zdobutky Ukrains'koyi Literatury za 1911," *Literaturno Naukovyy-Vistnyk*, I (1912), 107.

Rufinus has betrayed them. But when Priscilla's father, Pansa, who had bribed the guards, offers Priscilla and Rufinus a chance to escape, they refuse and are slaughtered with the Christians in the Roman circus.

Within the play we see the crossing of two conflicts. One of these conflicts is of a family nature: Priscilla, the wife of a prominent Roman, becomes an ardent Christian neophyte. Rufinus, reared on the philosophy of Plato, Xenon, and Epicurus, and adhering to the platonic ideology of Celsus, cannot grasp the quintessence of the Christian faith. As a rationalist, he bows only to the wisdom of philosophy and has neglected even the worship of the Gods. Though he has searched all his life for the truth, which has continually eluded him, Rufinus finds himself at the crucial moment without the help of faith. This is why Priscilla, who has found her highest ideal in the new faith, can ask him: "Whither is errant wandering thought to lead? Where is the source of argument? Where the anchor? Where will you cast it and what will it catch and hold, to halt the exhausted vessel despairingly seeking haven?"

The other conflict which permeates the play emerges from Rufinus' opposition to the autocratic authority of Caesar. Rufinus, who is an intellectual, a Republican, and a Roman patriot, cannot accept autocracy, which he believes will cause the downfall of Rome. For this reason he does not go into state service, although his patrician friends try to persuade him to do so. His attitude is expressed in his last words: "Farewell, my Rome, soon you also will perish."

Rufinus, a man of great intelligence and dauntless spirit, does not die for an ideal like Priscilla. Unable to accept the Christian ethic, he remains outside the world of his beloved wife and of his dear friend Gnaeus Lucius. The latter becomes a Christian because in the new faith, which teaches peace and brotherhood among men, he sees the salvation of Rome. In his tragic loneliness, Rufinus realizes that his love for Priscilla is the only stimulus in his life and that when she perishes his life will become meaningless. He decides to die in the arena. The thought of escape is both foreign and repugnant to him because, like the Girondist in *Try Khvylyny*, he considers the aimless life of an exile worse than death.

Searching for the genesis of *Rufinus and Priscilla*, some critics have attempted to found the play on actual biographical data. Muzychka, for instance, sees a parallel between Rufinus and Priscilla on the one hand, and Lesya's mother and father on the other, noting particularly their differing viewpoints on religion and social activities. Dray-

Khmara, however, rejects Muzychka's opinion. Another critic, Oleh Babyshkin, believes that to a certain degree Rufinus and Priscilla resemble the Kovalevskys, a family very close to Lesya Ukrainka. Kovalevsky's wife was condemned and perished in Siberia because she belonged to revolutionary circles; her husband, although a good patriot, was never a revolutionary.

Zerov insists that

... the nature of the conflict between the protagonists is so universal that many events from the life of the poetess may provide an analogue. It is not so much the conflict between the parents in the Kosach family, as the difference in approach to their mutual work, brought about by their diverse social upbringing. ... Rufinus and Priscilla do not resemble living people drawn from nature, but appear rather as representatives of different ideologies.[65]

There is little doubt that the play reflects the life and the temper of the reactionary years following the 1905 Revolution. The Roman crowd in the circus, expectantly awaiting a bloody spectacle, is a reminder of the drop in social morals of a society unable to appreciate the struggle and sacrifice for a great cause.

EVER AND AGAIN the poetess returned to her biblical and early Christian themes. In February 1909, while living in Telavi, she wrote one of her better dramatic poems, *Na poli krovy* (On the Field of Blood). The theme was not new. At that time Judas made frequent appearances in European and, particularly, in Slavic literature: Paul Heyse, in his play *Mary Magdalen*, portrays the figure of Christ's betrayer, and in Slavic literature Judas appears in the works of Leonid Andreyev and of Stanislav Przybyszewski. In their works we can discern a certain tendency to try to understand Judas' psychology and motivation and to justify his actions.

Lesya Ukrainka similarly concentrates on his psychology and gives a detailed analysis of the impulses leading to the treachery. With limited resources (apart from Judas there is only an old pilgrim in the play), but with a brilliantly organized dialogue, the author obtains the maximum artistic effect. Step by step she leads up to the motive behind the deed and completely reveals the soul of the perfidious Judas. The great value of this short dramatic poem rests in its monolithic simplicity, in the economy of words, in the simple harmony of composition, and in the logical and natural development of ideas.

The aged pilgrim asks for a drink of water from the man who is

[65]Mykola Zerov, "Rufin i Pristsilla," *Tvory Les'i Ukrainky*, VII, 31.

painstakingly working a stony piece of ground and draws him into conversation. Tilling the land he purchased for thirty pieces of silver Judas is at first not keen to talk and, in fact, would be very happy to get rid of the pious pilgrim whose every word reminds him of his heinous deed. When Judas does begin to speak, however, it is almost throughout in a monologue in answer to the questions which, from time to time, the old pilgrim asks him.

Both the style of presentation and Judas' reasons for betraying Christ are complex. At first, he attempts to degrade the dignity of his Teacher and to destroy His aura of divinity, in order to humiliate Christ and justify his own actions. His arguments sound extremely persuasive, although he suffers deep remorse while he tries, it would seem, to build up an unbreakable defence of his innocence. As the portrait of Judas comes into focus, it soon becomes evident that, in attributing to him both originality and intellectual superiority, Lesya Ukrainka has created a different figure from the one portrayed by her contemporaries and her predecessors.

Paralleling the progressive revelation of the soul of Judas, as the dialogue develops the attitude of the pilgrim to Judas changes. In spite of the plausible motivation, Judas fails to uphold his quasi-noble intentions. When forced to answer why he kissed Christ if not to betray him, Judas becomes entangled in his own argument: he explains that his kiss was motivated by love for his Teacher. But perceiving the pilgrim's repugnance for the betrayal of a beloved Teacher, he decides to change his line of argument; he says his kiss was cold. This completely repels the pilgrim, who curses him and leaves.

Considered ideologically, *Na poli krovy* is in line with Lesya's other works. Continually searching for the strong and the noble, she created heroes who tolerated no compromise of good with evil, nor any mediocrity in values. This poem was her dramatic answer to the concept of Judas in the literature of her time, which so often neglected moral issues for the sake of originality of idea and of literary effect. It is also a milestone in her use of psychology, a feature which increasingly becomes characteristic. Her heroes cease to be merely the mouthpieces of ideals or philosophical concepts and gradually take on the attributes of living human beings. As dramatic conflict develops, engendered by the nature of her characters, her philosophical concepts take firmer root on psychological grounds.

LESYA'S USE of psychology is most clearly marked in works dealing with the problems of marriage, particularly in the short dialogue,

Aisha and Mohammed, and in the one-act dramatic study, *Yohanna, Zhinka Khusova* (Johanna, The Wife of Khus). The former was written in Yalta, in April 1907, and belongs to those works in which she portrays a specifically human problem stripped of all social or political colouring—the problem of love.

It is quite possible that in writing *Aisha and Mohammed* Lesya Ukrainka was inspired by *Mohammed and Khadija* by Panteleymon Kulish. This dialogue on marriage takes place between Mohammed and the young and beautiful Aisha, who becomes his wife after the death of Khadija. We find Aisha suffering because Mohammed, still comparing her with his deceased first wife, does not give her all his love. She is tormented by the thought that the Prophet cannot forget Khadija, who was both ugly and much older than he. Reproaching him for this, she asks: "How is it possible to love such an ugly old woman who is already dead and to ignore a young beautiful living one who loves you?" The Prophet replies: "There was something in her . . . something eternal, Aisha."

In *Aisha and Mohammed* Lesya stresses the idea of an eternal love founded not on outward appearance but on spiritual understanding, on the close union of souls which survives beyond death. It is quite probable that Lesya Ukrainka's own personal life exercised a considerable influence in refining the delicate psychological texture of this theme.

Like *On The Field of Blood*, *Aisha and Mohammed* possesses all the virtues of a dramatic dialogue. The piece is constructed on logical premises and exhibits great economy of expression. In addition, the dramatist has satisfactorily co-ordinated her own opinions with the comments of the characters, giving expression to her most intimate feelings.

In June 1909, while in Telavi, Lesya wrote a dramatic study, *Yohanna, Zhinka Khusova*, a piece thematically related to *Aisha and Mohammed*. In it the dramatist portrays the tragedy of a wife in much gloomier tones. She has taken a traditional subject from a period of Jewish history when the new ideals of Christianity had begun to take root.

The action takes place during the Roman occupation after the death of Christ, and, specifically, in the home of Khus, a Jewish official. Called by the teaching of Christ, Johanna, the wife of Khus, leaves her home to follow Him, evoking the anger of Khus who cannot understand his wife's idealistic motives. After Christ is crucified the sorrowing Johanna returns home at the very moment when Khus, an opportunist eager to serve Rome, is making preparations to entertain Publius, a distinguished Roman, and his wife Martia. Johanna is subjected in her own home to extreme humiliation through her husband's mockery and insults. The dramatic tension rises to a powerful climax when, forced to dress herself in the garments of one of her husband's concubines, she is compelled to extend hospitality to the enemies of her people. The tension is further heightened by the conflict between the two different and mutually alien worlds. Khus is lacking in all moral values, and, while adulating his strong oppressors, he acts as a tyrant in his own home. The idealism which moved Johanna to follow Christ is completely beyond his comprehension; dissolute himself, he accuses his wife of loose behaviour. The idealist Johanna, seeking a higher form of life, is thus hurled by fate into the immoral home of Khus and turns into a lonely, defenceless and deeply humiliated figure. In her grief she lifts up her hands and cries: "Oh, Lord! how long this suffering? Master! why have you forsaken me?"

In her earlier dramatic works the characters speak in logical syllogisms; here the poetess builds up her dramatic tension by baring the soul of a human being. Miriyam, for instance, by logical reasoning reveals the tragic conflict and the granite strength of her principles, but only at the cost of the finer impulses of her soul. The anguished soul of Johanna is illuminated not by logical argumentation, but by the "realism," by the life-like psychology and the diverse personalities of the characters. We are acquainted with Khus' immorality long before Johanna, or Publius, or Martia appear; the stifling atmosphere of his home soon becomes apparent from the few comments of his proud and ambitious mother, Melkil.

Within the darkness of Khus' home we see Johanna's longing for the light of life, for the noble "world of truth, and goodness, and love, and freedom." Khus never hesitates to sacrifice everything, no matter where or when, in order to secure safety for himself, especially while under foreign domination. His crafty behaviour and his desire to change his name to a Roman-sounding one remind us of some of the poetess' fellow-countrymen who never failed, in times of political upheaval, to gain an advantageous position for themselves and who did not hesitate to betray the national and cultural traditions of their people.

The theme of the tragic destiny of a woman in her own home could also have been suggested to the dramatist by family life in Georgia where the women occupied a clearly subordinate position. One can hardly avoid seeing in Johanna's yearning for a "world of truth, and goodness, and love, and freedom," the poetess' own longing for the new world and the new man, a longing begotten by the sad reality of her times.

AFTER WRITING *The Azure Rose* Lesya began the search for a new dramatic style and a new genre. First she turned to the old Hellenic motifs, and, while staying during the winter of 1897–8 at the villa *Iphigenia* in Yalta, she completed the dramatic study *Iphigenia v Tavrydi* (Iphigenia in Taurus) which was initially planned as a dramatic poem in two acts. Abandoning this plan, the poetess reconstructed it into what she herself called a "dramatic *étude*," and, as such, included it in the cycle of her poems, *Kryms'ki Vidhuky* (Crimean Echoes). It is quite possible that her original plan to write a dramatic poem about Iphigenia was suggested primarily by Euripides, although the influence of Goethe's *Iphigenia* should not be underestimated.[66] It is also possible that, having failed to complete her original plan because of the great demands it made upon her, she limited herself to a dramatic *étude*. In the course of her work on *Iphigenia*, she came across Lord Byron's *Cain*, which made a deep impression upon her. She became over-critical of her own abilities and as a result abandoned her original plan to write *Iphigenia in Taurus* as a dramatic poem.[67]

The subject comes from the well-known Greek myth. When the Greeks set out against Troy, a hostile wind prevented their ships from leaving the shore. The priest saw in this the displeasure of the gods and prophesied that the goddess Artemis would relent only when Agamemnon had sacrificed to her his daughter Iphigenia. Artemis, however, did not intend the death of Iphigenia, and, when Iphigenia voluntarily stepped on the sacrificial altar to offer her life for the victory of Hellas over Troy, the goddess Artemis removed her to Taurus where the young maid became her favourite priestess.

The action of the piece takes place in the city of Partenit in Taurus, before the temple of the Tauridian Artemis. First, there appears a chorus of maidens praising the goddess Artemis in traditional strophes and antistrophes. Iphigenia appears to make her sacrifice to the goddess and together with the chorus praises her. As the chorus withdraws to the temple Iphigenia reveals in a long monologue her poignant longing for her native land.

Neither her heart nor her thoughts are with the goddess Artemis, but far away in sunny Hellas. Everything most dear to her, "family,

[66]Babyshkin, 47.   [67]*Ibid.*, 52.

fame, youth, love," she left there and she lives here, in Taurus, alone "like the shadow of a forgotten being." Memories of her loved ones— her sister Electra, her brother Orestes, and her betrothed Achilles— torment her soul. The autumnal landscape of Taurus only serves to remind her of the perpetual spring of Hellas and deepens her nostalgia. Iphigenia, although weakened by longing and sorrow, feels within her soul the sacred fire of Prometheus which had dried her tears when "she boldly walked to be sacrificed for the honour and glory of her native Hellas." In her moment of despair, the Promethean spirit forbids her to commit suicide and commands her to live in spite of her suffering. She accepts her fate "when for the glory of her native land / Such sacrifice Artemis does command." For the sake of the love she bears Hellas, which demands a sacrifice from her, she resolves to continue her sorrowful life as a priestess in the temple of Artemis in Taurus.

Indeed, this is a short study in the power of the Promethean spirit; Iphigenia suppresses her personal feelings for the sake of a higher ideal, that of serving her beloved Hellas. There is however no trace of "declared" patriotism. We see in the heroine a natural development of thought and feeling. The nostalgia, which evokes the thought of suicide, intensifies the tragic tone. And when it seems that the dreaded Fate Moira remains implacable, the sacred fire of Prometheus, left to mankind as the god's inheritance, revives Iphigenia's strength to live.

Already in this early work we note the Promethean spirit which was to predominate in the later dramatic works. Iphigenia is a beautiful prelude to the heroines of such dramatic works as *Boyarynya, Orgiya,* and most of all, *Cassandra.*

It was in the dramatic poem *Cassandra,* regarded by the poetess as one of her best dramatic works, that she fully developed a classical theme. While her *Iphigenia in Taurus* portrays only one episode from the myth which Euripides had already so superbly presented in his *Iphigenia Among the Tauri* and in *Iphigenia at Aulis,* Lesya's *Cassandra* stands out as an independent and original work. It is a meticulously wrought version of the antique theme so frequently met in ancient Greek literature and to which Western European authors also have devoted much attention.

Lesya Ukrainka took a long time to write *Cassandra;* the numerous variants that have survived in her notebooks indicate the prolonged attention she bestowed upon this dramatic poem. She worked on *Cassandra* during the two winters of 1901–2 and 1902–3 while staying in San Remo on the Italian Riviera. When almost complete the work was put aside for several years, and, it was not until 1907 in the Crimea, a land steeped in legends of antiquity, and after reworking the seventh and eighth scene and adding an epilogue, that she completed the final edition of the dramatic poem.

From earliest times tales of the Trojan war, particularly those about the fair daughter of Priam and Hecuba, have fired the imagination of poets. In the *Iliad* Homer speaks of her as the most beautiful daughter of King Priam but does not endow her with prophetic powers. Aeschylus in *Orestes* and Euripides in the *Trojan Women* mention her only episodically. Nor does Virgil pay much attention to her in *The Aeneid*, although in it she has acquired the gift of prophecy. Cassandra also appears as a motif in Seneca, the imitator of the Greek tragedians, and in the works of the French Classicists. As Alexander Biletsky remarked: "All the tragedians and the later compilers failed to enrich the legend of Cassandra with any new episodes and almost all of them end up by making Appollo bestow upon Cassandra the gift of prophecy when she promised to love him."[68] When she failed to keep her promise he punished her by seeing to it that no one believed the prophecies she made. Thus, when her brother Paris arrived with Helen in Troy and also later when the Trojan war broke out, she foretold disaster for the Trojans, but she was laughed at and thought to be mad. When the booty was divided after the fall of Troy, she was allotted to Agamemnon and with him came to Mycenae where both were slain by Aegisthus and Agamemnon's wife, Clytaemnestra.

Beginning with the second half of the nineteenth century we notice, particularly in the works of German authors, an attempt to make Cassandra the central figure of a tragedy as well as to introduce new motifs into this traditional classical subject.

It was Lesya Ukrainka's intention to end the first version of this dramatic poem with a scene depicting Cassandra's arrival in Mycenae and her tragic resolve to refuse the marvellous gift of prophecy, a scene which Aeschylus portrays in *Agamemnon*, the first part of the *Orestes* trilogy. She soon realized, however, that such an epilogue, following upon the tragic scene of the fall of Troy, would weaken the play's artistic impression on the reader. Consequently, in accordance with the author's wish, the epilogue is not included in the text of the play.[69]

[68]O. Bilets'kyy, "Trahediya Pravdy," *Tvory Les'i Ukrainky*, VI, 122.
[69]*Ibid.*, 123.

Lesya Ukrainka's conception of Cassandra may have been influenced by Schiller's famous poem "Kassandra," by Homer, and to some extent by Aeschylus, Euripides, and Virgil, in whose works the poetess found both superficial and detailed portrayals of the heroine. She may also have been influenced by Shakespeare's *Troilus and Cressida*, where Cassandra appears twice on the stage.[70] The poetess followed none of the existing patterns of this theme but worked out her own, developing some of the suggestions and details she had discovered in the classical sources. In her choice of characters she exhibits an impressive independence, limiting herself to a bare minimum of episodes that take up a great deal of space in other classical works. Lesya Ukrainka placed the main accent on the dialogue, which follows an antithetical pattern in the revelation of Cassandra's tragedy.

The central figure of the piece is Cassandra herself; all the other characters and the restricted action which takes place against the setting of the Trojan war off-stage provide only such background as is necessary to support the antithesis or to uphold the central idea.

The opening scene shows Cassandra and Helen, their first few comments revealing the gulf between them. On the one side is the Trojan prophetess who clearly sees the cause of her family's destruction, and on the other side, the beautiful Helen who has become the light-hearted mistress of Cassandra's brother, Paris. In her prophetic vision Cassandra sees the tragic consequences for Troy of Helen's arrival.

In the second scene Cassandra reveals to her sister, Polyxena, and to her sister-in-law, Andromache, the fate awaiting them. Polyxena is not to become Achilles' wife, and Andromache will lose her beloved husband, Hector. The scene unveils the tragic fate of Cassandra, a gentle maiden unhappy in her own love, whose gift of prophecy weighs heavily upon her destiny. To her closest and dearest ones she foretells the disaster which she continually sees in her visions.

In the third scene Cassandra's dark prophecy is realized. While Hector is fighting in hand-to-hand combat with Achilles, Andromache discovers that her husband's strength is weakening, and blames Cassandra for uttering the malicious words which affect Hector's fate. When word arrives that Hector has fallen in battle Cassandra, in her despair, begins to admit the possible validity of Andromache's reproaches. "Not fear, not shame, and not the sword, but with my truth I ruined my brother," she cries out in despair.

70Ibid., 127.

Cassandra's tragedy deepens in the fourth scene in which, together with herself and Polyxena, appears her former fiancé, Dolon. Commissioned by Cassandra's brothers to scout in the Achaean camp, he encounters Cassandra who sees his approaching death but, conscious of the omnipotence of Fate does not prevent him who is so dear to her from departing into the enemy camp. A Greek slays Dolon almost before Cassandra's eyes. Horror stricken she blames herself for his death. Her tragedy is that foreseeing disaster she is powerless to avert it; for Fate is ineluctable and implacable. Her divine gift turns into a curse; it leaves her passive to approaching evil and turns her into a lonely being despised even by her dearest ones.

In the fifth scene Cassandra is powerless to prevent the massacre of Œnomeus' troops. Œnomeus is the Lydian king whom her brothers, desirous of his aid in their war against the Greeks, wished to match with Cassandra against her will. She even draws upon her head the curses of her family and friends, who believe that her prophesies have destroyed the Lydians. It is quite true that Cassandra repulses Andromache and Polyxena from her; any dream, any illusion is better for Andromache than the grim truth continually foreseen by Cassandra.

The pattern of naked truth on the one hand, confronted with illusion and falsehood on the other is developed in detail in the sixth scene. Cassandra is presented as the exponent of a starkly grim veracity. At the same time, Cassandra's brother Helenus, a seer who never fails to make use of falsehood for his own ends, appears in dramatic contrast to the heroine. He is a man of pragmatic views who represents the concept of relativity of all values. According to him, truth does not beget language, but language begets truth. Following the line of this argument, Cassandra becomes the cause of every disaster. The philosophical content of this section is connected to the central motif of Schiller's ballad: *Nur der Irrtum ist das Leben, und das Wissen ist der Tod* . . . (Life is only in ignorance, and knowledge is death . . .).[71]

The seventh scene has more action than all the previous ones. Helenus announces to the Trojans that the Achaeans have abandoned the siege of the city and have left the gift of a horse for the Trojan gods. Cassandra foresees the fall of Troy, as well as the treachery of Sinon, the Greek left behind with the horse. When she disagrees with Helenus that the Greek prisoner should be spared, he gives her the sword to slay him. Cassandra, however, weakens and cannot bring the sword down on the neck of the Greek spy. Her clear prophetic

[71]*Schillers Werke*, I (München: D.V.Th.K.N.), 175.

perception on the one hand and her weak femininity on the other deepen her spiritual conflict and her tragedy.

All Cassandra's prophecies are fulfilled in the eighth scene: the Greeks destroy Troy and take the Trojans into captivity. Andromache's curses fall on her because her terrible forecasts have come true. Thus she triumphs over the false Helenus but remains despised as the exponent of unpalatable truth.

Two closely allied themes are interwoven in the play: the development and deepening of the tragic element, and the philosophical problem of truth, the problem of the power of the word. Cassandra's tragedy is that, although she is blessed with prophetic powers, she cannot take action to influence the turn of events. Her words remain far removed from deeds. Like Iphigenia, Cassandra is a true descendant of Prometheus and refuses to submit to the will of the gods who are only slaves of Fate. She becomes the embodiment of the lofty principles of the truth for which she suffers like Prometheus before her. Nevertheless, the mark of human weakness is still perceptible on her; she remains passive and hesitates at a crucial moment.

Such philosophical problems as the question of absolute truth, of principle versus pragmatism, and contingency and the relativity of ideas, the concepts of good and evil and the meaning of the power of the word, are also raised.

THE DRAMATIC POEM *U Puschi* took longer to write than did *Cassandra*. Lesya began to work on it in 1897. In 1899, while at the family summer home, she wrote the first, the third, and part of the second act. Then she abandoned the poem for several years. In 1907, when the doctors informed her of the critical state of her health, she began to concentrate on her unfinished literary works. While in the Crimea, during the months of August and September of that year, she completed *U Puschi* by re-editing the previously written parts and writing a judgment scene for the second act.

The idea and the plan of the drama came to her in 1895 during her stay with her uncle in Sofia. Drahomaniv had suggested that she should write a biography of John Milton, and acquainted her with the appropriate literature about the English Puritans and their colonization of North America. The proposed biography of Milton did not materialize but, strongly influenced by the works on Puritan colonization, Lesya conceived the idea of writing about an artist whose fate had tossed him about the world and forced him to live in the American wilderness. She started work on this drama after studying a number

of sources dealing with the life of the Puritans, chief among which
was *Milton und seine Zeit* by Alfred Stern (Leipzig, 1877–79), a
book which she had in her own library. In addition, she perused the
history of the colonization of North America, devoting special attention to Roger Williams, in whom Drahomaniv was particularly
interested. Richard Aron, the main character of Lesya's drama,
reminds one of Roger Williams, a New England public figure who
was sentenced to exile in 1635 by a Massachusetts court because of
his opposition to the State's interference with religious affairs. While
in exile he founded the city of Providence, an event which stimulated
the settlement of colonists in Rhode Island. Although the conflict of
U Puschi is not theological, "Richard's problem resembles in many
ways the aspirations of Roger Williams: freedom of conscience and
the individual's right to choose his own destiny."[72]

The action of this dramatic poem takes place in North America in
the seventeenth century: the first two acts in the Puritan colony in
Massachusetts; the last act in Rhode Island. Richard Aron is a talented
sculptor. In his youth he had studied art in Venice, where the Italian
masters predicted a bright future for him. In his quest for freedom
and in his desire to give unconstrained expression to his ambitions, he
departs for America with his compatriots. But Richard is frustrated
in his new Puritan environment: instead of freedom he finds spiritual
slavery. The Puritan leader Godvinson, whom the Puritans reverently
and submissively obey, sharply criticizes Richard for his free thinking,
lack of spiritual submission, and his artistic endeavours. Richard, for
whom freedom of spirit and conscience and freedom of artistic expression are the highest values, finds himself isolated in a Puritan colony,
misunderstood and condemned even by his own mother. The in-
tolerant Puritan society, roused by Godvinson, destroys his statues and
subsequently exiles him. Richard finds his way to Rhode Island,
where he is invited to teach, and there the last act of his tragedy
takes place.

The people in Rhode Island also fail to respect and appreciate his
talent and art, since they are interested only in pragmatic accomplish-
ments. Richard slowly loses faith in his lofty ideas on art and has to
witness the deterioration of his talent. He is painfully aware of the
contrast between his noble dreams and the bitter reality of Puritan
life. Inspiration deserts him. An old friend, an emissary from Venice,
urges him to return to Italy, but without success. Having lost faith

---

[72]P. Fylypovych, "Heneza dramatychnoyi poemy Les'i Ukrainky *U Puschi*," *Tvory
Les'i Ukrainky*, IX, 10.

in himself and deprived of his former artistic genius, Richard has reached an impasse in life. The drama ends with his impassioned and pessimistic plea: "When will the angel of death call me? I have a premonition that he will soon come."

Skilful stage direction, vivacity of dialogue, and an excellent handling of contrast combined with strength and harmony of diction are the chief merits of this drama. Here action predominates to a greater degree than in her earlier plays. Richard's monologues in the third act contain passages of remarkable lyrical beauty.

In *U Puschi* the playwright expressed her personal views on the relationship between life and art. She pictured life as an obstacle to the realization of an artist's aspiration and ideals. The harsh conditions under which Lesya wrote her works and the merciless censorship to which they were subjected in tsarist Russia are echoed in the play. The spiritual isolation of Richard is typical of the spiritual situation of the playwright herself. In many cases her plays were misunderstood by her contemporaries. *U Puschi* is full of echoes of Lesya's intimate and painful thoughts on the basic problems of life and art, reality and the ideal. The poet was plagued with these problems throughout most of her creative life.

WHILE SOME of her plays were written over the course of several years, some were completed in a remarkably short space of time. To such works belongs *Boyarynya* (The Boyar's Wife), which she wrote at Helwan on June 27th and 28th, 1910.

Boyarynya differs significantly from the rest of her plays in its character, and in the lack of usual subject-matter and symbolism. In it she speaks directly and realistically, turning her attention to the Ukrainian national theme—perhaps indirectly suggested by those critics who reproached her for excessive attention to foreign themes. The fact is, however, that Ukrainian themes were never alien to Lesya. She began her dramatic output with the *Blakytna Troyanda* and the dialogue *Praschannya*, the themes of which are taken from Ukrainian life. The action of *Lisowa Pisnya* takes place in the Ukraine, against the background of the Volhynian landscape and it is well known that she intended to write a series of works with Ukrainian historical and legendary figures as heroes. Her prolonged stay at foreign health-resorts, far from her native Ukraine, gave rise to a longing in her for those she loved, a longing that roused her interest in Ukrainian themes.

Boyarynya deals with the Hetmanate of Peter Doroshenko who, during the so-called era of "Ruin," attempted to unite the Ukrainian lands. After the death of Hetman Bohdan Khmelnyts'ky Ukraine had become an object of political intrigue between Moscow and Warsaw.

The heroine of *Boyarynya* is Oksana, a daughter of a well-known Ukrainian cossack. On marrying Stepan, a young Ukrainian, she leaves with him for Moscow where he is a boyar and a member of the tsar's entourage. Once in Moscow, Oksana comes into contact with a different and alien world. She, like other women in the Muscovite state, in the seventeenth century, is deprived of her freedom and her equality with men. Her subordinate position, the foreign environment, and strange and difficult customs awaken longings for her native Ukraine. The hostile attitude of the Muscovite world towards the Ukrainian national liberation movement under the leadership of Hetman Doroshenko deepens Oksana's feelings of estrangement and grief. As a result of her troubles Oksana falls seriously ill. Stepan suggests they should return to Ukraine, believing that this will improve her health. Oksana, however, rejects this plan to visit her fatherland where the liberation movement led by Hetman Doroshenko has already been suppressed by Moscow. In her opinion, Stepan has no right to return to Ukraine because during the bloody struggle for liberation he remained passive in the service of the tsar. Her fatherland remains for her a cherished dream and as she dies she bids farewell: "Goodnight, dear sun! You are setting in the west. . . . You see the Ukraine—greet her for me!"

In the drama Lesya Ukrainka expressed her deep patriotism and her grief at the unfortunate lot of her fatherland. Here we find her views on problems of her peoples' political independence, and cultural and national identity. Although *Boyarynya* has an historical colouring, one can easily detect ideas related to the problems of her own age. As Mykhaylo Dray-Khmara indicates:

In the person of Stepan one sees that typical Ukrainian public figure of the late nineteenth and early twentieth century who detaches himself from his people and loses his feeling of national identity; thus finding himself in a foreign environment whose culture he accepts, he rejects his native cultural traditions. In the person of Oksana one sees another type of public figure who for a long time struggles, agitates and protests for the principle of national self-determination, but who, on finding herself trapped in the wills of tsarist service, is unable to free herself and as a result dies in this strange and foreign land.[73]

Disregarding the fact that *Boyarynya* is a psychological rather than

[73]Mykhaylo Dray-Khmara, "Boyarynya," *Tvory Les'i Ukrainky*, VIII, 97.

an historical drama, one finds therein Lesya Ukrainka's thorough knowledge of the historical, cultural, and social environment of seventeenth century Ukraine. Certain motifs and details found in the drama indicate that the playwright was well acquainted with historical works, such as Mykola Kostomariv's work *Ruina* and *Istoriya Rusiv* of unknow author. Also evident is Lesya Ukrainka's deep knowledge of the Bible, a book which was her constant companion.

Although *Boyarynya* may seem to occupy a distinct place in Lesya Ukrainka's dramatic work, judged by its ideas and its expressive media, it is closely related to a number of her lyrical and dramatic works. The motif of nostalgia, which permeates *Boyarynya* and often repeats itself in her lyrics, is also strongly emphasized in *Iphigenia v Tavrydi*, *Vavylons'ky polon*, *Na Ruyinach*, *Try Khvylyny*, and *U Puschi*.

In all of these works much emphasis is laid on love for one's fatherland. Oksana epitomizes Lesya's feminine characters. They are endowed with tenderness and great strength of will, as well as profound and original thought combined with deep emotions.

LESYA UKRAINKA's next drama *Lisowa Pisnya*, a fairytale which she had long wanted to dramatize, was also on a Ukrainian theme. Written in Kutaisi in the summer of 1911, *Lisowa Pisnya* is based on the popular legends, stories, and folksongs familiar to her from youthful days in Volhynia.

The prevalent currents of neo-romanticism and symbolism which appeared in European literature at the beginning of the twentieth century and the rebirth of the Novalis cult of "living nature" in great measure influenced the creation *Lisowa Pisnya*. At the same time several other works appeared in Ukrainian literature containing popular songs, stories, and folklore. Two were novels: Olha Kolylyans'ka's *V Nedilyu Rano Zillya Kopala* (Picking Herbs on a Sunday Morning) and Mykhaylo Kots'ubyns'ky's *T'in'i Zabutykh Predkiv* (The Shadows of Forgotten Ancestors). And the young poet Aleksander Oles' used, in his dramatic poem *Nad Dnistrom* (Along the Dniester River), the same motif of the nymph which is also found in *Lisowa Pisnya*.

The nearest parallel in contemporary European literature to Lesya Ukrainka's fairytale is Gerhart Hauptmann's *Die Versunkene Glocke*. In both works a strong romantic undercurrent is evident; both works have folklore elements; the real is intermingled with fantasy; mystery and magic fill a world where the human being becomes one with nature and nature transcends the boundaries of the human order.

Lisowa Pisnya as well as *Die Versunkene Glocke* revolves around the same basic theme: fairies fall in love with men and enter the real world, where they suffer and eventually perish.[74] However, it would be incorrect to conclude that Lesya Ukrainka wrote her fairytale under the influence of Hauptmann. Comparative analysis reveals a marked difference between the two.

It was not only the contemporary rebirth of romanticism in literature that prompted Lesya to write *Lisowa Pisnya*. Nostalgia for her native country never ceased to haunt her. As her illness grew more acute, the more intensely did she recollect her youth, her carefree childhood days in the beautiful Volhynian countryside. In one of her letters to her mother she says that her nostalgia for the Volhynian forests remind her of Mavka, the forest nymph of popular Volhynian legend.

This was not the only story her mother had told her: there were many others and many of them found their way into *Lisowa Pisnya*. In her memoirs, the poet's sister, Olha Kosach-Kryvynyuk wrote: "In Lesya's *Lisowa Pisnya* there is not one character, not one belief, not one melody with which I am not acquainted; all of them are from Polissya and are familiar to me. I heard and knew them all while still at Kolodyazhne. . . ."[75]

Olha mentions a trip they had made in their childhood into a thick forest in which was a bottomless lake. During this journey they stayed at their "Uncle Lev's" and slept three nights in a hayloft, from which they viewed the landscape which Lesya was to portray. It was precisely here that, "while walking through the forest and round the lake, and sitting long hours by the camp fire, we heard from Uncle Lev many tales about the forest, the lake and the field spirits, their customs and their relationships with each other and with human beings."[76]

Her childhood recollections, together with the figure of Mavka remained in the poet's imagination for many years; and shortly before her death they found expression in this masterpiece of hers, which stands alone in Ukrainian literature. Here are reflected her love for the folklore of her native Volhynia and the weird denizens of the forests just as the dense Volhynian forest is reflected on the surface of the bottomless lake.

---

[74]Viktor Petrov, "Lisowa Pisnya," *Tvory Les'i Ukrainky*, VIII, 165.
[75]Ol'ha Kosach-Kryvynyuk, "Z Moyikh Spomyniv," *Lesya Ukrainka, Publikatsiyi, Statt'i i Doslidzhennya*, III (Kyiv: Vyd-vo an USSR, 1960), 339.
[76]*Ibid.*, 339.

Lesya wrote *Lisowa Pisnya* rapidly, caught up by her inspiration: "I myself am not indifferent to my literary creation, since it [*Lisowa Pisnya*] gave me many more pleasant and enjoyable moments of ecstasy than any other work."[77] In a confidential remark to her friend, Olha Kobylyans'ka, she admitted that inspiration for her last drama *Orgiya* fell far short of that which had gone into *Lisowa Pisnya* and *Kaminnyy Hospodar*. In fact, never again could she be as completely involved.

Lesya started to write *Lisowa Pisnya* in prose, but soon reworked it into verse form, which she immediately re-edited without setting it aside as she had done with her other works. The main features of the first draft, the basic idea of the plot, and all the significant scenes of the drama remained unchanged.[78] She had nurtured the idea of *Lisowa Pisnya* so long, and the theme lay so close to her heart that it literally "flowed" from her pen as a completed work.

She created a kingdom of mermaids, forest-nymphs, and forest and water spirits, the figures which popular mythology uses to personify the forces of nature. This mythical world is shown to be in close relationship with man, and the boundary between the real and the fantastic is blurred. In the meeting of these two worlds lies the action of the drama. The forest-nymph falls in love with Lukash, a man who plays the flute. Enchanted by his song, the forest-nymph acquires a human soul, leaves the forest, and goes to live with people as an expression of the depth of her love. She begins to experience suffering, her happy existence as a forest-queen having gone forever. The real world of people is filled with notions and ideas which are incomprehensible to her; pragmatism, scheming, and self-seeking are the order of the day. Meeting human beings and leading an every-day life, exemplified by Lukash's practical and calculating mother, Mavka endures unbearable sufferings which assume tragic proportions. She has sacrificed her former happy state for the sake of her boundless love for Lukash, but this love is thwarted and undermined. A peasant girl, Kalyna, whom Lukash's mother prefers as a daughter-in-law, comes between Mavka and Lukash. The spring, which saw Mavka's love develop, turns into late summer. Luxuriant nature gradually loses its beauty and Mavka notices something strange and incomprehensible in Lukash's behaviour. Autumn arrives and her tragedy deepens. Finally, nature and Mavka are enfolded in the deep sleep of winter.

The whole play develops like the four seasons of the year and is

[77] *Lesya Ukrainka, Tvory v pyaty tomach,* T.V. 611.
[78] Babyshkin, 230.

subjected to the process of change typical of nature. In this drama, human actions are synchronized with the life of nature, a theme that involves the romantic philosophical notion of "living nature." The story of Mavka, the forest-sprite who acquires a "psyche," is an attempt at the symbolic and mythical re-creation of nature.[79]

Lisowa Pisnya deals with the theme of pure love which transforms earthly desires into eternal ones. The tragedy of Mavka is acute because she becomes a martyr to love by acquiring a human soul and thus undermines Lukash's happiness. There is in *Lisowa Pisnya* a joyous affirmation of life. In its essence, life is eternal, indestructible as is nature itself; for after autumn and winter there comes spring again, where the end becomes a new beginning. All material things of life pass but eternal values such as love, beauty, and happiness remain.

Two years before her death, as the end of her life drew near, the problems of eternal life found explicit manifestation in this masterpiece. In *Lisowa Pisnya*, Lesya Ukrainka gave voice to her idealistic outlook and convictions.

The artistic strength which inspired Lesya during this period was reflected also in her dramatic technique. Here the metrics of the verse are employed according to the psychological disposition of the protagonists. Typically her verses are written in five-foot iambic metre and blank verse. Here, the frequent changes of metrical form and complicated structure reflect a high degree of emotion. As Babyshkin writes:

A mighty lyrical stream has drowned *Lisowa Pisnya*. As a lyric writer par excellence, Lesya Ukrainka has contrasted in this work a purely feminine tenderness, a sensitive human heart, genuine beauty of feeling, and a sublime dream of happiness and love . . . with staleness, coarseness, brutality and indifference to beauty. . . .[80]

The play is the embodiment of a philosophy of life, as revealed in its subject-matter. Manipulation of contrast is combined with deep lyricism and artistic perfection, making *Lisowa Pisnya* a masterpiece of Ukrainian literature.

THE RETURN to the Ukrainian theme in *Boyarynya* and *Lisowa Pisnya* was only a brief interlude in the creative process of Lesya Ukrainka. While living in Khoni (now Tsulukidze) in Georgia, she wrote a dramatic poem, *Advokat Martiyan* (The Lawyer Martian), which

[79]Petrov, 159.   [80]Babyshkin, 255.

again draws on historical material from early Christianity. It was as if, after a brief respite to get a breath of fresh air from nature and the historical past of her native land, she now returned again to the world of antiquity.

The action of this drama takes place in the third century when Christians were severely persecuted but nevertheless had already gained a large following in Roman society. Thus, as regards theme, this play is related to her works *V Katakombakh* and *Rufin i Pristsilla*. Critics often consider *Advokat Martiyan* as the acme of Lesya Ukrainka's works.[81]

The lawyer Martiyan is a deeply religious man but on the instructions of Christian leaders, he is forced to conceal his faith in order to defend the accused Christians during their trials. His daughter, Aurelia, and son, Valentian, have been brought up as Christians but because of the predicament in which their father finds himself they also are obliged to conceal this. Such a state of affairs disrupts Martiyan's family life. His wife, Tullia, who has found it impossible to put up with such an atmosphere in her home, has left Martiyan to live with a rich pagan as his wife. To retain his Christianity Martiyan has to detach himself from the world. His children live alone and are deprived of the warmth of ordinary family happiness and the opportunity to lead a Christian life whose essence they see not in passivity but in sacrifice and heroism. Consequently, they too leave their father. Aurelia goes to her mother without saying goodbye to him and Valentian, eager for action but deprived of opportunity to defend his faith, enlists in the army.

Thus, Martiyan, who has devoted his life to promoting the Christian cause, is left alone and forsaken. His tragedy, however, does not end here. When an impulsive Christian youth, Ardent, is hotly pursued by guards for demolishing a statue of Caesar, Martiyan denies him protection at his house for fear of betraying himself as a Christian. Yet Ardent's father when dying a martyr's death named Martiyan guardian of his son. Ardent deprived of help and protection curses Martiyan. The guards who question Ardent and search Martiyan's home frighten Ardent's young niece Lucilla to such a degree that she dies, leaving her mother in despair. Thus Martiyan is instrumental in the death of his niece and the bereavement of his sister.

Although Martiyan has suffered so much in the name of Christianity, he does not give way to despair but continues to work. But outside his work there is nothing worth while in life for him.

[81]*Ibid.*, 258.

The dramatic tension so successfully created and maintained in this play is based not only on the tragic motivation, but also on the powerfully portrayed contrast between Martiyan's unfortunate lot and his lofty ideals as a person and Christian. He is a virtuous man, a hero who remains faithful to his duty. The hardships he experiences in life he endures manfully, neither grumbling nor cringing.

The harsh political conditions in the Ukraine prompted the playwright to create a person endowed with the ideals necessary to undertake the task which faced this subjugated nation. Martiyan's unyielding spirit, his steadfastness of faith, and his readiness to sacrifice his life honourably for the sake of higher ideals are the marks of a person who, on finding himself in the political turmoil of the time, was able to lead a new life and realize the great idea of a new religion.

The *Lawyer Martiyan*, which consists of two parts, presents only a single episode in the life of the principal character. All the action takes place in one day but, in spite of its brevity, the work is a rare example of terse strength. There are no monologues in the play nor any superfluous words or scenes. Though the playwright spares words, she is generous in her stage directions. In them she portrays the background, the environment and the psychological atmosphere. The structure of the play is symmetrical and well-proportioned. These qualities make the *Lawyer Martiyan* one of Lesya's best achievements.

LESYA UKRAINKA's interest in universal themes led her to write, as we have seen, many works based on Biblical, early Christian, and classical plots. But, in May 1912, while living in Kutaisi, she wrote a drama the outline and details of which she had elaborated during the winter of 1911–12. The subject was the Don Juan story and it was under these circumstances that she composed *Kaminnyy Hospodar*, which, with *Lisowa Pisnya*, is the culmination of her dramatic creation.

At the beginning of the seventeenth century, Tirso de Molina wrote *El Burlado de Sevilla y Convidado de Riedra* which was largely based on medieval Spanish legends. This comedy became the model for numerous versions of the Don Juan theme in world literature.[82] During the course of the century the Don Juan theme spread to other countries outside Spain. First it reached Italy where it became a part of the repertoire of the *Commedia dell' Arte*. Then the Italian artists

[82]Laffont-Bompiani, *Dictionnaire des œuvres*, II (Société d'édition de dictionnaires et encylopédies), 84.

took it to Paris where, in 1657, they successfully presented a number
of their comedies. While in France, the theme was reworked by
Molière, who, in his comedy, *Don Juan, ou Le Festin de Pierre*,
portrayed Don Juan as a seducer and an idler. Here for the first time
Don Juan appears as a representative of a social *milieu*. Molière's
comedy was a model for a similar work written by Corneille, which
enjoyed great popularity on the Parisian stage. Hoffmann freely
imitated Mozart's *Don Juan* by writing a novel under the same title.
Hoffmann's work, besides its romantic elements, reveals a strong
tendency to interpret the theme along mystical and philosophical lines.

In German Romantic literature the Don Juan legend very often
approaches and even fuses with the Faust legend. Hence there is a
close similarity between the Romance hero and his northern counter-
part.[83] Both Faust and Don Juan are sinners with an unquenchable
desire to comprehend the supernatural. Both characters display a spirit
of revolt and pride and attempt to transgress the laws of society; the
former for the sake of knowledge, the latter for sheer enjoyment.[84]
In this manner the Romantics try to rehabilitate the Spanish sinner
and to forgive his former evil deeds in the light of his new striving
for the ideal.

Byron, however, approached the Don Juan motif quite differently.
In his epic satire, Don Juan, he departed from the traditional scheme
of the subject-matter. As Dashkevych writes: "Of the ancient legend
only the name has been preserved, a name which has an aristocratic
origin, an enchanting fascination of character and a general outline of
the literary type. Besides, there is a disregard for the generally accepted
moral code and a propensity for amorous adventures."[85]

The action of Byron's *Don Juan* takes place in the eighteenth
century. The supernatural element was jettisoned by Byron and the
negative features found in Molière's hero are modified, even purified
in his poem. Pushkin, on the other hand, developed the theme in the
manner of Hoffmann rather than of Mozart or Molière. His play
Kamennyy Gost' (The Stone Guest) represents a quite original version
of the old legend. Both Hoffmann and Pushkin made an attempt to
rehabilitate Don Juan; the latter giving mystical features to his hero,
whereas, the former concentrates on his frivolity and joyous living.

---

[83]Ye. Nenadkevych, "Ukrains'ka Versiya Svitovoyi Temy pro Don Zhuana v
Istorychniy Perspektyvi," *Tvory Les'i Ukrainky*, XI, 12.
[84]*Ibid.*
[85]Prof. Dashkevych, *Vstupna stattya do "Don Zhuana,"* III (Bayrona: Vyd.
Brockhaus-Yefron), 200.

The tendency to justify Don Juan's actions appears also in *Les Ames du Purgatoire* and *Namouna*, works by Prosper Mérimée and Musset, respectively. Following Mérimée's conception of Don Juan, Alexander Dumas père wrote *Don Juan de Marana ou La Chute d'un Ange* in which he developed the romantic motif of salvation for Don Juan's soul. Dumas' drama in turn influenced a talented Spanish poet, de Zorilla, whose *Don Juan Tenorio* ranks as an outstanding work of nineteenth century Spanish literature. De Zorilla depicts the salvation of the sinful hero through his genuine love for a girl. The influence of de Zorilla and of Hoffmann is also noticeable in Alexey Tolstoy's poetic drama, *Don Juan*. A German writer, Paul von Heyse, also treated this theme in a rather original manner in his drama *Don Juans Ende*, in which the old *roué* commits suicide because of a spiritual crisis brought about by the conflict between his passion and his fatherly love for a young girl. In this respect, his drama is closely related to the dramatic poem, *Don Juan*, written by another German, Nikolaus Lenau, in 1844.

At the beginning of the twentieth century, before the appearance of Lesya Ukrainka's *Kaminnyy Hospodar*, Bernard Shaw in his *Man and Superman* developed the Don Juan theme in his own paradoxical fashion. His hero tries to reach superman status by disregarding women, who, in his opinion, hinder man in his thinking and artistic expression.

Thus has the Don Juan theme undergone many transformations and variations depending on the author and literary style of this or that period.

Contrary to the opinion of certain critics who regard Lesya Ukrainka's treatment of the Don Juan theme as stereotyped and romantic,[86] *Kaminnyy Hospodar* is a rather original work. Working on the old motif of Don Juan, she introduced into her drama a number of new elements, created new episodes, and altered the configuration of certain characters. The chief figure of her drama is not Don Juan but Donna Anna who in previous versions occupied only a secondary role. Don Juan who formerly appeared as a seducer and a lover now appears in her version as a "bulwark of will power."

Comparing the last variant of *Kaminnyy Hospodar* with the earlier ones, one notices how thoroughly the playwright was freeing herself from the influences of other literary works dealing with this theme.[87] Certain episodes reminiscent of treatment by other writers were cut

[86]Laffont-Bompiani, II, 87.
[87]Babyshkin, 297.

out and Lesya carefully avoided following Pushkin's *Kamennyy Gost'* which was at hand for her to read.[88]

Her novel philosophical conception substantially changed the heroes themselves, and accounts for the fact that not one work of world literature dealing with the Don Juan theme was the prototype for *Kaminnyy Hospodar*.[89] The dramatic episode of Don Juan's courtship received a philosophical and social colouring in Lesya Ukrainka's work. Don Juan has no craving for blood; he is a gallant knight. Indeed, he has still not lost his charm and fascination for women, but he lacks the primitive impetuosity of his prototype deceiver. He finds his ideal in Anna, who is able to comprehend the loneliness of his free spirit. However, he betrays his ideal of freedom by following Anna's belief that happiness depends upon power. Both of them perish by the hand of Komador, Anna's deceased husband.

There is another original trait in Lesya Ukrainka's drama. Formerly, Anna's character had two specific functions: as a victim of Don Juan's rapacious nature and as a condemnation of his misdeeds. In Lesya Ukrainka's work however, Dolores, Don Juan's unfortunate fiancée, embodies the first aspect, and the second aspect is reserved for Donna Anna.[90] Moreover, it is evident that Dolores is closely related to a number of feminine characters portrayed by Lesya Ukrainska. Her faithfulness and devotion remind one of Priscilla, Johanna (*Johanna, Zhinka Khusova*), and Mavka (*Lisowa Pisnya*). Commander Don Gonzago, Anna's suitor and, later, husband, who in other versions of the Don Juan motif used to be replaced by Anna's father, also differs in Lesya's play from the traditionally ideal type of the latter. Pushkin, for example, in his *Kamennyy Gost*, depicted him as a despotic father. In *Kaminnyy Hospodar* he is master of the power which rules his life, an embodiment of duty combined with unflinching self-discipline, and faithfulness to tradition. Besides, he is a virtuous and a just man, a "knight of duty" as opposed to a "knight of will power" such as Don Juan.[91]

Babyshkin convincingly remarks that the most characteristic feature of *Kaminnyy Hospodar* is the way in which word-symbols develop into picture-symbols. A psychological atmosphere is created, and the essential plot of the drama is more realistically revealed. As the basic symbol of the drama, the playwright chose a stone, which symbolizes rigidity, inflexibility, conservatism, and immobility.[92] This

---

[88]A. Hozenpud, "Poetychnyy Teate," *Mystetstvo* (Kyiv, 1947), 221.
[89]*Ibid.*   [90]Nenadkevych, 36.
[91]*Ibid.*, 37.   [92]Babyshkin, 301.

stone motif is connected with the story of a princess who lives on a steep mountain, and is thus associated with Donna Anna who marries the Commander in order to satisfy her ambitions to live in a "lofty castle." Stony inflexibility is an essential attribute of the conservative Commander, who marries without love and thus secures "stony happiness." In the end, Don Juan perishes as the Commander's ghost crushes him with its stony right hand. The symbol of the stone was explained by Lesya Ukrainka: "The drama . . . is called *Kaminnyy Hospodar* because its basic theme is the victory of the Commander's callousness and obstinate formalism over his spiritually divided, proud, and egotistical wife Anna, and through her over Don Juan, 'the knight of the will.' "[93]

Lesya Ukrainka's treatment of the Don Juan theme is thus seen to be original however aware one may be of certain traditional romantic ingredients. Commenting in her letter to Ol'ha Kobylyans'ka on her work *Kaminnyy Hospodar*, Lesya Ukrainka stated that she wrote it oblivious of the fever which tortured her day and night. After she had completed it she fell ill, and when she had partially recovered she shortened, polished, and tried to condense its essence into a concise form by freeing it from lyrical inertness, compressing the subject-matter into compact yet energetic form, and endowing it with certain "stony features."[94]

To this assiduous polishing are due the fine artistic qualities of this drama, its well balanced structure, its dynamic power, and the concise dialogue. The evocative stage directions, the apt aphorisms, the semantic richness all help to make the drama a masterpiece.

THERE ARE certain motifs which pervade all of Lesya Ukrainka's works. The problem of art in the life of an artist and of a nation and its significance for the nation constitute one of the main motifs of her lyrics and especially of her dramatic poems. For its complete realization, however, this motif had to wait till her last play *Orgiya*.

She began to write this dramatic poem at Kutaisi during the summer of 1912 and completed it in Egypt during the winter of 1912–13. Her trip to Egypt across the Aegean Sea during the Graeco-Turkish war may have had some effect, but the main stimulus to the writing of *Orgiya* was afforded by the political and cultural conditions of her native land.

Orgiya is composed of two acts. The first is set in the house of the Corinthian bard Anteus during the Roman domination over Hellas

[93]*Ibid.*, 274.   [94]*Ibid.*

in the second century A.D. The tragedy begins to develop in the initial dialogue as Anteus, a Greek patriot, deeply wounded by Rome's occupation of his fatherland learns that his best student, Khilon, has rejected his teachings and entered the Roman school founded by Maecenas, hoping to promote his career.

The conversation between Anteus and his young wife Nerissa, whom he ransomed with his inheritance, discloses another problem in his life. Nerissa, until recently a slave, does not understand her husband's ideals. She is indifferent to Greek national culture which Anteus feels must be protected from the Romans. For the sake of glory and personal gain she is ready to surrender everything. She tries to ingratiate herself with Maecenas and win his favour. Following the inopportune request of Nerissa, whom Anteus genuinely loves although her views are alien to him, he agrees to attend a banquet at the home of Maecenas to which he has been invited by the sculptor Phaedon.

Phaedon then informs Anteus that he has sold Maecenas his sculpture of Terpsichore, the muse of choral singing and dancing. Anteus rebukes Phaedon for this as an act of treason against the national culture.

The second act reveals the banquet which Maecenas arranges at his home. The three most famous participants in the banquet, Maecenas, the Prefect and the Procurator, discuss important questions which deal with Greek and Latin languages, the primacy of Greek culture with respect to Roman, and the problem of Roman domination over the Greeks. Soon after Anteus makes his appearance, the drama reaches its height. Anteus refuses to sing a wedding song which, in the opinion of Maecenas, symbolizes the wedding of Hellas with Rome. He sings and plays a Bacchanalian song and the dancers begin to dance. Nerissa dances with them, although she had been forbidden by Anteus to attend the banquet. Maecenas, who is greatly impressed by Nerissa's beauty, her dancing, and coquettish behaviour, kisses her. And when at the invitation of the Prefect Nerissa approaches his bed, Anteus hurls his lyre at her and kills her. Realizing that she is dead, he takes a string from the lyre, chokes himself with it, and dies.

Chilon, who chooses to attend a Roman school and Phaedon the artist, are status-seekers, renegades, and prototypes of all those writers and artists who, as soon as Ukraine lost her independence, rejected their native language and sought positions and careers, losing all feeling for their national culture.

Lesya Ukrainka felt the political subjugation of her people very keenly. Her frequent trips to Western countries only strengthened her desire to see her people gain the freedom enjoyed by other nations. In a letter to her brother, Mykhaylo, written in Berlin in 1891, she talks about it in plain terms:

Never and nowhere did I feel so acutely how burdensome it is to be under the yoke. . . . I do not recall whether I ever experienced such difficult, unbearable and bitter desires as here in the free world. It affected me so often . . . that one can notice on my hands and neck the red traces of the yoke and the chains. Everybody sees these traces and I am ashamed before the free world. As you can see, my hands are chained, but my heart and thoughts are free, perhaps even more so than those of the people around me. It is for this reason that I find it so difficult, disgraceful and impossible to bear. When I return to the Ukraine, I shall certainly feel it even more keenly and lose my last moments of peace, which I still enjoy. . . .[95]

The thought of the liberation of her people and the preservation of Ukrainian culture lay close to her anxious heart. Harassed by these thoughts, she depicted such figures as Eleazar, Tirtsa, Cassandra, Richard, Boyarynya Oksana, and Martiyan, who make up a new group of characters, strong and majestic. They are capable of great deeds and sacrifice; they are the chosen ones, who, amidst a sea of opportunism and betrayal, are able to give a new direction to the events shaping national destiny. In her last play Lesya Ukrainka created Anteus, who chooses to die rather than betray the idea of national culture. He is representative of a new man whose task it is to destroy the power of the Roman conquerors and save Hellas' honour and culture.

Her last dramatic poem, written on the threshold of her death, shows many of those lofty literary qualities which appear so clearly in all the great works of her last years. It is marked in perfect composition, a classical dialogue and supreme mastery of contrast in ideas and characters.

[95]Yakubs'ky, "Orgiya," Tvory Les'i Ukrainky, III, XI.

Selected Works

Translated by VERA RICH

The Stone Host

A DRAMA

Dramatis personae

Commander Don Gonzago de Mendoza
Donna Anna
Don Juan
Dolores
Sganarel, *servant to Don Juan*
Don Pablo de Alvarez, *Donna Anna's father*
Donna Mercedes, *Donna Anna's mother*
Donna Sol
Donna Concepcion
Mariquita
The Duenna of Donna Anna
Grandees, grandees' ladies, guests, servants

ACT I

A cemetery in Seville. Magnificent mausoleums, white headstones, marble under cypresses, many brilliant tropical flowers. More beauty than sorrow. Donna Anna and Dolores. Anna in a pale dress with flowers in her plaits, all in gold veils and chains. Dolores in deep mourning kneels beside a grave that is adorned with fresh wreaths of living flowers.

DOLORES (*rising and drying her eyes with a handkerchief*):
　　　　Come then, Anita.
ANNA (*sitting down on a tombstone under a cypress*):
　　　　　　　　　No, not yet, Dolores.
　　　　It's pleasant here.
DOLORES (*sitting down beside Anna*):
　　　　　　　　　　D'you really find enjoyment
　　　　In this sepulchral beauty? You—the lucky!
ANNA: The lucky?
DOLORES:　　　Won't you, without any pushing
　　　　Wed the Commander?
ANNA:　　　　　　　　　Who d'you think would push?
DOLORES: Are you in love with your fiancé then?
ANNA: Does Don Gonzago, then, not merit loving?
DOLORES: I did not say so. But how strange the manner
　　　　You give an answer, Anna, to my questions.

ANNA: Because they are not ordinary questions.
DOLORES: And what is extraordinary in them?
        Anna, we are most true and faithful friends
        You can tell me the truth of everything.
ANNA: First give me an example then yourself.
        For you have secrets. I have none at all.
DOLORES: I? Secrets?
ANNA (*smiling*):   What's that? Have you really none?
        No, do not drop your eyes! Come, I shall look
        (*She looks into her eyes and smiles.*)
DOLORES (*with tears in her voice*):
        Don't torture me, Anita!
ANNA: Even tears?
        O Lord above! This is true passion indeed!
        (*Dolores buries her face in her hands.*)
        Forgive me, then!
        (*She takes in her hand a silver locket which hangs on a*
            black velvet ribbon round Dolores' neck.)
                      But what do you have here
        Inside this locket? Here perhaps are drawn
        The portraits of your parents now at rest?
        (*She opens the locket before Dolores can snatch it away.*)
        Why, who is this, this handsomest of knights?
DOLORES: My fiancé!
ANNA: I didn't even know
        You were betrothed! Why did I never see
        You with him?
DOLORES: And you will not see us so.
ANNA: He's dead?
DOLORES: No, he's alive.
ANNA: Betrayed you then?
DOLORES: No, he has not betrayed me!
ANNA: Oh, enough
        Of riddles! You don't want to—well, don't talk.
        It's not my way to probe into your soul.
        (*She wants to get up. Dolores takes her by the arm.*)
DOLORES: No, Anna, stay, sit down. Don't you then know
        How hard it is to budge a mighty stone?
        (*She places her hand on her heart.*)
        And in me here lies such a heavy one
        And long ago—it pressed out of my heart

All sorrows, all desires except for one,
You thought that I was weeping for my dead
Parents? O no, dearest Anita, no,
It was that stone pressed tears from out my heart. . . .
ANNA: And have you been betrothed for long?
DOLORES: From birth
It was our mothers that betrothed us then,
When I still lived in my dear mother's hope.
ANNA: Oh, it's all so perplexing!
DOLORES: No, Anita.
Maybe it is the will of heaven that I
Might rightly call him mine, although, he still
Does not belong to me.
ANNA: Who is he then?
How strange it is that I don't know of him.
DOLORES: He is Don Juan.
ANNA: But which one? Surely not. . . .
DOLORES: That one! The very same! Which other one
Of all the hundred thousands Juans there are
Could simply be referred to as "Don Juan"
Without a surname or an epithet?
ANNA: I understand now. . . . Yet, how can it be?
He's been out of Seville for many years. . . .
Wasn't he banished?
DOLORES: The last time that I saw
Him, we were on a visit to Cadiz.
Then he was living hidden in the caves. . .
Living off contraband . . . he sometimes went
Sailing with pirates. . . . Once a gypsy girl
Ran away from her camp, and oversea
She fled with him, and somewhere there was lost,
But he returned and brought back to Cadiz
Some Moorish lass that poisoned her own brother
For Don Juan's sake. . . . Later the Moorish girl
Became a nun. . . .
ANNA: It all seems like some tale!
DOLORES: But it's the very truth.
ANNA: And for what cause,
Say, was he banished? I did hear some talk,
But very muddled.
DOLORES: He, while still a page,

Challenged a prince of the true blood to fight
For the Infanta's sake.
ANNA: And the Infanta,
Did she love him?
DOLORES: Well, people say she did
But I don't think so.
ANNA: Why?
DOLORES: Were she in love
For his sake she'd have cast away Madrid
And all the regal Court.
ANNA: Is that so easy?
DOLORES: True love does not require an easy path.
And then a Rabbi's daughter from Toledo
Gave up her faith for him.
ANNA: And?
DOLORES: Drowned herself.
ANNA: Oh what a terrible fiancé, this!
And, really, he has not the best of taste.
A gypsy girl, an infidel, a Jew. . . .
DOLORES: But you're forgetting the Infanta. . . .
ANNA: Well,
With the Infanta all is not quite clear!
DOLORES: He, on his way to exile, led astray
A pious Abbess, she the granddaughter
Of the Inquisitor himself.
ANNA: Indeed?
DOLORES: Then afterwards the Abbess kept an inn. . .
A tavern for the smugglers.
ANNA: Well, in truth
He is not blameless, this Don Juan of yours! . . .
And yet it seems that you are proud of it—
You reckon up these rivals like proud trophies
Your knight had won for you in tournaments.
DOLORES: I envy them, I envy them, Anita!
Why am I not a gypsy, that I might
Cast off my own free will to follow him?
Why am I not a Jewess?—I would tread
Religion underfoot to be his slave!
A crown is but a little gift. Had I
A family, I would not spare their shame. . . .
ANNA: Dolores, think! Fear God!

DOLORES: Ah, my Anita,
        It is the Abbess that I envy most
        She gave up the salvation of her soul,
        She spurned off Paradise (*Squeezes Anna's arm.*)
                                Ah, Anna! Anna!
        You will never comprehend these envies.
ANNA: I would not envy them if I were you.
        Those poor, unhappy cast-offs. . . . Ah, forgive me,
        I had forgotten that he left you too!
DOLORES: He did not leave me and will never leave me.
ANNA: More riddles. What's the matter, then Dolores?
DOLORES: I went to visit him there in the cave
        Where he was hiding . . .
ANNA (*with burning interest*):   Well? What happened? Tell me!
DOLORES: He was all cut about. He'd tried to steal
        The wife of the Alcaide. But the Alcaide
        Killed her and wounded Don Juan grievously.
ANNA: But how could you manage to visit him?
DOLORES: I cannot understand it now myself . . .
        But it was something like a fevered dream . . .
        I saw him there, and, in the midnight brought
        Water to him, to wash and bathe his wounds,
        Tending until they healed. . . .
ANNA: What happened then?
        Was that the end?
DOLORES: That was the end. He rose
        And I left him and journeyed home again.
ANNA: How could you act so?
DOLORES: I so acted, Anna.
        Like the pure Sacrament. You must not think
        That I would let him lead me so astray.
        No, never in the world!
ANNA: And yet you love
        Him so sincerely
DOLORES: Anna, that's no frenzy!
        True love dwells in my heart, as does the blood
        Within the mystic chalice of the Grail.
        I am betrothed, and no one has the power
        So to besmirch me, not Don Juan himself
        And he knows that.
ANNA: How?

DOLORES: In my soul I feel it
    And he too has some sentiment for me,
    But yet that sentiment is not called love,
    It has no name. But when we said goodbye
    From my hand he plucked away a ring
    And said, "My most respected Señorita,
    If anyone should slander me to you,
    Say to them that I am your true betrothed,
    For with no other lady have I yet
    Exchanged a ring—I give you my true word."

ANNA: If he said this, then surely it must mean
    That it is you and you alone he loves?

DOLORES (*sadly shaking her head*):
    You cannot fool the heart with empty words,
    Only my dreams thus bind me to my love.
    For such a betrothed couple as we are
    Pleasant to dwell as blessed souls in heaven,
    But here—what hell-born tortures come from this.
    But you can never understand this, Anna,
    For you all dreams, all hopes are realized.

ANNA: "All dreams, all hopes"—that's taking things too far!

DOLORES: But why too far? Whatever do you lack,
    You have it all, high birth, and youth and love,
    Wealth also; and soon you'll have the respect
    That is befitting a Commander's wife.

ANNA (*gets up smiling*):
    But I don't see where "dreams and hopes" can be.

DOLORES (*with a wan smile*):
    For you such things will not be needed now.
    (*They walk together among the headstones.*)

ANNA: Who is there has no need of dreams, Dolores.
    I have a . . . childish . . . dream . . . it came, maybe
    Out of those fairytales which grandmamma
    Would use to lull me when I was a child—
    I loved those stories so. . . .

DOLORES: What is this dream?

ANNA: Ah, moods and phantoms! There appears to me
    A mountain sheer and inaccessible,
    And on this craggy mountain a stern castle
    Perched like an eyrie. . . . In that castle dwells

A young princess . . . and no one has the power
To climb the precipice and come to her. . . .
There valiant knights together with their steeds
Perish in their attempt to scale the peak,
And blood in crimson rivers flows about
The mountain foot. . . .

DOLORES: O, what a horrid dream!

ANNA: In dreams all is permissible. And then . . .

DOLORES (*carried away*):
 One happy knight climbed up the mountainside
 And won the hand and heart of the princess.
 But see, the dream already has come true,
 For, Anna, that princess must be yourself.
 The dead knights represent those gentlemen
 Who courted you of old without success
 And that most happy knight is Don Gonzago.

ANNA: No, my Commander is the mountain's self
 And there shall be no happy knight for me,
 No, nowhere in the world.

DOLORES: That's just as well.
 For what have you to give to such a knight
 As a reward?

ANNA: A glass of lemonade
 To quench his thirst! (*Breaks off. In a different tone*)
      Dolores, look there, quickly!
 See how that light is flickering in the vault,
 Like someone covering and uncovering it. . . .
 What if there's someone there?

DOLORES: It is the bats
 Flapping around the votive lamps.

ANNA: I'll see. . . .
 (*She looks through the iron doors into the vault, takes
 Dolores by the arm and shows her something. In a
 whisper*)
 Look, there's a thief! I'd better call the guard!
 (*Breaks into a run. At that moment the doors open. Dolores
 cries out and faints.*)

DON JUAN (*coming out of the vault to Anna*):
 Please, señorita, do not run away!
 And do not be afraid! I'm not a thief!

(Anna comes back and stoops down to Dolores.)

DOLORES *(recovers consciousness. Squeezes Anna's hand)*:
    It's he! Anna, it's he! Have I gone mad?

ANNA: You are—Don Juan?

DON JUAN *(bowing)*:   The self-same, at your service!

ANNA: How did you get here?

DON JUAN: On a horse,
    And then on foot.

ANNA: O Lord above! He's joking!
    You certainly know how to use your head!

DON JUAN: The first time I heard such a compliment
    That I, not with my heart, however full,
    Reason, but with my head—still, Señorita,
    There are some thoughts in it, though only light ones.

ANNA: Well, what is there so heavy in your heart?

DON JUAN: That, Señorita, only she can know
    Who takes my heart into her dainty hand.

ANNA: Your heart's been weighed a good few times, no doubt?

DON JUAN: You think so?

DOLORES: Hide! If someone chanced to come,
    You would be lost!

DON JUAN: But I am lost already.
    I have received a glance from lovely eyes,
    So, if not lost, then where is my destruction?
    *(Anna laughs. Dolores draws her black veil over her face
    and turns her back.)*

ANNA *(waving him away)*:
    Be off! Get back into your house again!

DON JUAN: Only the fair hand of a woman can
    So lightly send a man into his grave.

DOLORES *(turning to Don Juan again)*:
    And are you really living in this tomb?

DON JUAN: How can I tell you? Here, I've had to stay
    All day and night—I don't need any more—
    But in this Court is stricter etiquette
    Than the Castilian Court, but even there
    I could not cope with all the ceremonies,
    Let alone here!

ANNA: Where are you going, then?

DON JUAN: I still do not know that myself.

DOLORES.   Don Juan
      There is a crypt beneath the church, hide there!
DON JUAN: It's hardly merrier down there than here.
DOLORES: You're always chasing merriment!
DON JUAN: Why not
      Chase after it?
ANNA: If someone should invite
      You to a masquerade—would you attend?
DON JUAN: I would attend with pleasure.
ANNA: I invite you.
      This evening we are having a masked ball,
      At my papa's house—Pablo de Alvarez,
      This is the last ball now before my wedding.
      All will be masked, except the older people,
      And my betrothed and I.
DON JUAN (*to Dolores*):
      Shall you be at the ball, too, Señorita?
DOLORES: I am in mourning, as you see, Señor. (*She goes aside.*)
DON JUAN (*to Anna*): In all my life I never have worn mourning,
      I gratefully accept the invitation. (*He bows.*)
ANNA: What will your costume be?
DON JUAN: I still don't know.
ANNA: A pity. I'd have liked to recognize you.
DON JUAN: Recognize me by voice.
ANNA: But are you sure
      That I'll be able to recall your voice?
DON JUAN: Then you can recognize me by the ring.
      (*He shows her the ring on his little finger.*)
ANNA: You always wear that ring?
DON JUAN: I always wear it
ANNA: You're very faithful
DON JUAN: Yes, I'm very faithful.
DOLORES (*entering from a side path*):
      Anna, I can see Don Gonzago coming.
      (*Don Juan hides in the vault. Anna goes to meet the
      Commander.*)
COMMANDER (*approaching with dignity. He is past his first youth;
      dignified and reserved, he wears the white coat of a
      Commander with great pride*):
      Are you alone here? Where are your duennas?

ANNA: They've gone into the church, because Dolores
      Doesn't like people watching when she visits
      Her family grave.
COMMANDER (*inclining his head with dignity to Dolores*):
                Indeed, I understand.
      (*to Anna*) And I have called already at your home
      I wanted to find out what kind of dress
      You will be wearing for the ball tonight.
ANNA: A white one. But why did you want to know?
COMMANDER: An airy nothing. Yes, a trifling thought.
ANNA: You'll recognize me in whatever dress
      I wear, for I shall not be masked.
COMMANDER: That's good.
      It somehow never came into my mind
      That you might wear a mask.
ANNA: Why didn't you
      In this case ever mention it before?
COMMANDER: I had no wish so to restrict your freedom
ANNA: How strange it is to hear when a fiancé
      Fears to impose the slightest of restraints
      Upon the lady whom he soon will bind
      With very different fetters to himself.
COMMANDER: I do not bind her, God does, and the law,
      And I'll have no more liberty than she.
ANNA: Gentlemen so not often speak this way,
      And if they do speak—who will keep his word?
COMMANDER: Now I no longer wonder, Señorita,
      That until now you did not wish to marry—
      What use is wedlock, if one is not certain.
ANNA: Are all young couples certain?
COMMANDER: Donna Anna,
      If I knew that we two were not quite certain
      Or if I were uncertain, or if you
      I would at once give back to you my promise
      Before it is too late. For once a solemn
      Promise is given . . .
ANNA: Ah! how terrible!
COMMANDER: It is not love that fears a solemn promise,
      You find that "terrible?"
ANNA: No, I was joking.
      (*to Dolores*) What did I tell you—he's a very mountain!

COMMANDER: Again some joke? You're very gay, today!
ANNA: Indeed what cause have I not to be gay
       When I can be certain of you, as of
       A stony mountain! Isn't this the truth?
COMMANDER (*offers Anna his arm in order to lead her. Anna*
       accepts):
       Yes, Donna Anna, I have told you this
       So you make no mistakes.
       (*They walk. Dolores follows a little behind them.*)
ANNA (*to Dolores in an unexpectedly loud tone*):
                      And, do you know,
       I thought him better looking in the portrait
       Than in real life.
       (*Dolores looks at her in silence.*)
COMMANDER: Who?
ANNA: Dolores' betrothed.
COMMANDER: And who may that be?
ANNA: Up till now, a secret
       But he will be this evening at our ball.
       (*Exeunt all three. Enter Sganarel, Don Juan's servant. He*
       looks around and approaches the vault.)
SGANAREL: You can come out, sir!
DON JUAN (*coming out*):   What! You here already?
SGANAREL: Greetings from Donna Sol. She does not wish
       That you should visit her, in case of rumour,
       For her duenna's very stern. She'd rather
       Slip away by herself for a few minutes
       And come down here alone.
DON JUAN: Indeed? So quickly?
SGANAREL: Is this not to your satisfaction?
DON JUAN (*inattentively*):   Get me
       A fancy costume for a masquerade,
       But something dashing.
SGANAREL: How did you find out
       That Donna Sol goes to the masquerade
       Given for the Commander's bride? It seems
       That you are planning that you'll meet her there
       And bring her here.
DON JUAN (*following up a different train of thought*): Who?
SGANAREL: Donna Sol, of course,
       Who else d'you think? Wasn't it for her sake

We came here to Seville?

DON JUAN: I do not know.
We'll have to see.

SGANAREL: But if you miss each other,
Whatever shall I do with her down here?

DON JUAN: Nothing at all! You'll go off to the tavern,
And she back to her husband.

SGANAREL: Eh, my lord.
I would have made a better show of knighthood,
Were you the servant and were I the lord.
(*Exit. Don Juan hides in the vault.*)

ACT II

A patio in the mansion of Señor Pablo de Alvarez, arranged in Moorish style, planted with flowers, bushes and small trees, surrounded by buildings, with a gallery under arches which spreads out in the middle into a verandah and a loggia; the roof of the gallery is flat with a balustrade like an oriental roof and spreads out in the middle in the same way as the gallery beneath; to both floors of a gallery a flight of stairs lead up from the courtyard, they are wide and low at the bottom, narrow and steep above. The house and gallery are brightly lit, and in the courtyard there is no light. In the foreground of the courtyard there is an arbour, covered with grapevines. Don Pablo and Donna Mercedes, the parents of Donna Anna are talking with the Commander in the courtyard. In the upper gallery a few guests are walking, not many as yet, and among them is Anna.

COMMANDER: Will you permit me to invite the most
Beautiful Donna Anna for a moment?

DONNA MERCEDES: Anita, Come down here! It's Don Gonzago!

ANNA (*leaning over the balustrade and looking down*):
And cannot you come up and greet me here?
Ah, a true mountain cannot climb a mountain!
(*She quickly runs down, laughing.*)

DONNA MERCEDES: Anna, you are laughing much too loudly.

DON PABLO: And such jokes don't appeal to me at all
You must remember this . . .

COMMANDER: No, do not scold
My bride for this; the wedding is so near,
And she must not be sorrowful for that.
I'm used to Donna Anna's jokes.

DONNA MERCEDES: Come, Pablo

We must go up and welcome all our guests.

COMMANDER: Please stay a little. At home in Castile
Fiancés never were alone together.
But I shall not delay you. Donna Anna,
I pray you to accept this trifling token
Of my great reverence and love for you.
(*He takes a pearl tiara from under his coat and bows before Anna.*)

DONNA MERCEDES: Ah, what magnificent pearls!

DON PABLO: But Commander,
Isn't this really a too-costly gift?

COMMANDER: For Donna Anna?

ANNA: Ah, so that is why
You asked me earlier about my dress!

COMMANDER: I am afraid that maybe I chose wrongly,
I thought, however, if the dress is white,
Then it should be white pearls, too . . .

ANNA: Don Gonzago
You wish to be entirely free from faults.
And that's not right at all—it is oppressive.

DONNA MERCEDES (*whispering to Anna in a low tone*):
Anna, collect your thoughts! At least say "thank you!"
(*Anna silently makes a deep ceremonial curtsy to the Commander.*)

COMMANDER (*holding the tiara above her head*):
Permit that I myself may place these pearls
On this proud, lovely head, now humbled in
Its first deep reverence before me here.

ANNA (*quickly standing up straight*):
For otherwise you couldn't reach so high?

COMMANDER (*putting the tiara on her head*):
As you see, I have reached it.
(*The courtyard fills with a crowd of guests, masked and un-masked, in various costumes. Some have come down from the upper gallery and others through the gate into the courtyard. Among those who enter through the gate is a masked lady in a black, wide, very full-skirted domino, with her face completely covered by a mask.*)

VOICES FROM AMONG THE GUESTS (*coming down from the gallery*):
                              Where's our host?

Where is our hostess?

DON PABLO: Here we are, dear guests.
DONNA MERCEDES (*to the newcomers*):
        How splendidly and brightly do such guests
        Adorn our home.
AN ELDERLY LADY GUEST (*from among the new guests, whispering
        to another elderly lady*):
                        She's probably counted up
        How numerous we are, and what we're costing.
THE SECOND LADY (*to the first, in the same manner*):
        O yes, she's quick enough to count the cost
        But somewhat slower with her invitations. . . .
A YOUNG LADY GUEST (*to Anna, greeting her*):
        Anita, dearest, what a stylish gown.
        (*more quietly*) Only for white, dear, you're a wee bit pale.
ANNA: Oh, that is nothing, it's the latest mode.
        (*more quietly*) I can lend you some powder if you wish
        Because, my dear, even your forehead's flushed!
THE YOUNG LADY: There's no need, thank you!
        (*She turns and moves away, adjusting her mask and hair
        to hide her forehead.*)
A YOUNG WIFE (*whispering to another young wife, and indicating
        Anna's dress with her eyes*):
                                        What a lovely dress!
THE SECOND YOUNG WIFE (*ironically*):
        That's her only pleasure now, poor Anna! . . .
AN OLD GUEST (*to Don Pablo*):
        Well now, Don Pablo, surely now at last
        The King will bid you take your place at Court,
        With such a son-in-law . . .
DON PABLO: His Majesty
        Values men not by sons-in-law, but service.
THE OLD GUEST: And recognition often comes too late.
DON PABLO: Well, late or not, you've had your share of it!
        (*turning to another gentleman*)
        You, Count? I am delighted! What an honour!
        (*The host, hostess, Commander and guests go into the house
        through the lower entrance, the masked lady "Black
        Domino" stays behind unnoticed in the shadow of the
        bushes. Soon Anna with some young ladies appears on
        the verandah. The servants hand round lemonade and
        other cold drinks.*)

DON JUAN (*masked, in Moorish dress with a guitar comes through the gate into the courtyard, stops opposite the verandah and, after a short prelude, sings*):

> In my land, my native country,
> Stands a lonely crystal mountain,
> On this mountain, on the summit,
> Shines a diamantine castle.
>> Anna, ah my sorrow!
> And there grows amid the castle
> Blossom in a bud enclosed
> On its tender petals resting
> Cold hard pearls instead of dew drops,
>> Anna, ah my sorrow!
> On that lovely crystal mountain
> None the steps and none the pathways,
> In that diamantine castle
> None the portals, none the casements
>> Anna, ah my sorrow!
> But comes one who needs no pathway,
> Needs no steps and needs no portal
> He'll fly down to greet the blossom
> From the sky, for love has pinions.
>> Anna, ah my fortune!

(*During the song "Black Domino" comes out a little from the bushes, listens and, at the end, hides herself.*)

COMMANDER (*coming out on to the upper verandah at the end of the song*):
What kind of singing is this, Donna Anna?

ANNA: What kind? I don't know! Probably it's Moorish.

COMMANDER: That wasn't what I meant.

ANNA: Well, then, what was it?
(*Not waiting for a reply, she takes from a servant a glass of lemonade and goes down to Don Juan.*)
Perhaps you would like some refreshment, maybe?

DON JUAN: Thank you, but no. I never drink sweet things.
(*Anna throws the glass into the bushes.*)

COMMANDER (*following Anna*):
Did you like the song, then, Donna Anna?

ANNA: Did you?

COMMANDER: I didn't like it, not a bit.

DON JUAN: Señor, I didn't please you? What a pity!
      I thought it would have been the very thing
      For a near-bridegroom to hear songs of love.
COMMANDER: In your song the refrain was out of place!
DON JUAN: It is a pity I could not omit it,
      But Moorish style demands that it be there.
ANNA: You chose the song to suit the costume, then?
      (*Enter through the gate a crowd of young gentlemen. They
      see Anna and surround her.*)
VOICES FROM THE CROWD: O Donna Anna, Donna Anna, grant us
      Your favour! For this evening is the last
      That you shall have a maid's unfettered will.
ANNA: What is it that you ask me, my good sirs?
1ST KNIGHT: We ask you that you will yourself decide
      Who shall attend on you and in which dance?
ANNA: And I, myself, must ask? . . .
2ND KNIGHT: No, do not ask,
      You have to order us, for we shall be
      Your slaves for this one evening.
ANNA: Very well,
      Though not for very long, for I don't know
      What your good ladies have to say about it.
      Maybe you're safe from them behind your masks?
3RD KNIGHT (*removing his mask*):
      All stars grow pale before the sun.
ANNA: Indeed,
      This compliment does not require a mask
      Being so dignified with hoary age.
      (*The knight puts on his mask again and steps away from
      the group.*)
      (*to the young men.*)
      Well, then, stand in a row, I shall select.
      (*They all stand in a row, Don Juan among them.*)
COMMANDER (*to Anna*):
      Is this the custom in Seville?
ANNA: It is.
COMMANDER: And do I have to stay?
ANNA: No.
      (*Exit Commander.*)   Gentlemen,
      Are you all ready? (*to Don Juan*) How is it that you,
      Votary of the changing planet, stand
      In line, does custom really let you dance?

DON JUAN: For her surpassing custom, I break custom.

ANNA: For that I'll dance with you the first of all.

    (*Don Juan bows in the Oriental manner, placing his right hand on his heart, lips and forehead, and afterwards folds his arms across his chest and bows his head. In these movements the gold ring flashes on his little finger.*)

DON JUAN: One dance?

ANNA: One dance. You will not have another.

    (*to the young men*)

    Now I shall point to you, good gentlemen,

    And each one, please, take note which is your turn.

    (*She quickly points to each of the young men in turn but one young man is left out.*)

YOUNG MAN: And I? And I? Which turn am I to have?

ONE OF THE GROUP: The last one, evidently. (*Laughter. The young man stands in confusion.*)

ANNA: My Señors

    I gave the first place to the Musselman

    Since in God's kingdom, he will be the last.

    But you are a good Catholic, I'm sure,

    And are not frightened of the last place here.

YOUNG MAN: For the first time I'd like to be a Moor.

DON JUAN: Eh, but your compliment is out of order,

    Maybe it's fated you should save your soul!

ANNA (*clapping her hands*):

    My subjects! That's enough. It's time to dance!

    (*She runs upstairs, followed by the young men. From upstairs one can hear music. The dances start, and spread on to the upper verandah and gallery. Donna Anna is in the first couple with Don Juan, then the other young men take their turn. The Commander stands on the corner of an alcove leaning on the buttress of a wall, and watches the dance. "Black Domino" watches from below, and without being observed comes out into an illuminated place in front of the verandah. Don Juan, having finished the dance, leans on the balustrade, notices "Black Domino" and she, at the same time laughingly hides in the shadows.*)

SUNFLOWER MASK (*entering from the side, confronts Don Juan and seizes him by the arm*):

    You are Don Juan! I know it!

DON JUAN: How I wish
    That I knew you so well, my lovely mask.
SUNFLOWER MASK: You know me! Don't pretend! I'm Donna Sol.
    (*She unmasks.*)
DON JUAN: Forgive me. In the sunflower, hard indeed,
    To know the sun.
DONNA SOL: You're laughing at me now?
    Haven't you had enough of jokes?
DON JUAN: What? Where?
DONNA SOL (*gloomily*):
    I have just come back from the cemetery.
DON JUAN: Did someone see you?
DONNA SOL: "Someone" wasn't there!
    But "no one" was for sure!
DON JUAN: Well, what's the problem?
    Isn't the masquerade a rendezvous
    Far jollier than in a cemetery?
DONNA SOL (*clasping her hand to her belt*):
    Oh! I forgot to wear my dagger, too.
DON JUAN (*bowing, hands her his stiletto*):
    Señora, if you please!
DONNA SOL (*brushing away his hand*): Away!
DON JUAN (*putting back the stiletto*):   How fickle!
    What is your wish, most beautiful of ladies?
DONNA SOL: You don't know?
DON JUAN: No, indeed, I do not know.
DONNA SOL: But you remember what you wrote to me?
DON JUAN: I wrote you: "If you find your husband loathsome,
    Then cast him off from you, and run away."
DONNA SOL: With whom?
DON JUAN: Is someone really necessary?
    Well, then, with me. I'll be an escort for you.
DONNA SOL: Where to?
DON JUAN: Cadiz!
DONNA SOL: Why there?
DON JUAN: What need of "why?"
    Is your escape to freedom worth so little?
DONNA SOL: Did you invite me to this rendezvous
    Just to say this?
DON JUAN: And for what cause did you
    Come to the rendezvous? Were you then seeking

A little sweetening for the bitter pill
Of married duties? Then you must forgive me
I never learned how sweetmeats are prepared!

DONNA SOL (*approaching the steps of the verandah*):
Nevertheless, you'll still pay me for this!

BLACK DOMINO (*coming out into the light, confronts Donna Sol. In an unnatural, disguised voice*):
Your husband will allow you take the payment?
(*Donna Sol at once runs out of the gate. "Black Domino" tries to hide in the shadows, but Don Juan blocks her path.*)

DON JUAN: Who are you, mournful mask?

BLACK DOMINO: I am your shadow!
(*She dodges away from Don Juan, hiding behind the bushes, goes into the arbour and hides there. Don Juan, losing sight of "Black Domino," goes to the other side looking for her. On the upper verandah, Donna Anna is dancing the sequidillas.*)

A KNIGHT (*when Anna has finished dancing*):
Donna Anna, you've indeed been dancing
Upon the hearts of all.

ANNA: Indeed? It seemed
To me that I was dancing on the floor.
Or are your hearts in truth as hard as that?

2ND KNIGHT (*approaching Anna, invites her to dance*):
Now it's my turn!

ANNA (*clapping her hands*): Señor, excuse me please!

2ND KNIGHT: I shall wait. But whose turn comes after mine?

ANNA: Open to anyone!
(*She gets up and mingles with the guests, then comes down to the courtyard by the lower stairs. Donna Anna approaches the arbour. "Black Domino" runs out of it, quite silently, and hides in the bushes. Anna falls weakly on to a wide bench in the arbour.*)

DON JUAN (*approaching her*):
You're here? Excuse me, do you feel unwell?

ANNA (*sitting up straight*):
No, only tired.

DON JUAN: Will you go up again?

ANNA: Why? Ah? With other people I'm most tired.
Exhausted by unending wit this evening.

DON JUAN: I was not thinking about wit.
ANNA: What else?
DON JUAN: I wondered what it was could make you try
          To find yourself a prison on a mountain?
ANNA: A prison? What I dream of is a castle
          And castles always stand upon a peak
          That way they're greater and more hard to capture.
DON JUAN: I have a great respect for what is hard
          To capture, if it's built, not upon stone
          But something living.
ANNA: To stand on something living,
          Why, nothing can, for it will quickly buckle.
          But for the soul that lives in pride and lordship,
          Freedom and life are set on a high mountain.
DON JUAN: No, Donna Anna, there you have no freedom
          From the high mountain peak a man can see
          Free boundless space, yet he himself is chained
          Into a little area—one step
          Too far—he plunges into the abyss.
ANNA (in thought): Where in the world is there true freedom,
          then? . . .
          Maybe it is in such a life as yours?
          Yet among men you slink like a wild beast
          Among the hunters in the chase; a mask
          Is all that can protect you.
DON JUAN: But the chase
          Is mutual between us. What's a mask—
          Only a hunter's craftiness. Straightway
          It is no more!
          (He unmasks and sits down beside Anna.)
                         Believe me, Donna Anna,
          Only he's free from all society's
          Fetters, who's cast out by society.
          And I have forced society to this.
          You have seen one who, going in pursuit
          After the true clear voice of his own heart
          Would never ask, "But what will people say?"
          Look, I am such a one. And this the world
          Has never been a dungeon cell to me.
          With a light felucca I skimmed over
          The sea's expanse, like a migrating bird.

I learned the beauty of a distant shore,
And the lure of a country yet unknown.
In freedom's light, all lands are beautiful,
All waters have the power to mirror heaven,
And every wood is like the groves of Eden.

ANNA (*quietly*): Yes . . . that indeed is life!

    (*A pause. Upstairs once more there is music and dancing.*)

DON JUAN: How strange! more music . . .

ANNA: What's strange in that?

DON JUAN: Why, when some creature dies,
Old and worn down by sorrow, all lament.
But here they lay young freedom in its grave
And all are dancing.

ANNA: But you too, Señor,
Were dancing.

DON JUAN: Ah, but if you only knew
What I was thinking then!

ANNA: Indeed?

DON JUAN: I thought
"If only, keeping her still in my arms
I might upon my horse bear her away,
Right to Cadiz!"

ANNA (*getting up*):   But do you not permit
Yourself too many liberties, Señor?

DON JUAN: Ah, Donna Anna, you no longer need
Those paltry miserable fences which
Are meant to guarantee and to defend
Womanly dignity. I'd not use force
To make attempts upon your honour. Do
Not fear, I don't eat women!

ANNA (*sitting down again*):   Don Juan, know
I do not fear you!

DON JUAN: Well, that's the first time
I heard such a statement from a woman's lips.
Do you, perhaps, bolster your courage so?

ANNA: I never yet, in all my life have been
Let down by courage.

DON JUAN: Are you still sure of this?

ANNA: Why not?

DON JUAN: Then answer me in truth,
If you've known freedom, even for an instant.

ANNA: In dreams!
DON JUAN: And day-dreams?
ANNA: Yes, in day-dreams, too.
DON JUAN: Then what prevents you from achieving these
        Proud day-dreams in your life. Step only once
        Beyond the threshold, and the whole wide world
        Is open to you! I am ready, too,
        To help you both in fortune and misfortune,
        Even if you should close your heart to me.
        For me it is the dearest thing to save
        Your proud, free spirit. O Donna Anna,
        So long have I been seeking you.
ANNA: You sought me?
        But you knew nothing of me until now!
DON JUAN: Only your name it was I did not know
        Only your countenance, and yet I sought
        In every woman's countenance to find
        Some small reflection of that bright refulgence
        Which spreads its radiance from your proud eyes.
        If we must part and go our separate ways
        There is no sense in all of God's creation.
ANNA: Wait for a moment! Don't bewitch my thoughts.
        With burning speeches. I do not lack courage
        To venture so out into the wide, wide world.
DON JUAN (*rising, extends his hand to her*):
        Come then!
ANNA: Not yet. Here, courage is not all.
DON JUAN: And what prevents you, now? Is it these pearls?
        Or that ring, maybe?
ANNA: Those least of all!
        (*She takes off the pearl tiara and puts it on the bench. The
        ring she holds on her open palm.*)
        Now put that ring of yours beside this one!
DON JUAN: What for?
ANNA: Don't be afraid I'll put it on!
        I want to throw them both away, into
        Guadalquivir as we cross on the bridge.
DON JUAN: Oh no, this ring I cannot give you. Ask
        For anything you like . . .
ANNA: I'm not prepared
        To ask you anything at all. I wanted

Only to find out if there truly lives
In the whole wide world one person that is free,
Or is it all only "the Moorish style."
And you, yourself, for this belauded freedom
Will not give up even a little circlet.

DON JUAN: I'll give you all my life!

ANNA: The ring!

DON JUAN: O Anna,
This ring is not a token of true love.

ANNA: What is it then? A fetter ring? Don Juan,
Does it not shame you to confess to it?

DON JUAN: I gave my word of honour I would wear it.

ANNA: Ah, word of honour. (*She stands up.*) Thank you, good Señor
For bringing back that word into my mind.

DON JUAN (*falling on one knee*):
Ah, Donna Anna, I implore you!

ANNA (*with an angry movement*):   Cease!
Enough of comedy! Get up at once!
(*Turning round she sees the Commander who is approach-
ing the bower from the house.*)
Ah, Don Gonzago, will you please escort me
Upstairs again.

COMMANDER: Please tell me, Donna Anna,
What is the name, I pray, of this Señor.

ANNA: This knight is the fiancé of Dolores,
And dares not to be known by other names.

DON JUAN: Indeed, I have a name—it is Don Juan,
A name renowned through all the land of Spain.

COMMANDER: You are that outlaw whom the King deprived
Of honour and all privilege. How dare you
Enter this honourable house?

DON JUAN: Kings give
Privilege, and can take it back again.
But like my rapier honour is to me,
For it is mine alone, and none can break it!
Or is it that you wish to try, maybe?
(*Draws his rapier and stands "on guard."*)

COMMANDER (*folding his arms*):
It is not fitting a Commander's honour
To duel with outlaws! (*to Anna*) Come, let us go in.
(*He takes Anna's arm and moves off, turning his back on*

> *Don Juan, who follows behind the Commander, want-*
> *ing to run him through with the rapier. "Black*
> *Domino" runs out from the shadows and seizes him*
> *with both hands.)*

BLACK DOMINO (*in a normal voice which may be recognized as that of*
      Dolores):
      Attacking from the back's dishonourable!
      (*Anna turns round, Don Juan and Dolores run out of the*
      gate.)

COMMANDER: Do not look round!

ANNA: There's no one left there, now!

COMMANDER (*letting go of Anna's arm and changing his quiet tone*
      for a fierce one):
      How did he come to be here, Donna Anna?

ANNA: I tell you, as fiancé of Dolores!

COMMANDER: And what was all that kneeling on one knee?

ANNA: To whom?

COMMANDER: Why, he of course, in front of you!

ANNA: Should *I* have knelt? And if not, what's the problem?

COMMANDER: And you could really let him?

ANNA: Lord above!
      Whoever asks permission to such things?
      Or maybe the Castilian etiquette
      Insists that one approaches ladies so:
      "Permit me, ma'am, to kneel upon one knee!"
      Here every lady'd laugh at such a thing!

COMMANDER: You're good at turning things aside with jokes!

ANNA: Have pity! If each time I sent away
      A suitor I must pour out bitter tears.
      Long since my eyes would have lost all their lustre!
      Is this the way you'd wish for things to be?
      Is it surprising to you that for him
      I don't stretch out my hands, weep bitterly,
      Ashamedly confess before you here
      Unlawful love which, like a raging storm,
      Swept unresisted through this heart of mine.
      I'd have been like Isolde in the tale,
      A pity I am not attuned for this,
      Just now, I feel inclined to the fandango,
      Ah, I can hear—they're playing it, tra-la!
      Let us go, Don Gonzago, I will fly

Like a white billow into the gay dance.
And you will stand quite tranquil, like a stone
Because the stone knows that the petulant wave
Will end the dance forever—at its side.
(*The Commander takes Anna's arm and leads her up to the dancing.*)

ACT III

A cave on the seashore in the neighbourhood of Cadiz. Don Juan sits on a rock sharpening his rapier. Sganarel is standing near him.

SGANAREL: Why are you always sharpening your rapier.
DON JUAN: Such is my habit.
SGANAREL: Yet you fight no more
        Duels.
DON JUAN: For I've no one I can fight.
SGANAREL: Aren't there sufficient people?
DON JUAN: All these people
        Are not fit for my rapier.
SGANAREL: Maybe the rapier
        For someone is not fit?
DON JUAN (*angrily*):   You!
SGANAREL: Forgive me, sir!
        It was a thoughtless joke. I can't recall
        Whence all these foolishnesses came to me,
        As if something were pushing me!
DON JUAN: Be off!
        (*Exit Sganarel, smiling. Don Juan goes on sharpening the rapier.*)
        Notched it again! Ah, only fit for breaking!
        (*He throws away the rapier. Enter Sganarel quickly and quietly.*)
SGANAREL: Sir, let us run away!
DON JUAN: What is it now?
SGANAREL: We are found out. I saw, not far away
        Some monk was wandering about.
DON JUAN: Well then?
SGANAREL: No doubt a spy from the Grand Inquisition,
        Or an assassin with a poisoned dagger!
DON JUAN: I don't fear spies! I have grown used to them
        And I've a rapier longer than a dagger!

Bring on the monk! The business will be shorter!
Tell him Don Juan, the universal sinner
Wants to make his confession.
SGANAREL: Very well!
You're not a child, and I am not your nurse!
(*Exit. He quickly returns, leading into the cave a monk,
        who is shortish, thin and dressed in a "cloak of invisi-
        bility"—a black cloak, which covers all the face—only
        two slits being left for the eyes.*)
DON JUAN: My father, or perhaps I should say—brother,
To whom am I indebted for this holy
Visit?
(*The monk makes a sign with his hand that Sganarel
        should go.*)
                              Sganarel, you have leave to go.
(*Seeing that Sganarel is in no hurry to go he whispers to
        him.*)
See, this monk has a woman's hands!
SGANAREL: Confound them!
(*Exit, with a wave of his hand. Don Juan places his rapier
        on the stone. From under the monk's hood there appears
        at once the face of Dolores.*)
DON JUAN: Dolores? You? Once more here in this cave . . .
DOLORES: I have come here to save you once again.
DON JUAN: To save me once again? Why, who has told
You that I might have been in need of saving?
DOLORES: I knew it for myself.
DON JUAN: I'm still not weak,
As you perceive, but powerful, happy, free!
DOLORES: You wish that you might appear so to be!
DON JUAN (*laughing, for a moment, then quickly raising his head
        with a stubborn movement*):
I see, my Señorita, that your garb
Has tuned you to a monkish way of speech.
But I shall not make my confession now.
My sins are not for a young lady's ears.
(*Dolores silently takes out two parchment scrolls and gives
        them to Don Juan.*)
No, forgive me, Dolores, I did not
Wish to insult you; that is not my way.
What's this that you have brought me?

DOLORES: Read it through!
DON JUAN (*glancing quickly through the parchments*):
          A Royal Decree . . . also a Papal Bull
          All of my misdeeds are forgiven me.
          And all my sins. . . . How is it? For what reason?
          However did you come to get these papers?
DOLORES (*lowering her eyes*):
          Do you not guess the reason?
DON JUAN: O Dolores,
          Indeed I understand. Once more you placed
          A debt upon me. And you know, indeed,
          It is my way to settle debts in full.
DOLORES: I have not come here as a debt collector,
DON JUAN: So I believe you. Yet I am not bankrupt,
          Once I gave to you a pledge—a ring,
          I'm ready now to settle the whole debt
          No more an outlaw; a grandee of Spain
          Am I, and now it is not a disgrace
          To marry me.
DOLORES (*with a sigh*): O God, O Holy Virgin!
          I had expected it might happen so . . .
          But now it's happened, and I have to bury
          This my last dream . . .
          (*Her voice breaks down in a fit of suppressed weeping*)
DON JUAN: Have I offended you?
          In what, Dolores?
DOLORES: Don't you understand?
          You think that when a Spanish grandee throws
          A wedding ring to a hidalgo's daughter,
          Like purse of guineas to the money lender
          That her heart ought to blossom into flower,
          And not pour forth its blood.
DON JUAN: Ah, no! Dolores!
          And you, too, have to understand that I
          Have never been indebted, since my birth,
          To maiden nor to woman.
DOLORES: Is this true?
          You, Don Juan, never, not in any way
          Wronged womankind?
DON JUAN: No! Never. In no way.
          For every time I gave them everything

That they were able to take in: a dream,
A brief few hours of happiness, excitement
And there was no one that could take in more,
While others found it far beyond their dreams.

DOLORES: But you would have been able to take more?
(*a pause*) But this time you won't be required to pay
And so take back again the "golden pledge."
(*She wishes to take off the ring from her right hand.*)

DON JUAN: No, this belongs to you by holy law.

DOLORES: And I, myself, belong to me no more,
This body which you see is no more mine,
The very soul within it is the smoke
Of incense offerings which burn before
God for the sake of your soul . . .

DON JUAN: What's all this?
I cannot understand your words at all.
You, like a slaughtered sacrifice of blood,
So are your eyes. . . . And this Decree . . . this Bull . . .
However did you get them? I entreat you
Tell me.

DOLORES: Why is it that you want to know?

DON JUAN: I still, perhaps, may cast away these gifts.

DOLORES: You'll not be able to cast them away,
I know. And how they're got—it's all the same.
It's not the first time that for you a woman
Perishes! Were it but the last time!

DON JUAN: No,
Tell me! If you won't say, I may conclude
That you obtained it by some shameful means—
An honourable method needs no veiling.

DOLORES: "Shameful" . . . "honourable! . . . How far now
From me these words are. Well then I shall tell you!
For this decree I have paid with my body.

DON JUAN: How?

DOLORES: I cannot put it any more plainly,
You understand the customs of the court,
There everything is paid for, if not money
Then . . .

DON JUAN: O my God! How terrible, Dolores!

DOLORES: Terrible for you? I did not expect that.

DON JUAN: But for you?

DOLORES: I have nothing left to fear.
    Why should I be frightened for my body
    When I was not afraid to give my soul,
    Even, that I might pay for the Bull.
DON JUAN: But who pays with the soul?
DOLORES: All women do,
    When they fall in love. And I am happy
    That with my soul I can buy out a soul,
    Not every woman has this happiness.
    The Holy Father will release your soul
    From torments of perdition on condition
    That I embrace atonement everlasting,
    For all your sins. Within a convent of
    The strictest rule, I shall become a nun.
    The vow of everlasting silence, fasts
    And scourgings I shall offer up to God.
    Juan, I shall have to renounce everything,
    Even my dreams and memories of you!
    Only about your soul may I remember,
    Neglecting my own soul. My soul shall even
    Go to eternal torment for your sake.
    Farewell.
    (Don Juan stands silent, dumbstruck. Dolores moves away
        but at once stops short.)
        No, still once more! For the last time
    I want to gaze once more into these eyes!
    For they will never shine for me again
    In that sepulchral darkness which will be
    Known as my life. . . . Take back your portrait, then,
    (She takes off the medallion and puts it on the stone.)
    I have to think only about your soul
    And nothing further.
DON JUAN: What if I should say
    That one brief moment's happiness with you
    Here upon earth is worth far more to me
    Than joy eternal without you in heaven?
DOLORES *(ecstatic, like a martyr undergoing torture)*:
    I do not ask you not to tempt me thus.
    This half-delusion. . . . If but to the end
    It might deceive this ever-watchful heart
    O Blessed Virgin! Grant that I may offer

This sacrifice on his behalf! O Juan
Speak to me, speak those words of truest love!
Be not afraid that I might still accept them.
Here is your ring.
(*She takes it off and tries to give it to Don Juan, but her
hand falls weakly and the ring rolls down.*)
DON JUAN (*picks up the ring and puts it once more on Dolores'
hand*):
No never shall I take it
Back again. You must wear it, or else give it
To the Madonna as an offering
If you so wish. To look on such a ring
Would be permitted to a nun. This ring
Will not rouse sinful memories.
DOLORES (*quietly*): It's true.
DON JUAN: And this of yours I'll never give away,
No never!
DOLORES: For what purpose will you wear it?
DON JUAN: The soul has its requirements and its customs
Just as the body. I had hoped you would
See this without unnecessary words.
DOLORES: It's time for me to go now . . . I forgive you
For everything that you . . .
DON JUAN: Stop, do not darken
All my bright memories of this last moment.
Why this forgiveness? Now, indeed, I see
That I remain in debt to you for nothing
For truly you, through me, have reached the height
Of a most pure and a most lofty summit!
So is forgiveness due to me for this?
O no! Maybe you made a slip of the tongue!
In a heart ever watchful such a word
Could not be born. You have no need of such
Words, since you have become so high above
Honour and shame. Is this not true, Dolores?
DOLORES: It seems that no more words are necessary! (*She starts to
go.*)
DON JUAN: Dolores, stay a moment. . . . In Madrid
Did you call on Señora de Mendoza?
DOLORES (*stopping short*):
You . . . you are asking me for news of her?

DON JUAN: I see that you're not ready for the convent.
DOLORES (*suppressing her feelings*):
    I saw her, yes!
DON JUAN: And she is well and happy?
DOLORES: It seems that I am happier than she is.
DON JUAN: She has not forgotten me.
DOLORES: O no.
DON JUAN: How do you know?
DOLORES: I feel it in my heart.
DON JUAN: That's all I want to know.
DOLORES: I'm going now.
DON JUAN: You do not ask for what reason I
    Needed to know this?
DOLORES: No, I do not ask!
DON JUAN: Isn't that rather hard for you?
DOLORES: I never
    Looked for an easy path! Farewell forever!
DON JUAN: Farewell forever. I shall not betray you.
    (*Dolores at once covers her face with her hood and leaves
       the cave without looking back. Sganarel enters and
       stands looking reproachfully at Don Juan.*)
DON JUAN: Well, what a lovely soul it is I've tempered.
SGANAREL: Whose soul? Your own?
DON JUAN: That's a stinging question,
    Though unintentional!
SGANAREL: You think so, sir?
DON JUAN: Well, what do you think?
SGANAREL: That I've often seen you
    As anvil and as hammer, but have never
    Seen you as smith.
DON JUAN: But that you soon shall see.
SGANAREL: Pity! The chance is lost!
DON JUAN: What's that? Lost, where?
SGANAREL: Your destiny has gone to be a nun, sir!
DON JUAN: So you were eavesdropping?
SGANAREL: You didn't know?
    He who has servants ought to realize
    That always he's in the confessional.
DON JUAN: But to admit the fact so shamelessly! . . .
SGANAREL: One has to be the servant of Don Juan!
    And sir, you are renowned for your plain speaking!

Don Juan: Well, don't keep chattering. My shadow's gone,
    My destiny is waiting in Madrid,
    Saddle the horses. We shall go at once.
    To win this destiny. . . . Quick! Off with you.
    (*Exit Sganarel. Don Juan takes the rapier in his hand and
    runs his hand down the blade, testing the edge, and
    smiling.*)

ACT IV

The mansion of the Commander in Madrid. Donna Anna's boudoir, a
large room opulently furnished but in dark tones. High narrow windows
with balconies reach almost to the floor. The shutters are closed. Donna
Anna in a grey dress with black half-mourning sits at a small dressing
table arranging her jewels in a box and trying them on, looking in the
mirror.

Commander (*entering*): What you dressing up for?
Anna: I am choosing
    Jewels for tomorrow. For I'd like to go
    To the bull fight tomorrow.
Commander: In half-mourning?
Anna (*exasperated, pushing away the jewellery*):
    Oh, all this mourning! When's it going to end?
Commander (*quietly*):
    This one will run for eight days more.
    In honour of an uncle, that's not long.
Anna: The strangest part of it is that in all
    My life I never even met this uncle.
Commander: That's not the point at all. You now belong
    To the noble house of de Mendoza.
    Therefore you must honour the memory
    Of all your kin.
Anna: God grant them all long lives!
    For now we are in mourning for an uncle,
    Last time it was an aunt, before her came—
    If I've not got it wrongly—our third cousin,
    Or was it a fourth cousin that had died?
Commander: With whom, then, are you angry?
Anna: I just wanted
    To recollect how many days it was
    That I've been out of mourning since the time
    That I've been married to you.

COMMANDER: A whole month.
ANNA (*ironically*): Ah, a whole month? Indeed, that's quite a while?
COMMANDER: I cannot understand your irritation.
        Surely you do not wish, for vain enjoyment
        To cast aside all honourable customs
        Hallowed by time?
ANNA (*getting up*):   What do you mean to say?
        Do I not keep these honourable customs?
        When have I acted in a shameful manner?
COMMANDER: There must not even be a hint of shame,
        But for us even the least deviation
        Would be a step towards the abyss. Remember
        That a Commander's coat came down to me
        Not for the asking, not for pay or violence,
        But for honour's sake. We de Mendozas
        Were all from olden days knights without fear,
        All ladies without blemish. Is it fitting
        That you'd be prone to vulgar criticism
        Tomorrow, when . . .
ANNA (*irritated*):   I shan't go anywhere.
COMMANDER: There is no need at all to stay shut in.
        Tomorrow morning we must go to church.
ANNA: I did not mean to go to church tomorrow.
COMMANDER: Nevertheless, we really have to go.
        Fra Iñigo is going to preach the sermon.
ANNA: But he's the dullest preacher in the world!
COMMANDER: I quite agree with you. But the Queen likes
        These sermons. So the whole Court goes along,
        To hear them too. If you should be missing
        From all the grandees' ladies, they would notice.
        (*Anna sighs without speaking. The Commander takes from*
           his pocket a smoky-crystal rosary.)
        I've brought you a half-mourning rosary.
        Soon I shall get you one of amethysts.
ANNA (*taking the rosary*): Thank you, but why all this?
COMMANDER: You must prevail
        Over all the ladies by your splendour.
        And please, moreover, when we go to church,
        Do not permit Donna Concepcion
        To sit beside the Queen. By right, that seat
        Belongs to you. Be sure you don't forget

That everywhere the first place is for us
Since we can occupy it worthily
And no one has the right to take our place.
Not just the honour of the de Mendozas—
The banner of my Order guarantees this.
But when not just Donna Concepcion
But the Queen also wishes to forget this,
Then I without delay will leave the Court
And all my knighthood will go after me.
Then let His Most Catholic Majesty
Hold up the crown even in his own hands
So that it doesn't tremble! I'll be able
With courage to defend my knightly rights,
For it is only needful that they be
All everyone, hence we must need not only
Honour, but the least rules of etiquette
However petty. Even if they seem
Boring, senseless, purposeless to you. . . .

ANNA: O Holy Patience!

COMMANDER: Yes indeed one must
Pray with sincerity to Holy Patience,
When one wishes to remain on top
Of rights which ask of us some special duties.
Rights without duties are but anarchy.
(*Anna sighs again.*)
You sigh? Nevertheless you knew quite well
What obligations would await you here.
You chose your destiny quite consciously
And your repentance now has come too late.

ANNA (*proudly*): Even in my thoughts I don't repent it.
I recognize that you are right. Forget
My whims and fancies—they are all quite gone!

COMMANDER: These are the words of a true grandee's lady,
Once more I recognize my own true spouse.
Forgive me, for a moment I was
Unsure of you—and I felt so alone
And all the struggle seemed too hard for me
To gain that rung which has to place us still
Higher.

ANNA (*excited*): What rung? Above us, after all,
Is just the throne!

COMMANDER: Yes, just the throne. (*a pause*) Long since,

      I would have told my plans to you, had I
      Seen you can live with the same thoughts as mine.
ANNA: And you did not perceive this?
COMMANDER: I regret it.
      But now I hope that every step of mine
      We two shall make together. The highest crag
      Only receives an honourable crown
      When the she eagle builds her eyrie there.
ANNA: The eagle?
COMMANDER: Yes, only an eagle can
      Upon a sharp and slippery mountain crag
      Build for herself a permanent abode,
      And live there without fearing aridness
      Nor arrows of the sun, nor threat of thunder,
      But the reward for this is lofty height . . .
ANNA (*interrupting*): In the pure mountain air, free from the scents
      And odours of the sychophantic lowland.
      Thus?
COMMANDER: Yes, give me your hand.
      (*Anna gives him her hand, and he presses it.*)
                    And so, goodnight.
ANNA: You're going out?
COMMANDER: Yes, to the Chapter Council.
      If I'm late back, please don't wait up for me.
      (*Exit Commander. Anna sits down, musing to herself.*
        Enter Mariquita, a chambermaid.)
ANNA: You, Mariquita? Where is my duenna?
MARIQUITA: She suddenly was taken quite unwell,
      She had to go and rest. But if you need her
      I'll go and call her, all the same.
ANNA: No, leave her,
      Let her rest. You can plait my hair for me
      For the night, and then go.
MARIQUITA (*plaiting Anna's hair*):   I have to tell
      The Señora something, but I thought I'd wait
      Till the Señor had left the house.
ANNA: Quite pointless!
      No secrets do I have from the Señor.
MARIQUITA: O no, of course not! Truly my Señora
      Is filled with holy virtue. And I said
      That to the servant when I took the flowers.
ANNA: What servant? What's that about flowers?

MARIQUITA: Just now
    Some servant brought some granadilla flowers
    From somebody for the Señora.
ANNA (*angrily*):   Never!
    Granadilla flowers, you say? For me?
MARIQUITA: I don't know. . . . He said so. . . . It is the truth,
    But rather impudent, for granadilla
    Flowers are a sign of passion. I shan't say
    More, for it's common knowledge.
ANNA: Mariquita,
    I have to know from whom this insult came!
MARIQUITA: The servant gave no name, he only said
    Giving the flowers: "These are for Donna Anna,
    From her faithful Moor." (*Anna cries out suddenly.*)
                 Señora knows
    From whom they came?
ANNA (*embarrassed*):   These flowers are not required . . .
MARIQUITA: I'll bring them just to show you.
ANNA: Not required!
    (*Mariquita not listening runs out and returns in a moment
        with a bouquet of red granadilla flowers.*)
ANNA (*waving them aside and turning away*):
    Throw them away!
MARIQUITA: I'd have liked to have them
    If the Señora doesn't want them. Really
    They are the choicest blossoms.
ANNA: Yes, yes . . . take them . . .
MARIQUITA: Tomorrow I'll wear flowers all over!
ANNA: Go!
MARIQUITA: Shouldn't you have the windows open here,
    It's very close
ANNA (*in thought, not attending*): Open them.
MARIQUITA: And the shutters?
ANNA: No, they might see in from the street.
MARIQUITA (*opening the shutters*):   O no,
    For the whole street is quite deserted now.
    For this is not Seville! Ah, in Seville
    All the streets now will ring and sound with songs
    And the air whirls in the swift Madrillana
    But here the air is stony. . . .
ANNA (*nervously*):   Ah, enough!

(*Mariquita, while speaking, has leaned out of the window.
    She looks to all sides and suddenly makes a movement
    with her hand as though throwing something.*)

ANNA (*noticing the movement*):
    What's that for, Mariquita?
MARIQUITA (*innocently*):   What? Why, nothing?
ANNA: You threw a flower to someone?
MARIQUITA: Not at all!
    I chased away a moth. Does the Señora
    Have need of something else, maybe?
ANNA: No, nothing.
MARIQUITA (*bobbing a curtsy*):
    I wish you pleasant, pleasant dreams.
ANNA: Goodnight.
    (*Exit Mariquita, but as she goes she leaves behind the
        bouquet of granadilla flowers. Anna glances at the
        door and with a trembling hand she takes the bouquet
        and looks at it longingly.*)
ANNA (*quietly*): From her faithful Moor . . .
    (*Don Juan quietly and with agility climbs through the
        window, throws himself on his knees before Anna and
        covers her hands with kisses.*)
ANNA (*letting the bouquet fall in ecstasy*): You!
DON JUAN: I'm your knight,
    Your faithful Moor!
ANNA (*recollecting herself*): Señor who gave you leave?
DON JUAN (*rising*): What is this hypocrisy for, Anna?
    For I have just seen how you were holding
    My gift of flowers.
ANNA: That was an accident!
DON JUAN: I pray for blessings on such accidents.
    (*Stretches out his hands to Anna, who makes a movement
        of defence.*)
ANNA: I beg you, go away, leave me alone!
DON JUAN: Are you afraid of me?
ANNA: It is not right
    For me thus to receive you . . .
DON JUAN: What weak words!
    Of old I did not hear such things from you!
    O Anna, Anna, where now are your proud
    Day-dreams of old?

ANNA: Those girlish dreams were but
     A fairytale.
DON JUAN: Yet don't we, you and I,
     Live in a fairytale? The tale was born
     Midst tears and laughter in the cemetery,
     Bloomed in a dance and grew mature in parting . . .
ANNA: And it is time for it to end.
DON JUAN: Yet how?
     Shall the true knight set free the fair princess
     From the stone prison, and begin no mere
     Fairytale but a song of joy and freedom?
ANNA (*shaking her head*):
     Cannot the fairytale end with the knight
     Simply returning home again because
     It is too late to rescue the princess?
DON JUAN: O no. In fairytales such things don't happen.
     That happens only, maybe, in real life,
     And in a worthless life at that!
ANNA: I have
     No need of anything from you. I ask not
     That you should rescue me or comfort me.
     I've no complaints to make to you,
DON JUAN: O Anna,
     Don't I see for myself. (*gently*) These lovely eyes
     Once gleaming proud with scintillating sparks
     Now they are ringed about with blackest mourning,
     And all their radiant fires have burned away.
     These tender hands that once were gentle flowers
     Have now become like carven ivory,
     Like the hands of a martyr. This slim form
     Was once like an impetuous wave, but now
     Is like the form of caryatids, who
     Support a strong burden upon their heads.
     (*He takes her hand.*)
     Beloved, cast away this dreadful burden,
     And rend the stony garment!
ANNA (*weakly*):   Ah, I cannot. . . .
     That stone . . . not only burdens with its weight,
     It turns the soul to stone. This is the worst!
DON JUAN: No, no! This is a dream, a stony nightmare.
     I will awaken you with fire of love.

(*He seizes her in an embrace, she leans her head on his
shoulder and shakes with sobbing.*)
Ah, you are crying? These tears call for vengeance!
(*Far off a key is heard turning in a lock, then on the stairs
are heard the heavy slow steps of the Commander.*)

ANNA: That is Gonzago's tread. Quick! Get away!

DON JUAN: Escape, No. Now I have the chance I need
Not to give way nor yield before his might.

COMMANDER (*enters and sees Don Juan*):
You? Here?

DON JUAN: I? Here? Yes, Señor de Mendoza,
I have come here to offer you my thanks
For magnanimity once shown me. Now
I am your equal. Surely you know that?
(*The Commander silently draws his rapier, and Don Juan
his. They start fighting. Donna Anna screams.*)

COMMANDER (*looking round at her*):
I order you, be silent!
(*Don Juan stabs him in the neck—he falls and dies.*)

DON JUAN: It is ended! (*He wipes his rapier
on the Commander's coat.*)

ANNA: What have you done now?

DON JUAN: What? I have defeated
An adversary in a duel of honour!

ANNA: But this will not be taken as a duel.
You will be punished as a murderer.

DON JUAN: It's all the same to me.

ANNA: But it is not
The same to me, that people should remark
Me as a double widow—for my husband
And for my lover!

DON JUAN: But I have not been
Your lover yet!

ANNA: Yes, we know this is true.
But who would credit it? I do not want
With name of traitress and a brand of shame
To have to stay here in this hornets' nest.

DON JUAN: Then let us flee together!

ANNA: Are you mad,
That means you'll drag a stone along with you.
Go away! Leave me! Otherwise at once

I'll scream and shout you wanted to dishonour
    Me and to this end treacherously slew
    The Señor de Mendoza.
Don Juan: Donna Anna
    You can say that?
Anna: I certainly shall say it.
Don Juan: And what if I should tell them that you were
    My mistress and accomplice in the murder?
Anna (*firmly*): That is not chivalrous.
Don Juan: And you, Señora?
    What about the way you mean to act?
Anna: I shall only act in self-defence.
    And if you leave this house at once, I shall
    Tell everyone, and they will all believe
    That thieves broke in—and that will settle it.
    (*Don Juan remains standing in uncertainty.*)
    Well? Surely you've no more to think about?
    (*Don Juan without speaking, climbs out through the win-
        dow. Anna watches from the window for a while until
        he has got away, then she takes the jewellery from the
        box, throws it out of the window and shouts loudly.*)
Anna: Help! Murder! Help! For God's sake someone, come!
    (*As people rush into her boudoir, she falls as if fainting.*)

ACT V

A cemetery in Madrid. The monuments are mostly made from dark stone
in a heavy style. At the side is a granite chapel of ancient construction. No
plants, no flowers. A cold, dry winter day. Donna Anna in deep mourning
walks solemnly carrying a silver wreath. Behind her walks an old duenna.
They both come up to a grave with a monument to the Commander, a
large statue with a Commander's baton, and with the left hand resting on
a sword with an open scroll over the hilt. Anna silently kneels before the
grave, places the wreath at the foot of the statue, takes out her rosary and
begins to murmur prayers.

Duenna (*waiting until she has said one decade*):
    I venture to request that the Señora
    Would give me leave to go, just for a moment.
    Quite near, just over there, beside the gate
    To ask my kinswoman to lend some gloves
    To me. I left my own at home, alas,
    And it is biting cold.

ANNA: It is not proper
        That I should stay out here all by myself.
DUENNA: My kind Señora! For the Lord's sake, please
        I'm old, and my rheumatics are so bad.
        Does the Señora see, my hands are swollen?
        Indeed I have not slept a wink from pain.
ANNA (*looking at the duenna's hands*):
        Yes, they are badly swollen. All right, go!
        But don't delay!
DUENNA: I'll hurry. My Señora
        Is a very angel of compassion.
        (*Exit. Hardly has she gone when Don Juan appears from
        behind the nearest monument. Anna jumps to her feet.*)
DON JUAN: And so at last I see you!
ANNA: So, Don Juan!
        You have bribed my duenna, I presume?
DON JUAN: No, I just seized my chance! But if I had,
        You would be held responsible.
ANNA: I would?
DON JUAN: You would. For who is it that forces me
        To roam the cemetery by the hour
        Watching for you? And only due to this
        That I had the good luck to see how here
        Under the duenna's grim protection
        You read your insincere prayers on the grave
        Of the "unforgotten one."
ANNA (*stops him with a movement of her hand*): Wait! firstly
        No one is forcing me to anything.
        Secondly, my prayers are true and are sincere
        Because I was, although unwittingly,
        The cause that brought about my husband's death
        Who loved me and respected me.
DON JUAN: Señora,
        All hail to you! Such truly great achievements.
ANNA: In what?
DON JUAN: Why, in hypocrisy
ANNA: I must not
        Listen to such speeches. (*She quickly moves away.*)
DON JUAN (*catching her arm*): Donna Anna!
        I shall not let you go!
ANNA: Then I shall scream.

DON JUAN (*letting go of her arm*):
      I beg and pray you listen to me then.
ANNA: If you will drop that bully's tone of voice
      Then I shall let you. But speak quickly, please,
      For someone will come, and I don't want
      Them to see us together.
DON JUAN: I am wondering
      Whatever are these willing fetters for?
      I thought the stone had split apart already.
      The burden fallen and the person living.
      But no, it has grown harder still, that stone
      Your clothing. And your house, like a strong tower,
      During a siege. The doors with bolts and bars,
      The jealous shutters will not let go in
      Either a glance or sunbeam. All the servants
      Stern, armed, and incorruptible.
ANNA: That means
      That there have been attempts to bribe them.
DON JUAN: Anna,
      Does not despair have its own privileges
      For after all, when I came openly
      I only heard "Señora's not at home!"
ANNA: Think for yourself, is it the proper thing
      For a young widow, still in mourning, too,
      To entertain a knight of such repute
      As you, and all alone.
DON JUAN: O Anna, Anna.
      It seems that now I start to lose my reason.
      Is this you? Really you? The self-same beauty,
      But words, what words! Who was it taught you them?
      Who changed the very soul in you?
ANNA: Don Juan
      No one has changed the very soul in me.
      From birth it always has been proud, and so
      It has remained. I therefore shut myself
      Into an inconquerable fortress
      That none may dare to say "Aha, indeed
      The pretty widow's having fun—the bonds
      Are broken!" Surely you could not bear that?
DON JUAN: But Anna, don't I have my rapier?

ANNA: Indeed—will you depopulate Madrid?
         And with your rapier could you cut away
         All sidelong glances, sniggering and whispers,
         Raised eyebrows, whistles, shrugging shoulders which
         Would meet and follow me in every place?
DON JUAN: Anna, let's run away!
ANNA: Ha ha!
DON JUAN: It's funny?
ANNA: Had I not laughed, then certainly I'd yawn.
         Surely you'd not prefer that?
DON JUAN: Ah Señora!
ANNA: Now its the third time that I've heard these words.
         And it can get quite tedious.
DON JUAN: I see,
         You are indeed stone, without soul or heart.
ANNA: Though not without good sense, you must admit.
DON JUAN: Oh, I admit you've that!
ANNA: Then tell me why
         We ought to run away now? What's the point?
         When you seduced young girls and stole away
         Wives from their husbands, then it was not strange
         That it turned out you ran away with them.
         And he who's banished is a fugitive
         Of course. But why is one to send oneself
         To banishment? For what cause? Just to take
         A widow who's dependent upon no one.
         Think for yourself, is it not farcical?
         And what would I be to you, if I fled
         With you, into the world now. Certainly
         Only a toy for a short while.
DON JUAN: Oh, Anna
         There is no one that I loved as I love you!
         To me you seem to be a holy shrine.
ANNA: Why are you labouring then, senselessly
         To pull the shrine down from the pedestal.
DON JUAN: Because I want to have it here alive
         Not just of stone.
ANNA: The stone is necessary
         If one wants to build on firm foundations
         One's life and happiness.

DON JUAN: But do you really
        Still put your faith in stony happiness?
        Is it not true that I saw for myself
        How you were choking underneath these stones.
        Have I not felt here on my shoulders,
        Hot burning tears. For these tears, after all,
        He (*pointing to the statue*) has paid with his life.
ANNA: And guiltlessly.
DON JUAN (*steps away from her surprised*):
        If this be so. . . .
ANNA: In truth, he was not guilty
        Of this captivity. He bore an even
        Greater load all his life.
DON JUAN: He willed it so.
ANNA: And I took on that life of my own free will,
        But it was easy for him so to suffer,
        Because he loved me. It is happiness
        Indeed to place high on a shining summit
        The one you truly love.
DON JUAN: As for these summits . . .
        You know quite well my thoughts upon that theme. . . .
ANNA: What is a thought against the light of joy?
        Would I find dread the stern captivity
        Of this strict etiquette and ritual
        If I but knew that safe within my fortress
        My true love was awaiting me? That locks
        And jealous shutters are there but to hide
        My luxuries and state from prying eyes.
DON JUAN: You Anna now as if with red-hot iron,
        With cruel words put my heart to the torment.
        You paint a picture of true happiness.
        To say once more: "No, this is not for you!"
        But how am I to win you? For your sake
        I am suffering this secret shame.
        I live like a poor soul in Purgatory
        Among strange people, even enemies,
        A life uncoloured, and, I'd say, unworthy,
        Because it makes no sense. What do you want?
        Must I place underneath your feet my freedom
        That I have tended with such lavish care?
        But will you then believe me? From despair,

Even this thought is beating at my mind
Insistently.

ANNA: But only from despair?

DON JUAN: Do you really want to place compulsion
Between the two of us? Aren't you afraid
That it would suffocate our living love
The child of freedom.

ANNA (*pointing to the statue of the Commander*):
                              He would say of old
"It is not love that fears a solemn oath."

DON JUAN: At such a moment have you nothing else
To say to me, except these memories
Of him?!

ANNA: What am I then to say to you?

DON JUAN (*seizing her hand*):
No, this must end! For otherwise I swear
I shall go at once and give myself
Up to the law.

ANNA: Is this some kind of threat?

DON JUAN: No, not a threat; a groan of mortal anguish
For I'm expiring under stone oppression!
My heart is dying. O save me then,
Or kill me outright!
(*He presses both her hands, trembling all over and looking
into her eyes.*)

ANNA: Give me time, I must
Think it over. . . .
(*She ponders. From the gate there approaches the pale
Donna Concepcion, a stately grandee's wife, with a little
girl and a duenna. Anna fails to see them, as she is
standing with her back to the path. Don Juan is first
to see the new arrivals and lets go of Anna's hands.*)

LITTLE GIRL: Good day, Donna Anna!

DONNA CONCEPCION: The Señora is praying, don't disturb her!

ANNA (*embarrassed*): Good day, Donna Concepcion, good day
Rosina dear . . . I have such dreadful trouble
With my duenna. She went off to fetch
Her gloves, and is late back, and to go home
All through the town alone. . . .

DONNA CONCEPCION: But Donna Anna,
Here is a knight, he can escort you home.

(*to Don Juan*) I didn't even know, Señor de Marana,
That you were kin to Señora de Mendoza!
You ought to comfort her, at least a little,
Else otherwise she may fall ill from grief.
(*to the little girl who has run on ahead*)
Rosina, wait a moment! (*to Anna*) My respects!
(*Don Juan bows. Donna Concepcion gives him the merest
    nod and follows the little girl to the other side of the
    cemetery, beyond the chapel. The duenna follows,
    looking back several times curiously at Anna and Don
    Juan.*)

ANNA (*to Don Juan*): Now you had better go and kill this lady
Only, alas, it will not be the end
Of labour for your rapier. . . . Rejoice!
There's no more need to free your fair princess,
She'll tumble from the summit by herself.
(*She clasps her head in despair.*)
I know! This is what you were hoping for,
Lying in wait in here to ambush me,
That, struck by shame, I out of deep despair
Would fall into your arms, an easy prey.
But this will not occur.

DON JUAN: I swear to you
I did not want it, and I could not want it.
I do not seek unworthy victories.
How can we put this right? Tell me the way,
I will do anything you want, in order
Not to have to witness your despair.
(*A pause. Anna thinks.*)

ANNA: Come to me tomorrow night for supper,
I shall receive you. Even have some guests
It might be better if we meet in public,
I might perhaps. . . . Ah, my duenna's coming.

DUENNA: Señora, please forgive . . .

ANNA: You're not to blame
That you're too old for service.

DUENNA (*plaintively*):   Oh! . . .

ANNA: Let's go.
(*She nods to Don Juan without speaking. He bows deeply,
    Exeunt Anna and Duenna.*)

SGANAREL (*coming out of the chapel*):
        Well then, can I congratulate you, sir?
        You've had an invitation to take supper?
        And yet you don't seem very glad. . . . It's true
        To eat in that house. . . . They might lay for you
        That gentleman's own dishes . . . (*points to the statue*).
DON JUAN: Well, what of it?
SGANAREL: Yes, but supposing that Señor appeared
        Tomorrow at the table, facing you,
        Then. . .
DON JUAN: Do you think that I would be afraid,
        You know, I've met him several times already.
SGANAREL: That's nothing. A dead man is far more dread
        Than a live one, to Christians.
DON JUAN: Not to me.
SGANAREL: Nevertheless, you won't invite him to
        Tomorrow's supper.
DON JUAN: For they don't invite
        The host himself.
SGANAREL: At least they should inform him.
DON JUAN: Well go then, and inform him straightaway.
        I see that you have studied etiquette
        Since you have been servant to a grandee
        And not to a banished felon.
SGANAREL: How should I
        Inform him? In your name?
DON JUAN: Why, yes, of course.
SGANAREL: Why should I go? It's simpler if you do.
DON JUAN: You worried about etiquette, and now
        You want simplicity? Eh, Sganarel,
        Now you're getting rabbit-hearted here.
        Madrid, it seems, has not done you much good.
SGANAREL: And has Madrid not done you any harm?
DON JUAN: Well, well, go along straightaway and inform him!
SGANAREL (*moves off, then stops, looking back at Don Juan*):
        But what if I should bring you back an answer?
DON JUAN: Of course you must. That's just the thing I hope for.
SGANAREL (*going to the statue he bows deeply and recites with a jeer,
            but also with a tremble in his voice*):
        Immovable-in-strength and mighty sir

Deign to receive the greeting of Don Juan.
The Señor de Marana from Seville,
The Marquis de Tenorio, and grandee.
My master has received the noble honour
Of your wife Donna Anna's invitation,
And must appear tomorrow at the feast
In your own house. But if it doesn't please you
My master will refrain from such a visit.

DON JUAN: Well, the last part's superfluous.

SGANAREL: It isn't!
For why inform him otherwise? (*exclaiming*)
                             Look sir,
He gives an answer, and in writing, too!

DON JUAN: What answer? Where?

SGANAREL: "Come to me. I await thee!"

    (*Don Juan approaches Sganarel, who points to the scroll in
        the left hand of the statue.*)

DON JUAN (*after a pause*):
Well, maybe I have got a motto, too.
(*They depart from the cemetery.*)

ACT VI

A banquet hall in the Commander's mansion. Not very big but beautifully decorated with carved cabinets, sideboards with valuable plate, suits of armour, etc. In the middle is a long table set for a ceremonial supper, around it stand oak chairs in a heavy style. On one wall opposite the end of the table there is a large portrait of the Commander, with black drapery over the frame; opposite the other end is a long narrow mirror that reaches the floor. The chair which stands in the place of honour has its back to the mirror and faces the portrait. A servant opens a door from the adjoining room; other servants are getting ready to serve at the table. Donna Anna leads in a group of guests, mostly elderly, dignified, proud, and in dark clothing. Anna herself is in a white dress, piped along all the seams with black crepe.

ANNA: Will you all be seated please, dear guests.
    (*to the eldest guest, pointing to the place of honour*)
    And this is your place.

ELDEST GUEST: No, my kind Señora,
Forgive me, I won't sit there. Let it stay
Empty. In that way it will seem to us

That our dear host has merely been delayed
And still may come in time to join the party.
This is the first time that we meet without him
And it is hard to accept the thought that all
His trace is covered by the slab of death.

ANNA (*having seated herself at the end of the table, under the portrait
of the Commander, opposite the place of honour which
has been left empty, she makes a sign to the servants
to serve the guests who are all in their places*):
My gentlemen and ladies, be at ease.
Help yourselves, I beg you, and excuse me
If anything is not the way it should be
At a widow's party. It is hard
For a lone widow to maintain at home
That knightly manner, which the honour of
The house requires.

DONNA CONCEPCION (*quietly to her neighbour, a younger lady*):
As if the honour of
The house requires banquets amid full mourning!
When other matters are thought unrequired.

DONNA CLARA (*Donna Concepcion's neighbour*):
But so far Donna Anna has kept honour
In all particulars.

DONNA CONCEPCION: Dear Donna Clara,
I know the things I know!

DONNA CLARA (*with a sidelong glance at Anna*):
You don't say? Surely?

SERVANT (*on the threshold*): The Marquis de Tenorio!

ANNA: Ask him in!
(*Don Juan enters and steps on the threshold. Nodding a
welcome to Don Juan, Anna turns to the guests*):
Permit me, honourable company
To introduce the Señor De Marana
And Marquis de Tenorio. (*to Don Juan*) Señor,
Please take your seat.
(*Don Juan looking round for a seat takes the place of
honour. Seeing the portrait of the Commander opposite
him, he shudders.*)

ANNA (*to a servant*): Give the Señor some wine!
(*The servant gives Don Juan a goblet that is bigger and
better than the others.*)

A GUEST (*neighbour of Don Juan*):
   I recognize this goblet. It is fitting
   We should recall him who once drank from it.
   (*He raises his goblet to Don Juan.*)
   Be then his knightly spirit in this house
   Eternally remembered!
DON JUAN (*touching the guest's goblet with his own*):
         Rest eternal!
AN OLD LADY (*the wife of a grandee, who is sitting on the right of
   Donna Anna, in a low voice, to her hostess*):
   I don't know much about the de Maranas
   Is he Don Juan?
ANNA: His Christian name in full
   Is Antonio-Juan-Luis-Urtado.
OLD LADY: Ah then its not the same.
DONNA CONCEPCION (*listening to this conversation smiles ironically,
   and says quietly to her neighbour*):
         Yes, that's the same!
AN OLD GRANDEE (*to his neighbour, a younger grandee*):
   Do you know by chance how de Marana
   Surpasses us that, without pause for thinking
   He took the place of honour?
YOUNGER GRANDEE (*gloomily*): No, indeed.
OLD GRANDEE: Probably its because his honour's new,
   And ours has long grown old.
YOUNGER GRANDEE: Most probably.
DONNA CONCEPCION (*to Don Juan loudly*):
   Please pay attention, Señor de Marana,
   I couldn't really ask you yesterday,
   I didn't like to interrupt your converse
   When you were comforting poor Donna Anna
   Beside her husband's grave—but none the less
   I'd like to know in what precise degree
   You are related to her? A first cousin?
DON JUAN: No, we have no kinship.
DONNA CONCEPCION: Oh, indeed?
   But what a good and tender heart is yours!
   It is commanded, true, in Holy Writ,
   "To comfort the afflicted. . . ."
ANNA (*raising her voice a little*):
   Permit me now to give an explanation

Why I arranged, in this unusual manner,
This supper party *(to Don Juan)*
                                   Ah, forgive me,
You wanted to say something.
DON JUAN: Oh no, please
Continue speaking to us, Donna Anna.
ANNA *(to the knights)*: Beloved relatives, tell me, in truth
If ever I detracted from the honour
Due to your family name.
KNIGHTS: No, not at all!
ANNA *(to the ladies)*: My dearest kinswomen, you will know best
How a young lady often needs advice
And strong protection in this hostile world.
And where's advice, protection to be found
For a young widow, who's not called by God
Into the blest vocation of a nun.
For the protection which was given me
By widow's weeds, alas, is far too thin
For people not to touch me with the thorns
Of condemnation, though I'm innocent
So tell me then from whom and where am I
To seek protection.
DONNA CONCEPCION: It is far the best
When there's no need to seek for it at all.
DON JUAN: Still better not to tolerate the thorns
Nor to allow them freedom to destroy.
ELDEST GUEST *(looking at Don Juan in a penetrating manner)*:
Our kinswoman has complete freedom to
Do anything that does not stain the honour
Of the proud name of de Mendoza. But
Should anyone hinder our kinswoman
From holding high that honour, let him know
That in our family there are many knights,
And all their rapiers at the lady's service.
DON JUAN: She has no need of many rapiers,
So long as I still have this one to wield.
(He draws his rapier half-way from the scabbard.)
ELDEST GUEST *(to Anna)*:
And do you find one rapier enough
For your defence?
DON JUAN: If rapier will not do,

Then I'll find other methods of defence.

ELDEST GUEST (*to Anna*):

And does he have the right to say this?

ANNA: Yes.

ELDEST GUEST: It seems we are not needed in this house.

(*He rises and the other guests follow his example.*)

The Señor Marquis, as you see, has not
Decided yet what form defence will take.
He'll decide far more easily alone
Than in public eyes. The chosen date
They will announce not later than tomorrow,
Or we, ourselves, will guess what it must be.

(*He bows to Anna, and, following him, all the guests depart
from the hall. Donna Anna and Don Juan remain
alone.*)

DON JUAN: Well, so the gates of stone at last have closed

(*He laughs bitterly.*)

How strange the ending of the fairytale
The knight has joined the princess in the prison.

ANNA: Is it so bad an ending that you gain
As well as the princess a strong proud fortress,
Why should we think of it as a prison, not
A nest, an eyrie for a pair of eagles.
I built this nest, myself, upon the crag
Toil, torment, terror—I have conquered all,
And I have grown accustomed to my height
Why should you not dwell also on the summit
For, after all, you have a winged spirit.
Are you afraid of abysses and crags?

DON JUAN: Only of those things am I afraid
Which break the freedom.

ANNA: But you have no freedom,
For long ago Dolores took it from you.

DON JUAN: Oh no! Dolores did not break my freedom
Though for my sake she crucified her soul
And stabbed the heart?

ANNA: And why did she do this?
In order to restore your social bonds
That formerly you used to find so hateful.

DON JUAN: Oh, certainly I'd not endure them long
If it were not for you. I'd soon have cut them
If I could find no other way to freedom.

ANNA: Who for a single moment willingly
    Accepts them, finds they bite into his soul
    Forever—I know this too well, believe me—
    No longer can one cast them from the soul.
    Yet, by the spirit's strength and resolution
    One may make from them a great chain of office
    Which binds even society like a slave
    And throws it at your feet. To have true freedom,
    I tell you, power's essential. . . .
DON JUAN: Even so,
    I, too, have had power over human hearts.
ANNA: So it might seem to you. And yet these hearts
    Only turned to ashes from your power.
    Turned into nothingness. The only one
    That remained safe and undestroyed is mine
    Because I am your equal.
DON JUAN: That is why
    I strove so hard to win you.
ANNA: And in vain
    Is it not better that we join our forces,
    To dominate the mountain with our strength,
    I have climbed up it with great difficulty.
    But you—you only have to take the ring
    From your little finger and give it me.
DON JUAN: And must I give Dolores' ring to you?
ANNA: Why not? At least I did not kill Dolores,
    It was you felled a corpse here in this house,
    That forever have to lie between us
    Like a threshold, impassable and dread,
    But I am ready to step over even
    This threshold, since I have been brave from birth.
DON JUAN: Many the things of which men have accused me,
    But so far all acknowledge I have courage,
    Both friend and foe.
ANNA: You have enough of it
    To cut yourself a way from out this house
    You will not fear the de Mendoza rapiers,
    Of that I'm sure.
DON JUAN: What will become of you?
ANNA: What's that to you? Have no concern for me!
    The worst disaster's better than assistance
    That's forced and insincere.

DON JUAN: Here, take my ring!
    (Takes the ring from his little finger and gives it to Anna.)
ANNA: Here is mine, too. And soon I'll give another
    To you that you can set the seal upon
    The acts of a Commander.
DON JUAN: What's that?
ANNA: Yes,
    I shall win you the rank of a Commander,
    Surely my chosen one will not stand lower
    In the eyes of the knighthood and the Court.
    All people know you were a faultless knight
    Even at the time when you were banished.
    And now you'll be a paragon of all
    The knightly virtues—it is easy for you.
DON JUAN: *(interrupting)*: In your opinion one may easily
    Drown in hypocrisy, that plumbless ocean
    Which calls itself the code of knightly virtues.
ANNA: Enough of words and empty speeches, Juan!
    What does it mean "hypocrisy?" Admit
    That you've not always acted quite sincerely,
    Sometimes you happened to pretend a little
    So to attract some lady's lovely eyes.
    So why are you so conscientious, now?
    It is, perhaps, the aim's too high for you?
DON JUAN *(in thought)*:
    So I would have to take the heritage
    Left by the lord and master of this fortress?
    How strange . . . the knightly champion of freedom
    Takes up the heavy stony battering ram
    To storm and conquer citadels and castles.
ANNA: You, knightly champion of freedom, were
    In banishment, a bandit.
DON JUAN: I'd no choice.
ANNA: Indeed? No choice? And where, then, was the freedom
    When you were compelled to strike and rob
    Lest otherwise people or hunger slay you?
    I don't see any freedom there!
DON JUAN: But power
    Was mine, admit it.
ANNA: No, I don't admit it!
    There was nothing but a "mutual hunt"

I remember well the name you called it.
And it is no great rank to be a huntsman.
So far you have not learned what power can mean,
To have not only one right hand alone,
But thousands armed and ready for the fray
Who have power both to strengthen and destroy
Universal thrones, and win them too.

DON JUAN: (carried away):
    That is a proud dream.

ANNA: (comes nearer to him, whispering):
                        Yes, to win a throne.
You must take over as your heritage
This dream as well as the Commander's baton
(She runs to the cabinet and takes out the Commander's
    coat. Don Juan shudders but cannot take his eyes away
    from the coat, enraptured by Anna's words.)
Juan, look, for this white coat is the dress
Of a Commander. It is not a vain
Costume for ornament. It, like a banner,
Unites about itself all valiant
Warriors who've no fear with blood and tears
To join the mighty stones of strength and power
And build eternal glory.

DON JUAN: Till now, Anna,
I have not known you. You're not like a woman,
Your charms surpass by far the charms of women.

ANNA: (approaches Don Juan with the coat):
    See how the coat will look on you.

DON JUAN: (wanting to take it, but hesitating):
                      No, Anna.
It seems to me that there is blood on it.

ANNA: This is a new coat that was never worn.
    But if it were? If there was blood on it?
    Since when have you been so afraid of blood?

DON JUAN: Yes, you are right, why ever should I fear it?
    Why ever should I not put on the coat?
    For I shall take all the inheritance,
    I am to be the master in this house.

ANNA: Ah, how you said that, in a different way.
    As soon as possible I want to see you
    In that guise which must be yours forever.

> (*She gives him the coat. Don Juan puts it on. Anna gives
> him the sword, the Commander's baton and the helmet
> with white plumes, taking them down from the wall.*)

Truly magnificent! Look in the mirror!

(*Don Juan goes to the mirror and suddenly cries out.*)

ANNA: What is it?

DON JUAN: Him! His face! (*He drops the sword and baton and
covers his eyes with his hands.*)

ANNA: Indeed for shame!
What dream or figment is it? Look again!
Don't let imagination run away!

DON JUAN (*fearfully uncovers his face and looks. With a voice
choking with unearthly fear*):
Where am I? I'm no more! It's he—the statue!

He staggers aside from the mirror to the wall, and leans against it,
shuddering with his whole body. From the mirror steps out the Commander, just as in the monument, only without the sword and baton. He
comes out of the frame, and with a heavy stony tread walks directly at
Don Juan. Anna rushes between Don Juan and the Commander. The
Commander with his left hand thrusts Anna to her knees, and places his
right hand on Don Juan's heart. Don Juan grows stiff with the stillness of
death. Donna Anna screams and falls face downward at the feet of the
Commander.

The Orgy

A DRAMATIC POEM

Dramatis personae

Anteus, *a singer*
Hermione, *his mother*
Euphrosyne, *his sister*
Nerissa, *his wife*
Chilon, *his pupil*
Phaedon, *a sculptor*
Maecenas, *a rich well-known Roman, a descendant of the famous Maecenas, the Prefect*
Atriensius, *a slave*
Procurator
Guests at the orgy, slaves, slave girls, dancers, mimes, chorus of panegyrists
The action takes place at Corinth under Roman rule.

ACT I

The garden in the home of the poet and singer Anteus, not very large, surrounded by walls with a gate in one wall; at the back of the garden a house with a portico in four columns and with two doors, one leading to the andronitis and the other to the gynaecium. Hermione, the mother of Anteus, sits on the threshold of the gynaecium, spinning. Knocking is heard at the gate.

HERMIONE (*without getting up*):
      Who's there?
CHILON (*outside the gate*): It's Chilon Alcmeonides.
HERMIONE (*calls in the direction of the other door*):
      Anteus, come out! A student's here to see you.
      (*She remains sitting, but pulls her veil a little closer.*)
ANTEUS (*young, but of manly appearance, enters through the door and opens the gate to Chilon*):
      Today, Chilon, you have come much too late.
      The students have all gone.
CHILON (*a very young lad, he speaks pantingly and with some embarrassment*):   Excuse me, but . . .
      But actually I have not come to study. . . .

ANTEUS (*pleasantly*):
> Then be a guest.
> (*He sits down on a bench under a tree and indicates to
>   Chilon the place beside him, but Chilon remains
>   standing*).
>   Why not sit down?
CHILON: I've business. . . .
ANTEUS: Is it so urgent that you can't sit down?
CHILON: It isn't that . . . but . . . please excuse me. . . . I
> Today must thank you for your teaching. . . . I
> Shall not come any more.
ANTEUS: Why? (*Chilon is silent.*)
>   It is true,
> It's not for me to question you this way.
> Evidently I did not satisfy
> You with my teaching. So, no shame to you—
> For it is I who ought to be ashamed.
CHILON (*earnestly*): No, no, my master. Do not think this way.
> Apollo be my judge, that I respect
> This teaching like the Sacred Mystery!
ANTEUS: Then I don't understand.
> (*He stops, then clasps his hand to his forehead.*)
>   Ah, yes, of course.
> (*He, too, is evidently embarrassed.*)
> Listen, Chilon . . . I'm prepared to wait
> Until you've finished all my course of teaching.
> Indeed I'd rather take no fees at all
> From you, if that is causing difficulty.
CHILON: But, master, you are not a wealthy man.
ANTEUS: Chilon, I shall tell you all in truth—
> Although you are still young to hear such things
> But explanations otherwise come hard. . . .
> Song, speech and music are my pay, you see,
> And I place higher value on my art
> Than on the money that it brings me in.
> I have not taught talent to anyone,
> Nor shall I—for the god alone can give it—
> So, when instructing ordinary people,
> Who never felt Apollo's sacred hand,
> I teach them how to find a little pleasure,
> How to pluck the strings in harmony

And to express their thoughts somewhat more clearly;
Then they pay to me a little money
And the account is settled. If the god
Sends to me a young man he has chosen,
For me to aid with my experience,
And I perceive that every lifeless form
Which I expound to him, once it becomes
Familiar to him sudden springs to life,
And the young genius in the ancient form
Resounds and sparkles with its own clear radiance
Like young wine in a goblet of old crystal,
Then I'm already paid in full, No, more—
I even feel some guilt, since I'm not able
To serve him as I'd like. You understand, now?

CHILON: Master . . .
(*He cannot speak for emotion, he hangs his head and covers
his eyes with his hand.*)

ANTEUS: When your genius has surpassed
All of the forms and all the learning which
I possess and can impart, then, lad,
By all means leave me, I myself advise you,
But only, for the sake of Lord Apollo,
Still do not give up learning. Go to Athens,
There you will find teaching that's far, far better,
Than any we can offer here in Corinth.
And then when you have finished all the schools
Still go on studying, find yourself teaching
In books and people and in all the world,
But never, never tell yourself, "Now I
Have finished all my learning."

CHILON: This advice,
Master, gives me renewed courage. I
Assure you, I shall not be giving up
All learning, though now I am leaving you,
I'm going to study in the school . . . (*He is silent again.*)

ANTEUS: Which one?

CHILON: The one Maecenas has established here.

ANTEUS: Latin?

CHILON: Well, everything is Latin now.

ANTEUS: What's that? Have you and I, our native language
As well, all turned to Latin?

CHILON: Well, I meant
          Roman, of course. I just mistook the word.
ANTEUS: If you've still not learned properly from me
          How to avoid mistakes, in that new school
          For certain there'll be still more such mistakes.
          But I do not know what it is you'll gain there
          Besides mistakes. In Latin poetry
          I myself have taught you, probably
          Everything that's really worth one's learning—
          I do not think the rhetors in that school
          Can give you anything that's new, for I
          Know them too well. Indeed I think that you
          Could teach them even now.
CHILON: I am quite certain
          The teachers there can equal you in nothing
          At all. But none the less, I am still forced
          To go to them.
ANTEUS: What, then, is forcing you?
CHILON: Master, if I should stay with you, then I
          Would become similar in fate to you.
ANTEUS: And for what reason does this fate alarm you?
          Am I then the lowest among singers?
CHILON: Not among singers, no . . .
ANTEUS: But among people?
CHILON: I did not say so, but it still is true,
          That in society you cannot find
          The place that's truly fitting to your talent.
ANTEUS: But how will you prevent this happening
          When you have finished at Maecenas' school?
CHILON: I may become a rhetor in this school,
          And then in an academy somewhere.
          Or I shall go to Rome. Conditions there
          Are very favourable towards the pupils
          Of this Maecenas. Still his family holds
          The power they wielded in the Augustan age.
          But in the meantime while I'm yet a student
          I still can join the choir of panegyrists
          Of Maecenas . . .
ANTEUS (jumping up in rage):
                              You? You're going to enter
          The choir of panegyrists? Join that mob

Of traitors, wicked sinners against talent?
O, it were better to be dumb forever
Cut off your hands, grow deaf, than fall so low,
And this was once my best, my finest pupil.
(*a pause*)

CHILON: Master, then receive my grateful thanks.
(*He takes some money from his pouch and gives it to Anteus.*)

ANTEUS (*waving him away*):
Go! I have taught you nothing! Get away
Out of my sight! (*Exit Chilon, hanging his head.*)

HERMIONE:				Anteus, and you didn't
Accept his money. Yet his father's richer,
A hundred times than we are. Willy-nilly
It's still your rightful earnings.

ANTEUS:						Mother dear,
I have earned nothing but the bitterest shame.

HERMIONE: There is no cause that you should feel ashamed,
Except for throwing out to the four winds
Your hard-earned wages. In the end, my son
We'll come down to the bread of poverty.
Will it be right to you, when all your poor
Family must go and beg for alms
From these same Romans whom you hate so much?

ANTEUS: We have sufficient bread yet of our own,
Do not offend the gods.

HERMIONE:					This is their will!
Certainly Aphrodite wished it thus
That I, not a rich daughter-in-law but
The daughter of a dancing girl, a slave
Was forced to welcome . . .

ANTEUS:					Still no end of nagging?

HERMIONE: It isn't nagging, son, just the plain truth.
Didn't you pay, as price for your Nerissa,
All that your father left you, and a good
Slice of your salary?

ANTEUS:					But do not blame
Just Aphrodite. All the gods of Hellas
Wished that I should buy out from slavery
A little child of the Hellenic race
It could have been your daughter, my dear sister

Who'd fallen into slavery.

HERMIONE: My son,
At least that isn't added to our troubles!
We have been able to buy out Nerissa.
But there's the dowry for Euphrosyne,
We can't provide one. Is it better
To be an old maid than to be a slave?

ANTEUS: My sister, without dowry is worth more
Than all the rich men's daughters.

HERMIONE: But who knows it?
At home with us she's not like Roman girls
Who wander everywhere. She's always in
The gynaeceum and at work. And if
She goes out for a festival, the way
She dresses, nobody would notice her.
(*Euphrosyne appears at the doorway of the gynaeceum,
but Hermione does not notice her and goes on.*)
Nerissa always gets herself up well,
Euphrosyne won't even wear one ribbon.

EUPHROSYNE (*young, but not girlish, wearing an everyday dress, she
seems to be in the middle of her work. She bows, then
embraces her mother*):
But mother dearest! What's the good of ribbons
If one has beauty, what need to adorn it?
If one has not, a ribbon will not help.
(*Smiling she kisses her mother, then stands up straight.*)
Mother, how am I to dress the pigeons?
I've finished boiling them.

HERMIONE (*standing up*):   No, leave them, leave them
I'd better do it, you don't know the way.
(*She hurries into the house.*)

EUPHROSYNE (*going to Anteus and putting her hand on his shoulder*):
Dearest brother, why are you so gloomy?
Was mother going on at you again?
Don't pay attention—that's old people's way.

ANTEUS (*replying not immediately, as though he has not heard what
she said. After a pause his words come out as though
involuntarily*):
Chilon has got ahead of me.

EUPHROSYNE (*surprised*):   What way?

ANTEUS: He's going to join the choir of panegyrists.

EUPHROSYNE: What are you saying?
    (*For a moment she is silent from surprise and anger.*
      Then she collects herself.)
                              Well, I'm not surprised,
    His kind is always flighty.
ANTEUS: But in talent
    Strangely enough, he far surpassed the others.
EUPHROSYNE: It seems to me, though, that Appollodorus
    Who fled to you from the school of Maecenas
    Surpassed that self-same Chilon in his talent,
    Not only in intelligence. I've heard
    How he can render the great speech of Haemon
    From the *Antigone*—indeed I could
    Only just about hold back my tears.
ANTEUS (*with a gentle smile, putting his arm round his sister's
      shoulders*):
    For you yourself are my Antigone
    It seems that I could even forgive Chilon,
    If what he did he had done to relieve
    A sister such as mine from bitter hardship.
EUPHROSYNE: But I would never forgive such a sister.
ANTEUS: Oh, you would not accept the sacrifice
    Nor any other. But my dearest sister,
    If I should wish for riches, it would be
    For your sake, yours alone.
EUPHROSYNE: And all in vain
    Because I do not want it. (*smiling*) Mother'd quickly
    Go and buy me a husband. That would be
    Quite certainly a most disastrous purchase.
ANTEUS: All right, not wealth! But if I only could
    Save you from miseries.
EUPHROSYNE: From miseries?
    Where do you see such things?
ANTEUS: That I *don't* see them
    Is due to you, my dear, and you alone . . .
EUPHROSYNE: And mother and Nerissa. . . .
ANTHEUS: No, you know
    That mother now has finished all her work
    While our Nerissa . . .
EUPHROSYNE: Ought to start her work.
    Is life in truth so sweet to you, that even

A honeymoon is something you find needless?

ANTEUS: I am ashamed, enjoying happiness,
When I remember that you pay for it
By your hard work. We have our happiness
But what, in the house of your birth, have you?

EUPHROSYNE: I have a brother. Even if forever
I live in spinsterhood, yet I shall never
Envy any wives or happy mothers
For their love serves only their families
But mine is for all Hellas. For in you
Anteus, is all our hope.

ANTEUS: Euphrosyne
How is it possible to place all hope
Upon one person?

EUPHROSYNE: Out of all the gods
Only Apollo has not ceased to love
Hellas, and in her there's still hope of life.
And while Apollo's reigning on Parnassus
The Muses will be there.

ANTEUS (*with a smile*):   Not without fame
Am I, with none but you to give me triumphs
For you are my true Nike!

EUPHROSYNE: Nike must
Know how to do her duty. Wait a moment.
(*She breaks off two branches from a laurel bush, joins them
     into a wreath and steps on to the base of a column in
     the pose of the goddess of Victory, Nike stretching out
     her hand with the wreath.*)
And now, come over here! Bend your proud brow!
(*Anteus approaches, smiling all the time, and bends his
     head in front of Euphrosyne. She smiling, and with
     tears of sincere emotion, puts the laurel wreath on her
     brother's head.*)

NERISSA (*young, straight, very dainty, prettily dressed, stands on the
     threshold of the gynaeceum*):
What's all this?
(*Euphrosyne, embarrassed, jumps down from the base of
     the column.*)

ANTEUS: It is Nike who has crowned
Her poet. And when, also, Charis will
Give him a pomegranate or a rose

Then he will be endowed with everything
That is right for mortal man to wish for.

EUPHROSYNE (*feeling somewhat ill at ease under Nerissa's cold
          looks*):
          Roses are flowering over there . . . (*to Anteus*). But Nike
          Has to go to the kitchen to help mother,
          Because today we shall have a real orgy
          We've bought some fish, and auntie's given us
          Some good wine and a pair of pigeons, too.
          And when I've baked some honey cakes, then even
          Maecenas well might envy us our orgy.
          (*With a somewhat forced smile she disappears through
          the doors of the gynaeceum.*)

NERISSA: Euphrosyne's a strange girl, always joking!

ANTEUS: Well, she is young. . . .
          (*Takes off the laurels from his head, holding them in his
          hand. As he speaks he sits down and puts the laurels on
          the bench beside him.*)

NERISSA: But probably I'm younger
          Although . . .

ANTEUS: Although "moody from time to time"
          You wanted to say that.
          (*Smiling he embraces her. She received his caresses with
          some reserve.*)
                                   Why what's the matter?
          Are you not well, or has someone upset you?

NERISSA: But don't you really know? Why all the neighbours
          Must long ago have learned by heart the speech
          About my ransom and Euphrosyne's
          Dowry, which mother trots out every day.

ANTEUS: What, every day?

NERISSA: Yes, it's the very truth.
          I can no longer look Euphrosyne
          Straight in the face.

ANTEUS: But dear Euphrosyne
          Doesn't blame you for anything.

NERISSA: I know.
          She isn't your Antigone in vain.

ANTEUS: Nerissa dearest. It is really naughty
          To eavesdrop, and then put the blame on others.

NERISSA: Eavesdrop indeed! This isn't such a palace

That you can't hear all that goes on in it!

ANTEUS (*roused a little*):

Only the Romans now own palaces.

You'd have done better, then, to wed Maecenas.

NERISSA (*gentler than before*):

I am not blaming you for being poor

But doesn't every woman really wish

That wealth and riches may come to her husband?

ANTEUS: Yes, and to her as well!

NERISSA: To her as well.

Is that a crime? I certainly was not

Born to walk all day long beneath a yoke

Just as your sister does.

ANTEUS: Well, but you don't.

NERISSA: D'you think it's any easier for me?

ANTEUS: If it weren't easier, you'd work as well!

NERISSA: People have slaves to do the work.

ANTEUS: Nerissa,

It's somewhat strange to hear you speak this way.

NERISSA: Because I was a slave myself, you mean?

Well, I could earn my living, too, in freedom

If only you would give me your permission.

Since now there's nobody who wants me here,

I'm in the way, like a high, awkward threshold,

And you're to blame for that.

ANTEUS: Well, dear, enough . . .

NERISSA: Why not let me go to the theatre,

I shall adorn your sister with bright gold

And be a darling daughter to your mother

For certainly I can earn more by dancing

Than you by song and teaching ever can.

ANTEUS: Nerissa, stop! It is your grief that's speaking.

And, surely, I'm to blame for that. Forgive me

(*Kisses her. She bends toward him like a sulky child.*)

My dearest one! My treasure! I'll not give,

I shall not give you to the shameless crowd.

You shall not go to them, to their false orgies

For the crowd does not know what's a true

Holy orgy, that divine creation.

NERISSA: Have you been to an orgy?

ANTEUS: Long ago,
When I was still a lad, there was still in Corinth
A bard's hetaereia, secret, of course
For any kind of guild must be a crime
To Roman minds.
NERISSA: Well then? Were your orgies
Very luxurious?
ANTEUS: You just consider!
We would all meet together in a house
Like this of mine.
NERISSA (*surprised*):   Ah, so. . . .
ANTEUS: And in our goblets
The water always dominated wine.
We only could have flowers in the seasons
When they are blossoming in field and garden,
But when Persephone to Tartarus
Returned, she robbed us of all decorations.
NERISSA: Can orgies really happen without flowers?
ANTEUS: We had them and they were exuberant.
NERISSA: But they took place quite secretly you say?
Then how were these exuberant orgies not
Heard in the street outside?
ANTEUS: Could people hear
From outside how our hearts were beating in us
Or could the light from fervent glances pierce
Through the stone walls and the thick draperies?
NERISSA: But what about your songs?
ANTEUS: Oh they were strong
In their inspiration, not in sound,
And in the muffled sobbing of quiet strings
We could hear the storms and tempests which
Were nurtured deep within the singer's breast.
We had wild curls, and they, like thyrsi, called
Exclaiming to the sight "Evoe, Bacche!"
And even if the goblets only held
Pure water, yet we still would go home drunk.
O how I've wished that you just once could be
At such an orgy. In the holy frenzy
You would dance, indeed, like a true maenad.
NERISSA: I have been to orgies many times.

ANTEUS: But not like these!
NERISSA: Maybe to better ones!
ANTEUS: That is not possible!
NERISSA: I do not know
          What yours were like, but these to which I went
          Often when I was still a little girl,
          They were like carefree dreams.
ANTEUS: It's very wrong
          To take a child along to such an orgy.
NERISSA: My mother *had* to take me there.
ANTEUS: I know.
          Forgive me, I was speaking thoughtlessly.
          I should have realized how heavily
          The heart of a poor dancing girl must beat
          When she is forced to take her only daughter,
          A little girl still half in babyhood
          To such a shameful spectacle.
NERISSA: My mother
          Never told me anything of this.
          I always went off to the orgy gladly,
          There I could eat my fill of dainty tit-bits,
          And sometimes toys would come my way because
          The guests would make a fuss of me.
ANTEUS: Don't think
          Of it. I'm shivering at the idea. . . .
          All this fussing was, for certain, dirty
          And every word they spoke was soaked in filth.
NERISSA: I don't know. Then I didn't understand
          Either dirty talk or shameless glances.
          But even when still small I understood
          Beauty, my heart beat faster from their praise,
          As a lyre string does, touched by the plectrum.
          On the high stage, the two of us appeared
          Like two rainbows, one large and one small
          On the bright highlands. The transparent veils
          Brilliant with colours in the light-curved bow
          Were spread across the cloudlets of the gold
          And fragrant dust clouds. Then it seemed to me
          That I was truly dancing in the clouds
          Of heaven, and from the earth there came
          Only bright blossoms winging up to me.

It was the guests who threw their flowers to us,
Carried away with passionate delight.

ANTEUS: But in these flowers, there hid, unseen, the cold
Serpent of debauchery and disgrace.

NERISSA: But I tell you that I did not know this!

ANTEUS: But still you do not know how Romans treat
The hapless dancing girls who are their slaves.
Do not forget what would become of you,
If you had grown up amid such orgies.
Remember what became of your poor mother
Who perished like a broken, cast-off toy,
In illness, in neglect and base contempt.

NERISSA: I recollect that I owe you my thanks.
Do not be afraid, I shan't forget!

ANTEUS: Nerissa, is this really necessary?

NERISSA: No, no, it is my duty to remember
That you have made into a human being
"The little monkey from Tanagra."

ANTEUS: Stop!
I do not like it when you speak this way.
And I cannot stand the common nickname
That the vulgar Romans used to give
To a fair and dainty child of Hellas.
They were just jealous that their Roman women
Were heavy and ungraceful beside you
My fair Nerissa "of the breeze-light foot."

NERISSA (thoughtfully):
And what is that to me, now?

ANTEUS: What, my dear?

NERISSA: That "breeze-light footedness" you speak about . . .
I'm not a dancer now.

ANTEUS: What's that, Nerissa?
Do you really not enjoy the praise,
Mine, and our friends' praise, modest but sincere.
Is it not enough to be at home
A hidden treasure, but a jewel so dear
That even Caesar cannot have a better.

NERISSA: "A hidden treasure"—I will tell you truly
That I am more sincere than you. You also
Are a hidden treasure, but I, Anteus,
Do not rejoice to know that your sweet lyre

Is not heard by the whole wide world, but only
By me and by a small group of your friends.
No! If I had the power, myself I would
Place you upon a lofty pedestal
Like the statue of Apollo-the-Cytharist,
Then let the world be filled with the sweet songs
Which you would create up there on high.
ANTEUS: Do you think perhaps, that inspiration
Can raise me up more than a pedestal?
NERISSA: O yes, I'm certain of it!
ANTEUS: Still a child! . . .
But if you are so fond of pedestals
Then be content, for our friend Phaedon has
Carved in your image a Terpsichore,
Set on a pedestal that's high enough.
NERISSA: And what is Phaedon doing with the statue?
ANTEUS: Bringing it here.
NERISSA: And leaving it?
ANTEUS: Of course.
It's a friendly gift to us from Phaedon. (*a pause*)
You're very quiet as if you're worrying.
What is it, my Nerissa?
NERISSA: I am thinking
How many "hidden treasures" more will be
Hid in this house as in a mausoleum.
ANTEUS: I do not like to hear such words from you.
NERISSA: Well, when the stone Terpsichore arrives
Then I shall take from her the role of silence.
ANTEUS: Nerissa, you have freakish moods today.
NERISSA: In that case I shall go! (*She gets up.*)
ANTEUS (*restraining her*):   No, no, my dearest!
NERISSA (*pulling away*):
Let me go! (*Knocking is heard at the gate.*)
Look, someone has come to see you.
(*Nerissa goes to the gynaeceum. Anteus opens the gate,
and lets in Phaedon, a young sculptor.*)
ANTEUS: Greetings, Phaedon! (*They clasp hands.*)
PHAEDON: I've just got a moment.
No time to stop.
ANTEUS: Why? Have you got some work?
PHAEDON: No, I have finished work for the time being.

But now I have new worries. I am going
To a lord's orgy at Maecenas' mansion.
ANTEUS (*surprised*):
    Were you invited?
PHAEDON: Yes, and you as well.
ANTEUS: You're joking, or else fooling?
PHAEDON: It's the truth
I tell you. I just dropped in to pass on
The invitation.
ANTEUS: Who gave it to you?
PHAEDON: When I was with Maecenas I received it.
ANTEUS: You were with Maecenas? Why?
PHAEDON: On business.
And d'you know, I never could have hoped
He was like that.
ANTEUS: Like what?
PHAEDON: So cordial
And it's surprising that a great lord speaks
Like that. . . .
ANTEUS: And what is it that's so surprising?
That an all-powerful lord lets on his threshold
A lowly artist? Or that the fact,
Perhaps, that sometimes, too, a Roman knows
A little of fine art?
PHAEDON: Oh, not "a little"
He's a great connoisseur, a really true one.
He was the one that first valued your work.
ANTEUS: He was the first one? But I had a school
Long before Maecenas came to Corinth.
PHAEDON: What is a school? The school is to your glory
Like a clay patera is to a sculptor.
ANTEUS: It must have been something like to glory
Since this fine lord heard something about me.
PHAEDON: To tell the truth it was blind chance that gave
Him news of you. One of your pupils came
Wanting to join the panegyrists' choir
And giving an example of his skill
He sang your epithalamy, the same
One that you composed for your own wedding.
(*Anteus makes a movement of disgust, but Phaedon, not
noticing it, continues.*)

I started a discussion with Maecenas
About the song, and then I told him who
The author was, and straightway he told me
To come and to invite you to his orgy.
And this indeed, means something, my dear friend!
ANTEUS (*restraining the annoyance caused by Phaedon's last remark*):
    Whatever business could you have with him?
PHAEDON: He bought a statue from me, not long back,
    And I went to deliver it to him
    Because the slaves might damage it in transit.
ANTEUS: What was the statue that you sold to him?
PHAEDON: Forgive me . . . I ought really to have asked
    For your consent. . . . But mighty lords don't like
    To have to wait for things . . .
ANTEUS: You sold Nerissa?
PHAEDON: A statue of Terpsichore, the goddess.
ANTEUS: If you knew how, you'd sell the goddess, too.
    Into a Roman house of prostitution!
PHAEDON (*getting up, offended*):
    You have no right to speak to me like that!
ANTEUS: Certainly you will not like this insult
    For you have sold your best work there, where all
    That's holy to us is despised, derided.
PHAEDON: (*interrupting*):
    Nobody there despises anything.
    There genius is prized, there glory given,
    Not only money. I did not betray
    My dear Terpsichore, I only placed her
    As in a temple, for men's admiration,
    Is she, maybe, too holy for a temple
    In your opinion?
ANTEUS: In my opinion, you
    Blaspheme, to call that Roman's house a temple.
    You sold yourself—for money or for glory
    Together with your handiwork.
PHAEDON: O Anteus!
    You want to work me up so that I go
    And buy the statue back again. For love
    Or money it is quite impossible
    Maecenas does not sell the things he buys.
    But maybe that was not my final spark

Of inspiration. Maybe I'll be able
To create something better, and exchange it.
ANTEUS: You'll just exchange sin for a far worse sin.
PHAEDON: I can't see what it is you want of me!
Am I, like you, to sit out all my years
With neither bread nor glory.
ANTEUS: It is right
Hellenes should suffer thus, if bread and glory
Can only be obtained from Roman hands.
PHAEDON: No Hellene, he, who does not wish for glory.
Our fathers have bequeathed this yearning to us,
It is our grandsires' heritage.
ANTEUS: Our grandsires
From Mother Hellas' hands received their garlands,
Our fathers, though, allowed her hands to be
Fettered, and this deprived their sons of garlands.
So, Phaedon, since Hellas herself has no
Glory, Hellenes are obliged to bury
Deep in their hearts their yearning after glory.
PHAEDON: And thus increase their country's lack of glory?
How may Hellas herself be glorified
When her children win no laurels for her?
ANTEUS: But not accept them from an enemy!
PHAEDON: Why not? Homer himself said, "Sweet the praise
Won from a foeman."
ANTEUS: On the field of war
Not in captivity!
PHAEDON: But glory's glory
Too, in captivity.
ANTEUS: Do not hope it!
They will allow us to bear our inglory
But Rome takes all the glory as her due,
And that Terpsichore which you have sold
Brings glory not to Hellas nor to you.
But to rich Rome that gathered all the treasures
From all lands, by the hands of that Maecenas.
Your work will give glory to his creation
But not to you, for you are but the slave
Whose skill adorns an orgy for the lords,
That orgy will always remain the lords'
Although it is the slaves' hands that prepare it.

PHAEDON: For slaves there is no honour in an orgy.
         But those who are invited there as guests
         As you and I are . . .
ANTEUS: Do not hope for this
         That I shall go with you to the orgy!
         You seek the favours of the mighty ones,
         But I'll remain "with neither bread nor glory"
         As you said, but maybe not without honour.
PHAEDON: In all sincerity, I beg you: go.
ANTEUS: Indeed. For oxen bear the yoke far better
         In pairs.
PHAEDON: I plainly see you don't believe
         That I can wish only what's best for you,
         But yet although you've wounded me intensely
         I still have not forgotten we are friends.
ANTEUS: What, I have wounded you and not you me?
PHAEDON: See, Anteus, I'll buy back Terpsichore.
         But you will not take back your wounding words.
ANTEUS: But you cannot buy back what you have done.
         You put your art to shame, you made a goddess
         Into a piece of mundane merchandise.
         Even if out of slavery returns
         Terpsichore—she'll be no more a goddess,
         The marble not divine but a simple stone.
PHAEDON: If it was once divine, then it will never
         Turn back to simple stone, a work of art
         Will be, no matter where, a work of art.
         Your lovely epithalamy resounded
         No worse there in the spacious Roman school
         Than here at home in your poor narrow house,
         If only you would sing it for yourself
         There in the echoing palace of Maecenas
         Accompanying it on a rich harp.
ANTEUS: Phaedon, please do not say such things to me,
         For, if you do, forever I shall hate you.
PHAEDON: Anteus, this is some strange obstinacy.
         It's not the first time Hellenes have received
         Foreigners' praise; what is disgraceful in it?
ANTEUS: Foreigners! Yes, but never conquerors,
         For conquerors only have praise to give
         When the conquered stoops and bends his brow,

Before him, and kisses the very dust
Beneath his feet
PHAEDON: It was so with the Persians,
And the barbarians from the East. But never
Was it demanded of us by a Roman.
ANTEUS: Was not demanded of us? Who, then, stepped
Upon us, as upon a bridge to reach
The temple of the universal glory.
Whom did we, from barbarity's abyss
Bear to the height? Did we not lay ourselves
As cornerstone for our conquerors' mausoleum
And we have to rejoice that we can go
Into their vast and echoing palaces
And play a tune upon a plundered lyre?
PHAEDON: Would it be better if the lyre were silent?
ANTEUS: Better, indeed.
PHAEDON: I think it worse, however,
It is far better to build mausoleums
Even if not for us, rather than be
Like the wayside plants beneath the feet
Of conquerors. The conqueror, if he wishes,
With his armed foot can quickly trample down
All our pride with our headstrong dreams. . . .
ANTEUS: What? Better that we trample it ourselves
So as to save the conquerors some work?
Does the high priest of beauty think and speak so?
Only one thing is left, that he should act so.
You have not sold yourself—still worse! You gave
Yourself, like wet clay into foeman's hands.
And who will breathe in you the living fire
When you're no more creator, but created.
Go and serve your dear Maecanas, then,
Forget the mighty testaments of beauty,
Forget the deathless image of Prometheus,
Warrior against the gods, forget the torment
Of truth's great champion, Laocoön,
Do not recall Antigone the heroic,
Electra the avenger. From your thoughts,
Cast Hellas out, like chained Andromeda
Cast out to feed the monster, wearily
Awaiting Perseus who will rescue her.

You are not Perseus, it is you who turned
To stone before the glance of Rome's Medusa.
You do not recollect the higher beauty,
Beauty of contest, even without hope.

PHAEDON: No beauty lives in powerless obstinacy,
But I see that I cannot speak to you
Of this. Goodbye. I'll go now.

ANTEUS: Farewell Phaedon.

PHAEDON: Are we parting, then no longer friends?

ANTEUS: I fear that we may meet as enemies.
 (*Exit Phaedon shrugging his shoulders.*)

NERISSA (*coming out of the gynaeceum as soon as Phaedon has gone*):
Anteus, I simply cannot understand you,
Why were you so harsh to Phaedon, how
Is he so guilty?

ANTEUS: Eavesdropping again?
In that case you should have paid more attention.
You have realized, perhaps, your image
Will stand there as a spectacle of shame
Set in the mansion of a conqueror.

NERISSA: What spectacle of shame? What conqueror?
Is this Maecenas guilty that his grandsire,
Or maybe his great-grandsire fought the Hellenes?
Now, too, Maecenas does not take away
Our treasures or our works of art by force.
He purchases them, for a good price, too.

ANTEUS: He pays in gold that's gathered in for Rome
From the conquered, namely, we ourselves.

NERISSA: Maecenas does not gather it himself,
Your father, after all, left you some money
You didn't ask who got it nor what way.

ANTEUS: I know it was acquired quite honourably.

NERISSA: Maecenas certainly must think the same
About his patrimony. He returns
A certain part of it to us, to Hellas,
And yet for this he's your worst enemy.
In your opinion, it would be the best
If all our works of art were lost in corners,
If artists lost their skill and power through hunger,
If moss grew on the marble, rust on harp strings,
If Hellenes would become barbarians
Lest they should serve the Romans in some way.

ANTEUS: There are enough to serve them, I shall not.
NERISSA: But no one is demanding service from you.
       Has Maecenas hurt you by inviting
       You to his reception through a friend?
ANTEUS: Reception? Do you still think that Maecenas
       Would invite a singer to his orgy
       Just to have a friendly conversation,
       And not to sing to entertain the guests.
NERISSA: And what if you did sing a little there,
       Your songs have been heard in that house already.
ANTEUS: Well, that's no fault of mine.
NERISSA: Yes, it's your "fault"
       You gave your pupils songs to copy out.
       That means that you yourself have sent them out
       Into the world. And that a Roman valued
       These songs more highly than your countrymen
       Is normal. Blame Maecenas, if you like!
       In Hellas, now, he, only he, is famous
       Who has been praised by Rome, and Corinth values
       Her singer only when she's losing him.
       If you went to Rome, though, with Maecenas,
       And gained the triumph you deserve so well—
       Because Rome knows how talents should be crowned—
       When you came back to Corinth afterwards
       Your native laurels would be spread before you
       Like primroses in spring, beneath your feet.
ANTEUS: I do not wish to trample native laurels.
       Triumphs in Rome would seem disgrace to me.
NERISSA: What are you waiting for?
ANTEUS: For recognition
       In my own land, unhelped by conqueror's grace.
NERISSA: When will that happen? When your life is over?
       Posthumous glory is the usual gift
       For singers like yourself. But while they live
       There is none to hear them, none to see them.
       As if they are deep buried in a grave.
       Plunging themselves deep in their thoughts and dreams
       Such singers stay, unmoving in one place,
       While over them rushes, impetuous,
       The coloured Bacchanalia of life
       And throws its flowers and laurel leaves to him
       Who best knows how to catch them in their flight,

For such as you only the faded leaves
Are left, only the funeral wreaths remain.
Do you think that you will vanquish Rome
By such a tomb-like immobility.
If I were you I would shine forth resplendent
With your bright genius and that of Hellas,
I would rule triumphant on all stages,
Would take by storm forums and porticos
Until my name had quite blocked out the sound
Of Caesar's name. Ah, that indeed would be
True victory.

ANTEUS: And everyone would say:
"What splendid bards our Rome is buying now!
Hellas has quite declined into her dotage."
(*He takes Euphrosyne's laurel wreath into his hand.*)
See, Nerissa, this one wreath alone
I gained in all my life, but it is dearer
Than all the triumphs which you praise so much.
If wreaths like this are called funereal
Then let death come as quickly as he will.
(*He puts the wreath on his head with a proud quiet smile.*)

NERISSA: Anteus, listen for I can no longer
Bear this. One may choke and suffocate
In the tomb-like air of this close house.
You or I must go out in the world.
I love you so much that I can agree
To live upon your glory, but I cannot
Live without glory of any kind
I am a Hellene.

ANTEUS: And you want to win
This glory among Romans.

NERISSA: Among Romans
Or others, it is all the same. I need
Glory, like bread, water or air. If you
Cannot provide me this necessity, then I shall go
To win it for myself, I do not want
To die for lack of it. I am still young.

ANTEUS: And by what method will you gain this glory?
NERISSA: The same as you, by practising my art.
ANTEUS: You still want to go back upon the stage?
       (*after a pause*)

Well, Nerissa, I shall tell you truly
If you are not called by a vain whim
But by the muse Terpsichore, I shall not
Dare to argue with the goddess. Maybe
You can in truth bring back to life for Corinth
The holy mystery of Dionysus.

NERISSA: O, not for Corinth, no, do not think that!
I am not tempted by Corinthian praise.
Maybe Nerissa living will outweigh
The stone Terpsichore Maecenas has,
When she today will dance for him in person
The dances of Tanagra.

ANTEUS: Are you raving?

NERISSA: No, I am not in frenzy yet.

ANTEUS: You cannot
Go to the orgy.

NERISSA: And why can't I go?
The Roman women can go everywhere,
Why can we not follow their example?
I'll go and say "My husband is unwell,
But so as not to disappoint Maecenas
He sent me, being his wife, to the reception!"

ANTEUS: You shall not go there!

NERISSA: Will you lock me in?
Then I indeed shall know with certainty,
That you have bought me into slavery.
Yet sometimes even slave women escape.
Put not your trust in your strong locks.

ANTEUS: Nerissa!

NERISSA: What is your will, my lord? (*a pause*)
                                   Decide it now.
Either it's you or I.

ANTEUS: O, if I had
The power to tear you clear out of my heart
And cast you, like a venomous reptile under
The Roman's feet!

NERISSA (*with a short petulant laugh*):
                    You cannot do it, then?
Well, then, you must give in. Maybe one day
You yourself will thank me for it. I
Shall not go back on what I said. If not

You, then I shall go and gain some glory,
Yes, and today; I've waited long enough.
ANTEUS (*after a heavy silence*):
Yes, I shall go. I shall be better off
Among the Romans than home here with you.
NERISSA: Go then. But first take off those silly twigs
From off your head—you're not going like that?
(*Anteus puts his hand to his head, takes off the laurels,
looks at them sadly, and puts them where Euphrosyne
stood when she crowned him.*)
EUPHROSYNE (*from the depths of the house*):
Nerissa! Call to Anteus! Come and dine!
The lavish orgy is all ready now!
(*Anteus quickly runs to the gate.*)
NERISSA (*catching him up*):
Where are you off to, then? You must get changed.
ANTEUS: Let me go. Euphrosyne will come
And I'll not dare to look her in the eyes.
(*He runs out of the gate.*)
EUPHROSYNE (*coming through the door*):
Where's Anteus, then?
NERISSA: He's gone off to the orgy.
He had an invitation from Maecenas.
EUPHROSYNE: Your sense of humour's odd!
NERISSA: I am not joking
See, there the faded household laurels lie,
Today he will bring fresh ones home to us
Received from connoisseurs. (*Holding her head high, she
goes into the house.*)
EUPHROSYNE (*clasping her head*): Can this be true?

ACT II

In the house of Maecenas, a descendant of the famous Maecenas who
lived in the time of Augustus. A large, sumptuous reception room decorated for the orgy, divided by an arch into two unequal parts. In the first,
smaller part (in the foreground) is arranged a triclinium for the host
Maecenas and his two guests of honour—the Procurator and the Prefect.
A low dais has been set up, covered with carpets, for the performances of
singers, mimes, and other artists; in the other larger part, at the back, there
are many tables surrounded either by couches in the Turkish fashion or
benches in the Roman fashion, where guests of different types and ages,

both Greeks and Romans, are sitting and reclining. The banquet has only just started and is going very dully, apparently because the guests hardly know each other, and feel ill at ease under the gaze of the triclinium of honour in the front part of the room. On the dais, a choir of panegyrists, among them Chilon, is ending its song.

CHOIR (singing):

> Light out of Light
> Nascent forever,
> So the illustrious
> House of Maecenas,
> From ray to ray shining
> Flows forth its ever
> Radiant light.

(When the choir finishes singing, Maecenas inclines his head to the
  coryphaeus and makes a movement with his hand neither
  exactly directing nor inviting the members of the choir to
  take their places at the banquet in the back part of the
  reception room. The choir take their places at the furthest
  tables at the very back. Slaves are serving drinks and dainties.
  Slave girls distribute flowers.)

MAECENAS (beckoning to a slave major-domo):

> Let the mimes perform here for the moment,
> And afterwards, the Egyptian "boneless maidens"
> Who do the acrobatic tricks with swords,
> Only be sure it doesn't last too long!
> Each must perform only for a few minutes
> And nobody must come on more than once.
> (to the Prefect and the Procurator)
> For, you can guess, these monkeys are not deaf
> To praise, clap once, and you'll be sure to have
> A mighty task to get them off the stage.

(Meanwhile the major-domo goes out and there start to appear on the
  stage mimes who perform short farces in dumb show,
  Egyptian tumbler girls, with swords, jugglers and juggler
  girls with bright balls, etc. The guests clap for them from
  time to time, sometimes throwing them flowers and sweets.
  Very little attention is paid to them by Maecenas and the
  guests of honour who talk together. Maecenas in a somewhat soft voice, the Prefect with an even, monotonous,
  somewhat drawling tone, the Procurator loudly and effort-
  lessly.)

MAECENAS: I must admit this orgy I've prepared
        Is somewhat reminiscent of the Kingdom
        Of Shades before Pluto's triumvirate.
        You won't believe how hard I've had to work,
        Somehow to overcome this cautious shyness
        And mutual distrust, to join together
        Into one kin, the two-fold branches of the
        Corinthian people—Greeks and Romans.
PREFECT: Friend,
        Already you've achieved a mighty work,
        You have a panegyrist's choir worth hearing.
        Even in Rome such aren't heard every day.
MAECENAS (*waving his hand*):
        Eh! What's this choir. The place, to speak sincerely,
        For poetry like this is in the kitchen.
        For truly they would rather have leftovers
        Than laurels . . . I crave your forgiveness, that
        I entertain you with such paltry shows.
        (*even quieter*) For such are suited only to the crowd
        But I hope I can make it up to you
        With something else. For I have found a singer,
        A true one. He is not, so far, well known,
        But that's shame to the Greeks, not to the singer.
        I shall show Corinth it is necessary
        To have a Roman to assess the worth
        Of art, for otherwise art goes to waste—
PROCURATOR: This singer will come soon?
MAECENAS: I do not know.
        I sent an invitation, but the answer
        He sent to me was not quite clear!
PROCURATOR: Well, really!
        Inviting them! You ought just to command them!
MAECENAS: Commanding is not fitting here. This Anteus
        Is not a slave but a free citizen.
PROCURATOR: Is he a Roman citizen?
MAECENAS: Well, no,
        But still he is of noble birth. In Corinth
        His family was renowned from ages past,
        In olden times some heroes came from them.
PROCURATOR: In the eyes of Greeks, all men are heroes,

If someone in a squabble flings a platter
And hits his neighbour's head—at once he's famous.
A discus-thrower! . . . (*he laughs*)
                              So, too, are their poets;
One botches Horace up in the Greek style
And straightway he is crowned, a laureate!
In the Athenian Academy.
You can buy laureates at two-an-obol,
One will be poet, one philosopher!
But watch out that you get your obol's worth.
MAECENAS: Do not forget, my friend, the gods above
Have no love for ingratitude. Remember,
In days of old Rome went to school in Greece.
PREFECT: Certainly it is a lazy scholar
Who does not finally surpass the teacher.
MAECENAS: Indeed, yet still the scholar must be grateful.
PREFECT: Rome has paid for tuition lavishly,
She gave to Greece peace and law, which Greece
Had never had, not since the dawn of time.
PROCURATOR: But Greece in the most famous of her schools
Has only taught to Rome some old wives' tales,
Which are a disgrace to our religion
And are an insult to intelligence,
Like a dog's tail, wagging without purpose.
That's all their learning. Never have the Greeks
Made or created more than that. They didn't
Even have a language of their own.
MAECENAS: What's that you're saying? Didn't have a language?
Friend, now you're telling us something unheard of.
PROCURATOR: Well, there was the Ionian dialect,
The Attic and I know not what besides,
Each writer had a jargon of his own.
But a strongly tempered speech like ours,
Single and universal, the Greeks never
Had, from the beginning.
MAECENAS: This is so.
PROCURATOR: As for their poetry, to tell the truth,
It cannot stand comparison with ours
That elegance of language, such as Horace,
No Greek has ever reached, nor ever shall.

MAECENAS: Nevertheless, it was a Greek who taught us
　　　　　To honour our native tongue. A Hellene captive
　　　　　Founded Latin poetry, not a Roman.
PROCURATOR: Because he had to take his master's language,
　　　　　The master surely's better things to do
　　　　　Than chop his native language up in trochees.
PREFECT (*to Maecenas*): My friend, you are not going to insist
　　　　　These stanzas were not botched and badly bungled
　　　　　And the language not in clumsy style.
MAECENAS: Who knows, my friend, from whence the spark was born
　　　　　Out of which first came fire upon the earth.
　　　　　Maybe it was but a trivial ember,
　　　　　Yet all the same we ought to pay it honour,
　　　　　And to respect father Prometheus, though
　　　　　He may be nothing but a common thief.
PROCURATOR (*to Prefect, indicating Maecenas*):
　　　　　Here, indeed, is a fruit of the Greek learning
PREFECT: Maecenas is a well known "Phil-Hellene"—
　　　　　He's almost ready to split off from Rome
　　　　　A Republic of Corinth. (*He laughs.*)
PROCURATOR:　　　　　　　　　Jokes are jokes,
　　　　　But still, from such Phil-Hellenism might
　　　　　Come some loss to Rome.
MAECENAS:　　　　　　　　　Don't be alarmed.
　　　　　For the old governess remembers well
　　　　　How much she needs support in her old age.
　　　　　If Rome should grow angry with Greece and cast
　　　　　Her off, then Greece would cry, "Behold, I perish!"
PREFECT: Our friend, indeed, is right; it is a pity
　　　　　That our liking for foreigners has led us
　　　　　Into a situation where we too
　　　　　Ourselves have turned into barbarians.
　　　　　We have now learned "Latin of Africa"
　　　　　From our black-faced "Roman citizens."
MAECENAS: Still, we can't do without barbarians,
　　　　　We are obliged now to renew the blood
　　　　　Worn out from labour, toil and dissipation.
　　　　　Would you rather wish that all our peoples
　　　　　Should employ barbarian tongues forever,
　　　　　Would that really be for Rome a glory?

PROCURATOR: Let them hold their tongues till they have learned
　　　Latin correctly!
MAECENAS:　　　　　　That's a bit too hard!
　　　To learn a language properly in silence—
　　　Even Demosthenes could not achieve it.
PROCURATOR: Then what is one to do?
MAECENAS:　　　　　　　　　What I am doing.
　　　To teach by favours, even gifts, all leading
　　　Foreigners to love and honour Rome.
　　　For her who truly loves will soon resemble
　　　The one beloved in body and in soul.
PROCURATOR: Phil-Hellenism made you soft. It would be
　　　Interesting to know how, for instance
　　　You'd get taxes in "by gifts and favours"
　　　You'd get a lot in!
MAECENAS (smiling):　　On this point I must
　　　Lay down my arms. In this you are the expert.
ATRIENSIUS (entering):
　　　The singer Anteus has arrived.
MAECENAS:　　　　　　　　Ah, call him
　　　Here. No, wait! When Anteus starts to sing,
　　　I'll give a sign, then let the dancing girls
　　　Come in. But not before then, understand.
　　　Watch me, Now go! (Exit Atriensius.)
　　　　　　　　　　These accursed slaves
　　　Time after time have spoiled all my arrangements.
　　　In their opinion, orgies are just farces.
ANTEUS (on the threshold):
　　　Greetings to you, illustrious lords.
MAECENAS:　　　　　　　　Hello there!
　　　But come up closer. Standing on the threshold
　　　Does not befit the darling of the muses.
　　　(Anteus comes nearer but there is no place for him at the
　　　　table, and he remains standing in front of the reclining
　　　　guests.)
MAECENAS (to the guests): This, my friends, is the most costly pearl
　　　In all the Gulf of Corinth.
ANTEUS:　　　　　　　You, Illustrious,
　　　Have placed excessive favours upon me,
　　　To Corinth, though, you gave too little honour.

MAECENAS: Why too little honour?
ANTEUS: For you cannot
        Count up all the pearls found in our gulf
        And estimate which one is the most costly.
PREFECT: To love one's native town is right and proper,
        But one must not forget the honest truth
        And gratitude. If, indeed, in Corinth
        There are so many pearls of art and learning
        Then this is the achievement of Maecenas.
MAECENAS: It is a rooster-style achievement, friend.
PROCURATOR: Whatever do you mean by this, Maecenas?
MAECENAS: Because I go searching in all the dunghills
        And there I scratch up all my costly pearls.
PREFECT: But still, you don't gobble them like a rooster
        But put them in a setting. (*Anteus silently moves away.*)
MAECENAS: Anteus, stop!
        Where are you going?
ANTEUS: Back where I belong.
MAECENAS: I see you are offended.
PROCURATOR: It is strange
        How sensitive these Greeks are!
ANTEUS: Yes, indeed,
        Strange that we have still not grown accustomed
        To letting conquerors freely call our country
        A dunghill, and call us ourselves, when we
        Are not put in a "setting," simply refuse.
MAECENAS: You, it is, puts thorns into my words,
        And not I. All my guilt must lie in this
        That somehow my tongue slipped, but it was made
        That way, created slippery by the gods.
        Blame Jupiter, then, or Prometheus—you
        Must know far more than I which one to blame.
PREFECT: And I, bypassing all the guilt and blame
        Will turn to the achievement. My Maecenas,
        This time I truly have a case to bring
        Against you.
MAECENAS: How?
PREFECT: It was not you, but I
        That first discovered this fine pearl.
MAECENAS: Indeed?
PREFECT: Moreover, my achievement is still greater,

Because I didn't gobble up the pearl,
Though gobble it I ought to, when I found it.
MAECENAS: I'd like to know better what you mean.
PREFECT: Oh, this is no great mystery. Once I
Uncovered, rather, covered up for good,
A secret bard's hetaereia in Corinth.
The youngest member of this guild, it chanced,
Was this same singer. When I had observed
His tender youth, I spared him. He alone
Is left now out of all that brotherhood,
Because there are no more hetaereias,
You know, left anywhere in all the world.
ANTEUS: You are mistaken, there is still one left.
PREFECT: Where?
ANTEUS: Up on Mount Parnassus. Nine and One
Take part up there in a most secret orgy
And hide themselves with thick and heavy clouds
From the eyes of the law!
MAECENAS: Ha, ha! Precisely!
PREFECT (*changing his drawling tone to a different, sharper one*):
It is not now "precisely" so, Maecenas
The "Nine and One"—that's Phoebus and the Muses—
Are not at all a secret hetaereia,
But a panegyrist's choir. They have to
Earn their nectar and ambrosia, too,
And so they have to sing their panegyrics.
ANTEUS: To whom?
PREFECT: Why, to Rome's genius, of course!
Parnassus and Olympus, all the holy
Mountains have now come beneath her power's
Imperium, only those gods can prosper
Who have the rank of Roman citizen,
Or, at the least, the favour of Maecenas
The universal, *he's* Rome's genius.
Whatever gods would not submit to him
Were driven out, or even crucified.
ANTEUS: And then what happened? Did they die of it?
MAECENAS (*quietly, leaning towards the Prefect*):
My friend, excuse me, but the vulgar crowd
Maybe could find this jesting sacrilegious.
PREFECT (*drawling again*):

May the gods forgive! But still a Roman
Could not let a Greek have the last word.
MAECENAS (*loudly, to Anteus*):
We have had quite enough of human speech.
Now it is time, Anteus, for you to use
The speech of gods.
ANTEUS: Illustrious, forgive me,
But the muse has no wish to help me. Maybe
Today she is not feeling very hungry,
And without her I'm like a stringless lyre.
MAECENAS: Has my friend really spoiled her appetite?
PREFECT: I shan't apologize for what is true,
As for the muse, who *today* is not hungry,
She must remember, even for the gods
Tomorrow only comes to those who earn it.
ANTEUS: Quite often he who cares not for tomorrow
Will have eternal fame. (*Voices are heard in the antrium.*)
MAECENAS: What's all that noise?
ATRIENSIUS (*on the threshold*):
Illustrious master, it is some Greek woman
Who came and asks permission to come in,
That she may stand upon the threshold here
And listen while the singer Anteus sings.
MAECENAS: Who is she? And of what estate.
ATRIENSIUS: She says,
That's she's the singer Anteus's wife.
MAECENAS: Let her in, then.
        (*Exit Atriensius. Nerissa appears on the threshold and bows
            without speaking.*
ANTEUS: Well, what's all this, Nerissa?
        (*Nerissa remains silent and shyly covers herself with her
            veil.*)
Go back home at once!
MAECENAS: Excuse me, Anteus!
I am the master here, I'll not allow
Anyone to drive away my guests
You are free to stay here or to go
But likewise is your wife free, while she still
Remains a guest beneath Maecenas' roof.
ANTEUS (*to Nerissa*):
Do you wish to stay here?

NERISSA (*quietly but firmly*):
                                    I am staying.
PROCURATOR (*quietly to Maecenas*):
        You're no fool about this—she is lovely.
        Wherever did he find himself this nymph?
MAECENAS: Such women are found only in Tanagra,
        Believe me, I'm an expert in such matters.
        (*to Nerissa*) Have you been married long?
NERISSA: Less than a month.
MAECENAS: Oh, Anteus, do you really need the muses
        To help you, while it's still your honeymoon,
        You should be able to sing like a god
        When this fair Grace is standing there before you.
        But why is she hidden beneath a veil?
ANTEUS: Such is the custom among Hellene women.
MAECENAS: But in my home we hold by Roman custom,
        And it has its own laws. You must permit
        Your wife, therefore, to unveil herself.
        (*Nerissa without waiting for Anteus to answer, unveils her
            face and shyly looks at Maecenas.*)
        By all the gods! Just look at her, my friends,
        She's the Terpsichore of marble which
        I purchased only yesterday from Phaedon.
        Can this be chance? No, chances such as this
        Cannot occur. (*to Nerissa*) Were you the model for it?
NERISSA: Yes, my lord.
MAECENAS: Well, can you also dance?
NERISSA: I don't know. . . .
MAECENAS: You don't know? Terpsichore
        Doesn't know, though she's the goddess of the dance.
ANTEUS: She means that she is not a dancing girl
        And therefore cannot dance outside her home.
MAECENAS: Then I shall visit you some day at home.
ANTEUS: I shall be honoured. But I do not know
        If you will chance to see Nerissa there,
        For in my home, mother and wife and sister
        Live all the time in the gynaeceum,
        And I daren't venture to invite you there.
MAECENAS: Your custom is not good.
ANTEUS: But it is hallowed
        By age. I did not set it up, Illustrious.

PROCURATOR: But still you keep it up quite willingly.
MAECENAS: Well, this is nothing strange. I understand
   Anteus, jealousy. I placed the stone
   Terpsichore not in the atrium but
   My own tablinum, lest she be profaned.
ANTEUS: For this, indeed, I owe you heartfelt thanks.
MAECENAS: Then show this gratitude in deeds,
   Namely in song (*to a slave*) Euthymus, go and bring
   To us the lyre which I have bought today.
   (*Euthymus brings a large, richly inlaid lyre.*)
   Anteus, this lyre's the gift of the whole world
   Its horns from bison of the German forests,
   The Africa elephant gave ivory
   For inlay and Arabia's land sent gold,
   The wood from the mysterious Indian jungle,
   And the mosaic from the land of Sinai,
   The strings, the finest in the world—Italian,
   And mounted in bright silver brought from Britain.
ANTEUS: Only it seems there's nothing Greek in it?
MAECENAS: All will be Greek when it belongs to you.
   For I shall give it to you as a gift
   If you would like to have it. Touch its strings.
ANTEUS: (*He touches the strings casually, not taking it from the*
   hands of the slave. The strings give quiet but strangely
   beautiful and clear notes. Anteus gives a start of
   admiration):
   What a strange and lovely tone it has.
   Give me the lyre, boy! (*He takes the lyre in his hands.*)
       Oh, how very heavy!
MAECENAS: You do not need to hold it for yourself.
   There is a slave for that. Euthymus, kneel
   And hold the lyre the way the singer tells you.
   (*Euthymus kneels and supports the lyre for Anteus.*)
ANTEUS: No, we must not permit it to get used
   To this; at home I have no slaves at all.
   And it will have to hang up in the air
   Upon the strap.
MAECENAS: The way of old-time rhapsodes!
   That's very pleasant! Hang it up, Euthymus.
   Up there where the big lamp is hanging now.
   (*Euthymus hangs the lyre on the large candelabrum, taking*

down the big lamp from the candelabrum. Anteus steps
on to the dais and touches the strings more strongly
than before. . . . Hearing the melody, Chilon and
Phaedon jump to their feet.)

CHILON (*to his fellow choir members who are sitting at the back*
tables, busily eating and talking):
My friends, be quiet! Anteus is going to play!

PHAEDON: Anteus! Sing us the epithalamy.
(*Anteus stops, lets his hands fall, and bows his head. A*
pause.)

MAECENAS: Anteus, what's the matter? Are you ill?
Or can't you, maybe, manage such a lyre?

NERISSA (*to Maecenas, calling from the threshold*):
My husband is not long up from an illness.
(*to Anteus, pleading and quietly*)
Anteus, you mustn't overtax your strength
Completely. Better if you would permit
Me to express your gratitude for you
To the Illustrious lord. Though not a dancer
I shall dance, as is Tanagran custom
As my mother taught me. They'll excuse us.

MAECENAS: I am quite willing, though it would be better
If you in your two persons would unite
Music and dance into a wedded pair.

ANTEUS: My wife is not aware of what she's saying
At all. I feel quite well and strong, and I
Shall play and sing to you—but without dancing,
For this I was invited and agreed,
But your dances, Nerissa, are not for orgies.
I hesitated as I had to seek
Suitable songs within my memory.

PHAEDON: Sing the epithalamy! That's fitting.

ANTEUS: No, it's not fitting. We're not at a wedding.

MAECENAS: Why not? Imagine in this house takes place
The nuptial feast of Hellas and of Rome.

ANTEUS: I see an orgy here before my eyes
And so the songs I think of are not bridal
But Bacchic, rather.

PROCURATOR: Well, that's even better.
(*Anteus approaches the lyre again. Maecenas signs to the*
guests to be quiet, the voices die away, only the clink

*of goblets can be heard as the guests go on drinking.
Anteus recites the first line solemnly, without music,
then suddenly without a prelude, begins to sing, accompanying himself loudly and confidently in the rhythm
of the Bacchic dance.)*

Do thou, O universal gift, assist me now!
  O chime! O chime! Play! Play!
Wake the spirit of orgy for us!
Give a voice to dumbness of slaves!
Do thou stir sluggish blood for us,
Grant a strong thrust to our hidden forces!

*(Maecenas gives a sign to the atriensius, dancing girls and corybantes
run in and begin the Bacchic dance.)*

We begin the Bacchic dance
Frenzied spring will transform the orgy
Cold and fear disappear from souls,
Like the mountain snow in the sun,
Dionysus! Reveal thy wonders.

*(He goes on playing in the same rhythm without words and does not
notice that Nerissa has unostentatiously joined the group of
dancers. Anteus then changes the rhythm to a slower,
different one in another key.)*

Quietly dancing,
Order harmonious
Peacefully summer comes shining
After the tumult of noisy spring
And in solemnity the feast is prevailing.

*(With the change of rhythm, the dancers stop, only Nerissa goes on
dancing always keeping behind Anteus. She dances quietly,
gently, smoothly, slowly. Anteus does not see her at all, and,
carried away by the music, takes up his former rhythm only
with still more force.)*

O chime! O chime! Play! Play!
Let us feel in ourselves young strength,
Make us drunk with trans-human force.

*(The dancing girls and corybantes once more encircle Nerissa with
the Bacchic circle, but Maecenas stops them with a sudden
movement and a shout.)*

MAECENAS: Stop, all of you and let Nerissa dance!

(*At the shout, Anteus stops, turns and cannot control
himself from surprise and shock at seeing Nerissa in the
forefront of the dancers. Maecenas, noticing this, clasps
his hands.*)

MAECENAS: Musicians! Come and play the Bacchic dance!
(*Enter musicians with double flutes, cymbals and drums.
They play the Bacchic dance. Nerissa, after an instant
of confusion, blinking her eyes begins a rapid dance
with the uncontrolled but beautiful movements of a
maenad. Some of the guests clap to the rhythm of
the music, others snap their fingers. Maecenas beckons
to Euthymus and whispers something to him. The
latter brings an ornate box and hands it to Maecenas.*)

ANTEUS: Nerissa, that's enough!
MAECENAS: No! dance on, goddess!
            Dance on, most lovely muse Terpsichore!
(*He takes from the box a diamond necklace, and holds it
high with both hands, enticing Nerissa to him. Nerissa,
without ceasing to dance, approaches Maecenas, her
eyes are burning, her movements are lithe and sinuous
like a wild beast. The guests get up from their seats and
crane forward, trying to get a better view of Nerissa.
They throw flowers at her and there is thunderous
applause.*)

VOICE FROM PANEGYRISTS' CHOIR: It is our muse!
PROCURATOR (*leering*):   The pretty little thing!
PREFECT: This muse most certainly won't die of hunger.
(*Nerissa approaches Maecenas and kneels before him on one
knee, leaning back as if ready to collapse with weariness
but a delightful and coquettish smile plays on her lips.
The procurator rushes to support her, but Maecenas
forestalls him, putting the necklace on her neck and
supporting her in the same movement.*)

NERISSA: Thank you, my lord! (*She tries to kiss his hand.*)
MAECENAS: Not so, immortal one.
            (*He kisses her on the lips. Nerissa rises.*)
PROCURATOR: (*moving up a little on the couch, and offering her a
            goblet of wine*):
            Come here, Bacchante, rest beside the tiger!
(*Nerissa goes to him. There is strained laughter in the

crowd. Anteus suddenly tears down the lyre from the candelabrum and hurls it at Nerissa with all his might. Nerissa staggers and falls to the ground.)

NERISSA: Help me! He has killed me! (*Anteus bends down to her and sees that she is dying.*)

ANTEUS (*quietly and almost peacefully*): Yes, I've killed her.

PREFECT (*calling the slaves*): Fetch the vigiles!

ANTEUS: Stay, let me finish.

(He takes a string from the lyre and turns to Chilon and Phaedon who are standing in the front of the crowd.)

Friends, I am setting you a good example!

(He strangles himself with the string, and falls dead beside Nerissa.)

Cassandra

A DRAMATIC POEM

Dramatis personae

Cassandra, *daughter of King Priam of Troy, a prophetess and priestess of Apollo*
Polyxena, *her sister, a young girl*
Deiphobus, *her eldest brother, the war leader*
Helenus, *another of her brothers, a seer and priest*
Paris, *her youngest brother*
Helen, *wife of King Menelaus of Sparta; she has eloped with Paris to Troy*
Andromache, *the wife of Hector, Cassandra's brother*
Leuké
Chrysé
Aethra   *slave women of Andromache*
Creusa
An old slave woman of Polyxena
Dolon, *a young Trojan, formerly betrothed to Cassandra*
Onomaus, *King of Lydia, Cassandra's suitor*
1st Watchman
2nd Watchman
3rd Watchman   *of the Guard of the Citadel of Ilium in Troy*
4th Watchman
Flautist
Citharist
Sinon, *a Hellene spy*
Agamemnon Atrides, *King of Argos, Supreme Commander of the Achaean army*
Menelaus Atrides, *his brother, King of Sparta*
Odysseus, *King of Ithaca*   *subordinate leaders of*
Diomede   *the Achaean army*
Ajax
Trojans, Trojan women, slaves, slave girls, Trojan and Greek warriors
The action takes place during the Trojan War in the Citadel of Ilium in Troy.

ACT I

A room in the gynaeceum (women's half) of the palace of Priam. Helen is sitting on a low, carved stool, spinning purple wool on a golden spindle;

she is richly dressed, and a circular silver mirror hangs from her girdle.
Cassandra comes into the room, wrapped in thought, looking straight in
front of her; her glance falls upon Helen, as if appraising her, and as if
seeing around her something further. Looking at her thus, Cassandra
stops short in the middle of the room and stands there without speaking.

HELEN: Sister, good day to you!
CASSANDRA: A *good* day, Helen,
        Because we are *not* sisters.
HELEN: Yes, I know
        Too well you find me hateful as death's self.
CASSANDRA: You and death, truly, are a pair of sisters.
HELEN: Cassandra!
CASSANDRA: Yes, call me by that name, Helen,
        Not "sister."
HELEN (*offended*): I shall never, never call you
        "Sister" again. Only, why do you not
        Call your own self "death's sister," for, indeed,
        There's far more likeness to death in your face.
        Yes, far more likeness there.
CASSANDRA: Take out your mirror!
HELEN: What is all this about?
CASSANDRA: Take out your mirror!
        (*Helen involuntarily does as she says, and holds out the
        mirror in her hand.*)
CASSANDRA: Look: there you are, and I—and there is no
        Likeness between us.
HELEN: Why, what are you saying?
CASSANDRA: If it were really true I look like death,
        Then I would look like you.
HELEN: Be off! Away!
        Why are you trying to call death upon me?
CASSANDRA: Why, is a sister forced to kill her sister?
        More often sister gives a sister aid.
HELEN: Is this the reason you have come to me,
        To rail and scold? Go on, then, burn and strike.
        It is your only pleasure, when I weep!
        (*Cassandra takes the mirror from her hand and holds it up
        to Helen's face. Helen knits her brow, but she does
        not weep nor turn away. Gradually her face becomes
        less gloomy.*)

CASSANDRA: And so, like death, you have no power to weep.
Look there: your countenance is calm again,
Once more that power is shining in your eyes,
That mighty power—all men must yield to it,
All mortal folk, and with them too, Cassandra.
(*She lets the mirror fall.*)
You walk—and all those old and worthy men
Will bow before you in a deep obeisance,
And solemnly will hail you: "Goddess-like!"
You glance—and mighty men are turned to stone,
And softly murmur: "The unconquerable!"
You kiss—at once the gaze will grow bedimmed
Of him, the youngest of all Priam's sons,
And the blood surges, strikes with a strong wave
Against the heart; both heart and speech are dumb,
And memory grows pale, and face grows pale,
He is yours wholly, there is nothing more
For him, not mother, father, dearest kin,
Nor native land. . . . Women of Troy, lament!
For Paris, the young prince is dead, has perished!
HELEN: Do you foretell the death of your own brother?
CASSANDRA: Long since, I ceased to reckon him as living.
HELEN: You hateful thing! I know that from his birth
You've been an enemy to Paris.
CASSANDRA: I
Loved him from birth.
HELEN: So why, then, did you tell
Father and Mother they should not receive him
Into their Court, when first he came back home
From the poor shepherd folk who hid him safe
Against the persecuting oracle?
CASSANDRA: It was no persecuting oracle.
To die or live among the shepherd folk
Would be the only happiness for Paris.
HELEN: Why should that be? Why can Deiphobus,
And Hector and Helenus, all your brothers
And all your sisters, and you too, Cassandra,
Live in the palace, whereas Paris must
Pine away in a shepherd's smoky hut?
CASSANDRA: And is it better to pine in a palace,

As Paris here with you in the women's bower?
Deiphobus and Hector and Helenus
Live, do not pine: Deiphobus in council,
Hector at war, Helenus in the temple,
Body and soul they live. But as for Paris?
He only lived when there he played his pipe
Among the flocks. Paris is quiet in council,
And arms himself as if he put on fetters,
The gods will never come to talk with him.

HELEN: But Aphrodite talks with him!

CASSANDRA: O no!
He is her slave, and no one talks with slaves,
She orders, he obeys, and that is all.

HELEN: It's only you who fights against the gods,
And that is why they punish you.

CASSANDRA: Indeed!
Their power's in punishment and mine's in fight.

HELEN: Was it for this you fought the Cyprian,
When she persuaded Paris he should sail
To me in Sparta? Well, you see, Cassandra,
The Cyprian has the victory over you.

CASSANDRA: Me, Helen? O no! Over you and Paris.

HELEN: But Paris did not listen to your words.

CASSANDRA: The deaf hear not—what victory is that?

HELEN: And who would listen to your prophecies?
You never mentioned from what signs you knew
The outcome of that journey.

CASSANDRA: I can know
Nothing besides the thing that I can see.

HELEN: And what were you able to see that day?

CASSANDRA: I saw him as a handsome youth set sail
With a joyful heart, to foreign lands,
Not a wise-minded envoy from the nation,
Not as a warrior in arms, nor merchant;
His shepherd's love locks and his carefree brow
Bore beauty and no mischief. And I cried:
"Ah, Trojan manhood, forge strong helmets now!
Threefold and fourfold lay the gleaming bronze!"
And after. . . . O, that was an hour of doom,
When he returned, and with him you came, Helen,

And I beheld you give to him that dread
Death-dealing kiss. . . .
HELEN: Cassandra! That's a lie!
For I did not kiss Paris then at all!
CASSANDRA: Nevertheless, I clearly saw it then,
That kiss, I saw it at the very moment
When on our native soil was lightly pressed
That fair white foot in its fine scarlet shoe,
Your foot, Helen. You wounded our poor soil.
HELEN: And you cried out against me: "Blood and death!"
And I shall not forget you for that, ever.
CASSANDRA: I did not cry these words against *you*, Helen.
I at that moment was a new-born child
And with a cry of pain met a new world.
I saw: Paris to us gave not a glance,
Greeting the Trojans only with his lips.
I saw, indeed, how in his every thought
That sandal of fine scarlet set its tread.
I cried out: "Bear the barley and the salt,
Behind the High Priest walks the destined victim!"
The wind was ruffling through the golden locks
Of your hair. "See, Insatiate Ares speeds,
Led by the Cyprian, like a stallion
Hot with desire. Prepare the hecatomb!"
I shouted, and I saw: upon the sea
Already the black warships with their prows
Cleaving the russet wave, the sails were straining . . .
Upon the helms of the Achaean soldiers
Dreadly the plumes were tossing . . .
HELEN: You're demented!
Did the Achaeans really sail that day?
We lived in peace for more than a whole year!
CASSANDRA: That day I *saw* the host of the Achaeans.
And now I see that Menelaus takes
You by the hand . . .
HELEN: Away from me, wild creature!
It is a lie! A lie! And it shall never
Be so! I'd rather dash myself to pieces,
Falling from the steep tower upon sharp stone.
CASSANDRA (*with conviction*):

Your husband comes and takes you by the hand,
And, hardly *takes*, now it is you who leads him.
You go ahead, he follows in your path . . .
And foreign seas and foreign lands your ship
Passes, bearing you homeward once again . . .
The fires are dead on the remains of Troy,
The smoke from Ilium vanished in the heavens . . .
And you sit on your throne, a mighty queen,
Spin for yourself upon your golden spindle
With purple wool and with a crimson thread,
Twisting it, twisting ever . . .

HELEN: It's a lie!

CASSANDRA: O goddess-like! O thou unconquerable!
         Daughter of Epimetheus!

HELEN: What's this now?
         What new stupidity is this? How can you
         Call me "Daughter of Epimetheus"?

CASSANDRA: Prometheus and Epimetheus were
         Sons of the one father and the one mother,
         Life and fire gave Prometheus to mankind,
         And he *knew* tortures must await him for it,
         Foreseeing tortures, he did not turn back—
         Of all the sons of Proto-Mother Earth,
         Moira brought down worst punishments on him.
         But Epimetheus nothing knew. His thought
         Was always chasing to catch up with action.
         He took to wife Pandora, the self-same
         Who gave to mankind death and bitter woe,
         And he was happy with her; nevermore
         Did anyone see him to be unhappy.
         Sons of the one father and the one mother,
         These Titans from the first were never brothers.
         And yet it was your wish Cassandra should
         Speak of you as her sister! Helen, no!
         I am not able thus to speak in lies.

HELEN: You only have to speak and it is lies!

CASSANDRA: So Epimetheus told Prometheus once,
         And he was happy. Mighty queen, good day.

                                             (*Exit.*)

ACT II

Cassandra's room. Cassandra is writing a "sibylline book" on a long parchment scroll. Beside her there is a large tripod with incense burning.

POLYXENA (*dressed in white, with red ribbons and pomegranate
             flowers in her hair*):
    Cassandra, sister, dearest, you don't know
    How happy I am! He's so very handsome,
    My own Achilles, my betrothed! So often
    I have seen from the walls how he would come
    Into the field, like glorious Helios shining.
    He's disagreed with the Atreidae, he
    Wants to make a firm peace with our father.
    Our marriage will be fruitful from the start—
    So say the Trojans and the Myrmidons—
    For from it strength and concord will be born,
    And so our holy Troia will not perish,
    Nor will the folk of mighty Priam die!
CASSANDRA: Forgive me, little sister, but I cannot
    Speak to you just now. Do you not see
    I have to write my scroll. I must be ready
    To hear the message of the bright-haired god.
POLYXENA: You shouldn't scold your sister so, Cassandra!
    I'm not to blame that it was I Achilles
    Chose, and not you, out of all us princesses,
    A maiden cannot choose herself a husband,
    The husband chooses her. I'm not to blame
    That you are not the darling of the Cyprian.
CASSANDRA: No, I'm not scolding you, Polyxena!
    (*She covers her face with her veil.*)
POLYXENA: Forgive me, darling, now I have upset you.
    In my own happiness, I quite forgot
    That the word "wedding" to my dear Cassandra
    Is harsh and bitter, since the time that Dolon
    Faithlessly jilted her.
CASSANDRA: Polyxena,
    Why are you talking about that! I knew
    Quite well that I should never be his wife.
POLYXENA: Why then did you accept his bridal gifts?

CASSANDRA: Because I loved him dearly. And those gifts
           Were all that Dolon could give to Cassandra.
           What have I to reproach myself in this?
           He gave them quite sincerely. I received them
           To have a memory of a moment's joy,
           For I knew there would be but few of them.
           Observe then, how the golden serpent on
           My right arm twines, circling it round and round,
           Just so does memory twist about my heart.
           (*She shows the bracelet on her arm, above the elbow.*)
           Dolon was not to blame. It is these eyes
           That are to blame; they would not say "I love you!"
           Although the heart pulsated with that love.
           And Dolon feared them. He himself once said
           That these two eyes had slain our happiness,
           Striking it down with hard and chilly swords.
           They were indifferent, unchangeable,
           Before the gods and before love. And Dolon
           No dole of victory won against those eyes.
           He did not know how he should turn their gaze
           From mysteries to living happiness.
           But I knew that in these two eyes of mine
           Lay my misfortune, but what could I do?
           Should I have blinded them? For where do men
           Take as bird-oracles the glance of love
           Of the cooing dove?
           (*Polyxena looks her in the eyes.*)
                         Polyxena!
           You must not gaze so deeply in my eyes,
           You must not speak to me, nor ask me questions,
           No, not the smallest question. You know well
           That you are dearest to me of all sisters.
           You must not speak to me!
POLYXENA: No, my Cassandra,
           You must not think that I'm your enemy
           Like all the rest. You're not to blame you're ill,
           And that the god has so befogged your thoughts
           That you can see evil in all around you
           Where there is not even a sign of it,
           And poison joy both for yourself and others.
           I'm very, very sorry, darling, for you.

(*She sits down on a stool at Cassandra's feet.*)
Please, dearest sister, comb my hair for me!
Mother told me that I must comb it out,
You see, it is unplaited, but I can't
Manage to get the flowers out at all.
(*She takes from her girdle a golden comb and a small round
       mirror.*)
Here is a comb
(*She gives the comb to Cassandra, who takes it obediently,
       and begins to unwind the ribbons and take the flowers
       from Polyxena's hair. Polyxena looks in the mirror.*)

CASSANDRA (*whispering*):
                         How fair she is, this dear
      Sister of mine! The vengeful gods have chosen
      The best of all to be their sacrifice.
      Far better if I now should take the blade
      Of sacrifice, cut off her life straightway,
      While she has still not learned of bitter grief.

POLYXENA (*catching sight of Cassandra's eyes in the mirror*):
      Cassandra, I am frightened of your eyes!
      What do you see? What are you whispering?

CASSANDRA: Nothing at all, no, nothing! You just said
      That I am ill. Yes, maybe it is true,
      Surely I'm ill, pay no attention to me. . . .
      I was remembering about our Troilus,
      He was so very like you in his looks, . . .
      Too much so, when he lay, slain by the sword . . .
      Peaceful, quiet, handsome. . . . Ah, Polyxena,
      Have you forgotten who it was that drove
      His sword into our brother Troilus' breast?

POLYXENA: Cassandra, why poison with memories,
      That was in war.

CASSANDRA: Oh yes, that was in war!
      To kill the brother, then to get betrothed
      To the sister. . . .

POLYXENA: Our brother died long ago,
      I hardly can remember him at all,
      And, after all, Achilles did not know
      Whom he had killed.

CASSANDRA: Nevertheless, *we* know.
      And certainly Achilles did not know

At the time when he sent ambassadors
Hither to seek your hand in marriage for him,
That Hector, your own brother, had himself
Counselled the firing of the Achaean ships!
At the same time that you wove in your tresses
These pomegranate flowers, our own Hector
With his war helm was arming his wise head.

POLYXENA: And so? He won't engage the Myrmidons,
So it will make no difference to Achilles,
Just as to me.

ANDROMACHE (*enters, running*): Sisters, have you heard?
My Hector, so they say, cut down Patroclus,
The great Achilles held Patroclus dear,
First of his friends . . .

CASSANDRA: O sorrow, blood and vengeance!
Hapless Polyxena, that is your bridal.
(*Takes a pair of scissors from behind the tripod and cuts off
Polyxena's hair.*)

POLYXENA: O-oh!

CASSANDRA: Where are your mourning robes, Polyxena?

ANDROMACHE: What have you done, mad girl?

CASSANDRA (*in a prophetic trance*):   Andromache,
A sister must wear mourning for her brother,
A widow for her spouse wear deeper weeds,
An orphan child in swaddling bands shall perish!

ANDROMACHE: You prophetess of doom, may you grow dumb!

POLYXENA: Why did you not tell me at once that some
Sorrow was near? Maybe I could have gone
Then, and warned Hector.

CASSANDRA: O Polyxena,
Always I can hear sorrow, can see sorrow,
But I cannot express it. I can never
Say: "It is here!" or "It is over there!"
I only know that it already is,
And there is no one now who can avert it,
No one, no, no one! If I only could,
Then I myself straight would avert this sorrow.

POLYXENA: But you could have done if you'd only told
Hector, today: do not go out to battle.

ANDROMACHE: You knew it then. So why did you not tell him?

CASSANDRA: If I had told him, who would have believed me?

ANDROMACHE: And how can they believe you, when you always
     Prophesy out of place and out of season.
POLYXENA: You always are predicting sorrow, but
     How and from whom it comes, you never say!
CASSANDRA: Because I do not know, Polyxena.
ANDROMACHE: Well then, how are we to believe your words?
CASSANDRA: It is not words, my sisters, I can see
     All that I tell you. I see: Troy is falling.
ANDROMACHE: How? At whose hands? Who is destroying it?
     The Atreids? Achilles?
CASSANDRA: I don't know,
     Sisters, I only see: Troy falls in ruins,
     And Priam's daughter's wedding to Achilles
     Is reddened with the blood of men of Troy.
     That shameful wedding feast will not save Troy.
     The quick prepare the wine to grace the bridal,
     The dead are crying out: "Blood, give us blood!"
     Oh, what abundance of black blood I see!
     And our own father clasps the knees of his
     Own children's murderer. . . . I hear a cry,
     Lamenting, weeping, howling, wailing, wailing. . . .
     Our mother! . . . I can recognize her voice! . . .
ANDROMACHE: O Gods omnipotent, avert her words.
     (*Cassandra clasps her head and stares, terrified, into space.*
     Polyxena falls weeping into Andromache's arms.)

ACT III

Andromache's gynaeceum. Slave women are spinning and weaving, some
are embroidering and sewing. Andromache is weaving a large white sheet,
walking around a high loom.

ANDROMACHE (*to the slave women*):
     Go to the gateway now, Leuké and Chrysé,
     You go too, Aethra, and come back in turn
     When you've looked on the battlefield and asked
     How Hector fares; and bring the news to me.
                     (*Exeunt slave women.*)
CLYMENE (*an old slave woman*):
     But why do you not go yourself, my lady?
     You would not feel so sad if you could watch
     Your hero making war upon the foe.

ANDROMACHE: I cannot go, Clymene. I'm afraid
        Of neighing horses and the clash of swords,
        The dust, the war cries and—the worst of all—
        That dread, death-dealing singing of the arrows.
        All that I hear and see, it seems to me,
        Must have arisen from primaeval chaos,
        When there were yet no human folk, nor gods,
        But only death reigning supreme, alone.
        But when I do not look upon fierce war,
        Then I am not afraid; then I believe
        No one can have the victory over Hector;
        He is the hero far above all heroes.
CREUSA (*a young slave girl*):
        My lady, that is true! Happy the wife
        Who can speak thus about her wedded lord
        And tell the truth . .
CASSANDRA (*appearing suddenly*): The truth and happiness!
        How easily you couple them, Creusa!
ANDROMACHE (*with unexpressed fear*):
        Cassandra, what's the matter? You forgot,
        It seems, your spindle, yesterday, with me?
        Find it, Creusa . .
CASSANDRA: Sister, there's no need.
        I have not come for spinning nor for weaving,
        I have my mourning robes. As for the shroud
        Of death, you span the thread long since, yourself,
        I only wonder: will you get it woven?
ANDROMACHE: Why do you speak like that? I'm only making
        A nice new sheet to go on Hector's bed.
CASSANDRA: That's what I said.
AETHRA (*entering*):   Our lord, out in the field,
        Met with Achilles.
ANDROMACHE: Oh! What happened then?
AETHRA: It seems that he has won a victory.
ANDROMACHE: Which of them won?
AETHRA: Our lord, against Achilles.
        Polyxena quite fainted in the gateway
        When she saw how it went against Achilles.
ANDROMACHE: The shameless wretch! She did not watch her brother,
        Only the Myrmidon?

CASSANDRA: Andromache,
        Moira has laid her hand on her. You are not
        The most unhappy woman in the world,
        So judge not the unhappy. There are widows
        In plenty, but not often must a woman
        Choose between love and brother.
ANDROMACHE: What was that?
        As if you're tipsy, you've mixed up completely
        The truth with some inventions . . .
CASSANDRA: Wine and water
        Mixed up together make a single drink.
        (*Leuké enters and stops short in silence.*)
ANDROMACHE: Well, Leuké?
LEUKÉ: Please don't send me to the gate,
        My lady . . .
ANDROMACHE: Well then, tell me what has happened!
LEUKÉ: Nothing has happened yet. . . . I cannot, no . . .
        Oh, mighty Ares too would turn in flight,
        Not only a mere mortal . . .
ANDROMACHE: What's this babbling?
        Who is it that's in flight?
LEUKÉ: Our lord . . . your husband . . .
ANDROMACHE (*threatening her with the shuttle*):
        It isn't true! How dare you? . . .
CASSANDRA: Your hand cannot
        Prevail against the strong right arm of Moira.
ANDROMACHE: Go, go, you prophetess of doom! It's you,
        You are to blame, if what she says is true!
        From Hector you have stolen all his nerve,
        You broke his spirit with your words of doom,
        You killed his faith and certainty. For never
        Did my dear Hector flee the battlefield—
        He carried hope, he bore forth victory
        And glory. But now you have killed his hope
        With your accursed words: "Vengeance and death!"
        Then bear the shame and infamy yourself
        That your unhappy brother won in battle!
CASSANDRA: If he won only them, I'd bid them welcome!
        (*She shudders and, unable to remain on her feet,
            she sits down on the nearest unoccupied stool.*)

Andromache, I wish with all my heart
These words of mine had had no truth in them.
ANDROMACHE: If only you had never spoken them,
And had not poisoned us, it would not be
An evil truth. His nerve would not have gone.
CASSANDRA: Andromache, I spurn, I spurn away
These words of doom.
ANDROMACHE: It is too late, Cassandra,
His nerve is gone.
CASSANDRA (*involuntarily*): Ah! his life too is gone!
Ah woe! What must be done? I see it now!
I see: Achilles, the swift footed, charges,
And Hector falls . . . sharp fear it is, and shame
That laid him low, and not Achilles' sword.
ANDROMACHE: No, you yourself are guilty of all this,
It was not fear, nor shame nor sword, but you,
You poisoner, when you proclaimed the truth! . . .
Oh, why do they not come? I can no longer
Wait for their news. . . . I shall go there myself. . . .
CASSANDRA (*restraining her*):
I cannot tell you, I can tell you nothing,
I shall not prophesy . . . I only see!
Go blind, you doom-foretelling eyes!
CHRYSÉ (*running in*):   Oh, woe!
Our lord has perished on Achilles' sword!
(*Andromache falls in a faint. The slave women cluster
round her, wailing.*)
CASSANDRA (*distraught with grief, she speaks as if in a trance*):
It was not fear, nor shame, nor sword, but I
Who with the truth I spoke destroyed my brother!
(*She covers her face with her veil.*)

ACT IV

Part of a square near the Scaean Gate, enclosed by the wall. On the right,
a little in the background, stands a temple; on the left, the Gate. It is
growing dark. Long shadows stretch across the square. A small group of
Trojans in the centre between the Gate and the temple are whispering
together in counsel about something. In the middle of the group is Dolon,
formerly betrothed to Cassandra; it is to him that most of those giving
counsel turn. Cassandra and Polyxena are crossing the square from the
temple; both are wearing black robes of mourning, Polyxena with her hair

shorn and her head uncovered, Cassandra with a fillet round her head and
a long black veil.

CASSANDRA (*restrains Polyxena and stands motionless*):
       Behold, behold, see what uncertain people
       Have gathered here. . . .
POLYXENA: But why are they "uncertain?"
       Agenor's there, Deiphobus, Helenus,
       And in the middle, Dolon!
CASSANDRA: Also Dolon!
POLYXENA: Why did you sigh and moan so bitterly?
CASSANDRA: It's nothing, no . . .
POLYXENA: You still cannot forget
       That he was your . . .
CASSANDRA: Polyxena, my dear,
       Now I give no thought to myself at all.
POLYXENA: To what, then?
CASSANDRA: (*clasps her hands entreatingly towards her*):
       O my dearest, dearest sister,
       I beg you, I entreat you, do not ask,
       Do not force me to speak! Perhaps, indeed,
       It is the truth my words are poisonous,
       And that my eyes murder the strength of men!
       Would I had blinded them, had plucked them out . . .
       Ah, that would be great happiness indeed!
POLYXENA: Cassandra, calm yourself! Where is the person
       Who would enjoy deformity, or wish it?
CASSANDRA: Here is one, standing right beside you.
POLYXENA: Sister,
       Let's go away from here!
CASSANDRA: No, I'll not go,
       I must stay here, for I must look on Dolon,
       Because no, never mind . . . just look on him.
       I shall not go . . . I cannot . . . but you go,
       However, where you like.
POLYXENA: I'll stay with you.
       Something might happen to you by yourself.
CASSANDRA: Cassandra has no care if something happens
       To her, or not—she only has to do
       Whatever fate assigned to her.
       (*Meanwhile the group has finished giving counsel and has*

*broken up. Dolon, left without companions, approaches
the two princesses)*

DOLON: Princesses,
I greet you. (*Wishes to proceed.*)

CASSANDRA: Dolon, stay!

DOLON: What does the gracious
Princess say to me?

CASSANDRA (*embarrassed, seeks for what she is to ask. The whole
time she is speaking to Dolon, she keeps her veil drawn
low over her eyes, so that her face is hardly visible*):
I . . . really, I wanted . . .
To ask you . . . did they meet with your approval,
The gifts of honour from our ceremonies
In Hector's memory? . . .

DOLON: (*somewhat surprised*): Yes, I am very grateful
For this favour and honour.

CASSANDRA: Why are you . . .
Why are you not wearing the shield tonight?

DOLON: What do I need a shield for? Prophetess,
Do you see something?

CASSANDRA: (*frightened*): No, no, Dolon, no!

DOLON (*thoughtfully*): It's true, I walk on an uncertain path,
Yet shield is but a hindrance to a scout . . .
And I must go by stealth into the camp
Of the Achaeans, spy out all by night,
Eavesdrop upon the councils, and return
Likewise, by stealth.

POLYXENA: Forgive me, it's not fitting
For maidens to intrude upon affairs
Of State—but I must ask, why did the senior
Officers choose such a young man as you?

DOLON: Because a young man has a suppler step,
Treads lighter and (*smiling*), can run away more quickly!

CASSANDRA (*in an undertone, to herself*):
If he *can* run away!

DOLON: What's that you said?
(*Cassandra is silent.*)
I know that I in no way have deserved
That you should waste your words on my affairs. . . .
I only wanted. . . . No, I have no right. . . .

Princesses, greetings to you. . . .
(*He bows, preparing to go.*)
CASSANDRA: Stay a moment
    What did you want?
DOLON: To ask you . . .
CASSANDRA: Ah, to ask!
    No, do not ask, I have no love for questions!
DOLON: Then I shall go my way . . .
CASSANDRA: Ask on, ask on,
    I shall reply.
DOLON: Then tell me, Prophetess,
    If I shall come back living from this venture?
CASSANDRA: Why do you think I am the one to ask?
    Go ask Helenus, have we such a lack
    Of seers here in Troy?
DOLON: It's too late now
    To go and seek them out.
CASSANDRA: But what do you
    Want with my prophecies? Cassandra is
    A byword throughout Troy. Who will believe her?
    No one at all!
DOLON: I do not know myself
    Why, but all the same I'd like to hear
    Cassandra's own answer upon this matter.
CASSANDRA: You would believe her?
DOLON: Maybe I'd believe.
CASSANDRA (*bitterly*): But only "maybe?"
DOLON: I've offended you?
CASSANDRA: Oh no, I'm used to always being doubted!
DOLON: But they all listen to your prophecies.
CASSANDRA: To pity!
DOLON: But I want to listen to them.
CASSANDRA: And if, suppose, I were to tell you this—
    I do not tell you, it is just "suppose"—
    That you must not go on reconnaissance,
    Would you obey me?
DOLON: No, I'll tell you truly,
    It would not be possible to obey,
    Although you prophesied clear death for me,
    For it would be dishonour to go back

In secret on my public resolution
Which I made, uncompelled, of my free will.
CASSANDRA: But you still want to know what will befall you?
DOLON: Yes, for I like to look fate in the eyes.
CASSANDRA: No, Dolon, that is not a thing you like,
        You never liked it. You are speaking vainly,
        You are too much a child to meet such eyes.
DOLON: A child? Princess, I am a man mature,
        Welcomed in council, fit and apt for war,
        I'm long past boyhood now.
CASSANDRA: Nevertheless,
        To bear fate's glances, your maturity
        Is still too little.
DOLON: I can see, Princess,
        That you have no desire to answer me,
        And I am only wasting time in vain,
        And there's no longer much time left to me.
CASSANDRA: (shudders at his words):
        Who told you that?
DOLON: We all agreed that I
        Must be back safe before the moon has risen.
CASSANDRA: The moon will rise early indeed tonight!
DOLON: Then all the more I have no time to lose,
        I seem to have wasted a lot already!
POLYXENA: You should have waited for a moonless night.
DOLON: War does not wait, Princess—and if we were
        To wait until we had a moonless night,
        Maybe the moon would shine upon the ruins
        Of holy Troy. Princesses, I must go,
        Farewell to you!
        (He goes to the gate without looking back, and disappears
            through it. Cassandra silently waves him goodbye, and
            when he has disappeared, she falls on Polyxena's
            shoulder, weeping bitterly.)
POLYXENA: What are you weeping for?
CASSANDRA: That was the last time I shall speak with him!
        What did I say to him? They were all cold
        Words, and unwelcome, they were like the hostile
        Swords that so soon will stab away the life
        Of my only, my belovéd Dolon! . . .

Why did I not fall down before his feet?
Why did I not implore the Olympian gods
That he should not go on this evil path?
Why did I not say: "Go not, you will perish!"
Why did I not restrain him with my glance?
He might take warning from ill-boding eyes
And maybe he . . . maybe he would believe me—
He said, himself, that maybe he would heed.
He is a child before the eyes of fate,
He would not dare to go into their fires,
If once he surely looked upon clear death.
Ah, even now. . . . My only happiness
Is dying there! . . .

POLYXENA: Cassandra! Recollect!
He is alive! What are you wailing for
So doomfully, indeed! It is not fit,
Someone might overhear you! Let's go home!

CASSANDRA: Let all the wide world hear! There is no force
Would keep me quiet. . . . Ah, you have yet to learn
How hard it is to lose your dearest love!

POLYXENA: Cassandra, that's enough! What are you saying?
Let's go, it's dark and eerie! I'm afraid!
It's late now. . . .

CASSANDRA: Late . . . the moon will swiftly rise
And light the field. . . . Out in the field my Dolon
Is all alone there like a cypress tree
Beside the crossroads . . . and he is so gentle,
So young and sensitive, he is not fit
For arms, but for the cithera and lyre,
And for the songs of spring. . . . O that these hands
Could aid him now against the heavy swords
That are raised over him. . . . Save him!

POLYXENA: Take heed!
Have you gone mad? You'll fetch everyone out!
That would put the Achaeans on their guard!

CASSANDRA: The Achaeans? . . . I'll be silent. . . . I shall not . . .
(*A long silence. Cassandra trembles violently, at first covering her face completely with her veil and standing motionless; then she unveils herself and speaks in a whisper, clasping both Polyxena's hands.*)

Let us go to the gate. . . . Please come with me. . . .
It's hard for me. . . . I am afraid of fate. . . .

POLYXENA: How can we go? It's dark upon the steps.

CASSANDRA: It is not dark enough, I can see all.
   (*She stretches out her hands into space.*)
O Artemis, O sister of Apollo,
O shining goddess, quench that torch of thine
Just for tonight, just for this single night!
Let the young lovers lose their dreams awhile,
They have their happiness. Is it for them,
For happy folk to dream more blissfully,
That you will take from my unhappiness
This last despairing dream of mine, the dream
That somewhere in this world my love walks still,
My love, my only love, though fate forbids!
If it is true, as people say of thee,
That thou thyself hast also known true love,
O by the name of that chaste love of thine,
Look on me, I beseech thee!

POLYXENA (*trembling*):   Dear, enough!

CASSANDRA (*stops short, then speaks in a changed voice*):
Yes, it is true, enough, what use are prayers?
What good are all the gods against stern fate?
They too are bound by the eternal laws,
They, just as mortals—sun and moon and stars
Are torches in the mighty fane of Moira,
Gods, goddesses, are servants in that fane,
Only the slaves of that unyielding Empress.
And to implore *Her*, that is work in vain,
She knows no pity, she can know no grace;
Deaf she is, and blind, as primal Chaos.
And to implore her slaves—that too is vain,
Degrading; and to be the slave of slaves
I have no wish!

POLYXENA: Control yourself, poor sister!
Would you enrage the gods at such a time?
Have they not punished you enough already
For your audacity? Do you want still
More punishment?

CASSANDRA: What more? The slave of fate,
The gentle Artemis can have no power

To light the moon a moment earlier,
Nor to snuff out the moonlight in the heavens,
But by the laws which fate assigned to her
When time first was. I fear no punishment!
Let us go to the gate!
(*They go together up the steps in the wall by the gate; while
they are going up silently in the darkness, the horizon
beyond the wall, the sky becomes slightly red.*)

POLYXENA: What's that? Is it a fire?
Has Dolon set the Achaean tents alight?

CASSANDRA (*on top of the wall*):
No, no. . . . It's not a fire. . . .

POLYXENA: What is it?

CASSANDRA: Wait!
Quiet!
(*A long silence. The sky grows steadily brighter, and the
full moon appears above the horizon. Cassandra covers
her face with her hands and stands as if turned to
stone.*)

POLYXENA (*clasping Cassandra to her*):
Oh, dearest! . . .

CASSANDRA: I'm afraid of fate. . . .
She's looking down upon us with so great,
So white an eye . . . (*pointing to the moon*)
Oh, she sees everything!
Nowhere is there a hiding place, nowhere!
Yet still I cannot see! O where is Dolon?

POLYXENA: He's down there, crawling across the ramparts slowly.
(*The two princesses stand motionless for a while, their
black figures sharply defined in the moonlight.*)

POLYXENA: Now he's got up . . . he's gone into the camp.

CASSANDRA: O woe, they come!

POLYXENA: Who? Where?

CASSANDRA: There's two of them,
They come, they come. . . .

POLYXENA: No, no, the moon's gone in
Behind the cloud, Dolon's dropped down again,
They do not see him.

CASSANDRA: But I do, I see! (*shrieks loudly*)
Dolon!

POLYXENA: You fool! He's heard you! Now he's up

And started running! Now they're after him. . . .
(*Cassandra tries to jump down from the wall; her sister
holds her back. They struggle.*)
CASSANDRA: Let go of me! Let go of me! Let go!
I must go to him and. . . . Let go!
POLYXENA (*shouts with all her might*):   Help, help!
Everyone, help! Come here! Guards! Help! Come here!
(*The watchmen come and help Polyxena to restrain Cas-
sandra.*)
CASSANDRA: Leave me be! Him, it's him you have to help!
1ST WATCHMAN: Who?
CASSANDRA: Dolon! They are murdering him out there!
2ND WATCHMAN: Where?
CASSANDRA: Out there, in the field. O help him, Trojans!
Run quickly!
1ST WATCHMAN: But, Princess, we cannot help,
There are but two of us. To run into
The enemy's camp would be our sure destruction.
CASSANDRA: But where are all the Trojans? Are they hiding?
Or dead? Hey, Trojans! Trojans! Where are you?
(*The Trojans begin to run into the square.*)
POLYXENA: Here come the people.
CASSANDRA: Let me go!
(*She struggles desperately, then draws back worn out with
the struggle and defeated by terror.*)
                                                        Too late!
DEIPHOBUS AND HELENUS (*Cassandra's brothers. They come forward
from the crowd and, taking her hands, try to drag
Cassandra from the gate.*)
Sister, let us go home!
CASSANDRA (*thrusting them off*): Away, away!
It is you that have killed him. (*Suddenly dropping her voice
and speaking in a tone of utter defeat.*)
                                                No, it is I. . . .
(*Humbly she allows herself to be led, and goes, hardly able
to walk, so that she is more carried than led. The moon
hides behind a cloud, and the dark group of people
leading Cassandra down from the wall is hardly more
than a shadow and melts into the deeper shadows
below the temple.*)

ACT V

Cassandra's room. It is empty.

DEIPHOBUS (*entering*):
      Cassandra! Sister! Where are you? Hey, slaves!
            (*Claps his hands and calls.*)
      Slaves!
      (*From the neighbouring room an elderly slave woman
          enters.*)

SLAVE WOMAN: What is it, my lord?
DEIPHOBUS: What's going on?
      Hasn't my sister any serving maids
      That there's no answer when one calls?
SLAVE WOMAN: Exactly!
      The Prophetess sent all her slaves away,
      Saying: "Enough already of royal habits,
      Time now to learn to labour without slaves,
      For soon it will be needed."
DEIPHOBUS: Now new fancies!
      Whose are you?
SLAVE WOMAN: I'm Princess Polyxena's.
DEIPHOBUS: Well, all the same, you go and call my sister!
SLAVE WOMAN: Which, sir? Polyxena?
DEIPHOBUS: No, no, Cassandra!
      But quickly!
SLAVE WOMAN (*goes, grumbling*):
          Quickly! Not a bit of patience!
      My legs are old, so what's the good of "quickly!"
                (*on the threshold*)
      And there she is, herself. Princess, come quickly!
      Your brother's waiting for you! (*Exit.*)
CASSANDRA (*with a distaff stuck through her girdle and a spindle in
        her hand enters spinning*):   Greetings, brother!
DEIPHOBUS: And now what fancy have you dreamed up, sister?
      You have sent all your slaves away, but you
      Yourself still ply the distaff.
CASSANDRA: It is better,
      Brother, to grow accustomed in good time
      To the inevitable.
DEIPHOBUS: That's slaves' talk!
      A princess never in her life should speak so.

CASSANDRA: And what does she say, then?
DEIPHOBUS: "Either to rule,
     Or else to perish!"
CASSANDRA: All of us will perish,
     And without ruling!
DEIPHOBUS: Sister, please be quiet,
     And do not vex me with your prophecies.
     This is real grief: brother a prophet, sister
     A prophetess, and nowhere to escape
     In one's own house from kinsfolk's prophecies.
     But you took up the distaff, that is good!
     To tell the truth, it is more fit by far
     For girls to spin than utter prophecies.
     So spin, and do not prophesy.
CASSANDRA: I, brother,
     Myself would rather spin the snowy wool
     Than prophesy black fate for all of us.
DEIPHOBUS: Spin on, spin on—a betrothed maiden needs
     Plenty of white wool for the wedding feast:
     For bridal raiment and as gift for guests.
CASSANDRA: Brother, you too, I see, have joined the prophets,
     Alas, untimely and without true sense.
     (*She turns away, offended.*)
DEIPHOBUS: Timely and with true sense. Dear sister, it
     Is not my custom to waste words in vain.
     So, if I speak, that means it's worth the hearing;
     And, though a prophetess, it's clear that you
     Yourself cannot foresee your destiny,
     So I shall tell it you: we have betrothed
     You, just a while ago, to Onomaus,
     The King of Lydia.
CASSANDRA: Too quickly, brother,
     You say to me that "We have just betrothed you,"
     For I am not a slave woman as yet,
     And I have my free will.
DEIPHOBUS: Not so, Cassandra,
     For every maiden, whether slave woman
     Or a princess, has to obey her kin.
CASSANDRA: Brother, I am no slave, nor a princess,
     For I am less and greater than them both.

DEIPHOBUS: I did not come in here for guessing games,
Nor yet for empty chatter. I say, plainly,
That you have been betrothed. King Onomaus
Demands you as reward for his alliance,
And for his aid against the enemy.
He boasts that he'll make war this very day,
With all the men of Lydia besides,
And that before the sun sets, he'll hew down
The forest of the armies of the foe.
"If this be true," we said to him, "Tomorrow
You shall lead home Cassandra to your tent."
CASSANDRA: And what of that! "If this be true." . . . Of course
It is not true!
DEIPHOBUS: I'd never have expected
That you, a Trojan girl, and Priam's daughter,
Could have so selfishly refused to give
Salvation both to Troy and to your kin.
The daughter of Atrides was far greater,
It is not worthless to compare the Hellene
Maidens as finer than our Trojan girls,
For from the former came Iphigeneia,
Far-famed, who gladly paid her maiden life
To win her people glory.
CASSANDRA: Brother, you
Know not the price of women's sacrifices,
But I will tell you: of all woman kind
Far-famed Iphigeneia did not make
The greatest and the hardest sacrifice.
So many harder sacrifices, though
Unfamed, are made by women who leave not
Even a name to them! If you had wished
That I should give my life in sacrifice,
Surely I would have offered it, but this—
I cannot, brother, I'm no heroine.
DEIPHOBUS: Yes, I can see it. You are sister to
Paris, yet not to Hector. Hector could
Lay down his life, leaving his spouse and making
His son an orphan to bring Troy salvation,
Or bring her honour. Paris, though, was ready
For Helen's sake to let his native land

Go to destruction. Such are you, Cassandra,
For the sake of that languid shade of your
Dolon, although indeed he had betrayed you,
You're ready to let us be drowned.

CASSANDRA: My brother!
Do not offend the shade of the departed!
You say Dolon was languid, he betrayed me?
Was it a languid man went forth to doom,
Forth to clear death, when not a single one
Of all my hero brothers dared to go?
Perhaps now Hector's dead, Deiphobus
Can show his bravery in words alone.

DEIPHOBUS: I am too old for spying. You, Cassandra,
However, are too young to judge your elders.

CASSANDRA: But truth is older than all elders, brother.

DEIPHOBUS: Leave it! The dead don't rise. That's not the point!
The point is surely what you're bound to do
For Troy's salvation and her happiness.

CASSANDRA: How do you know that this will bring salvation?

DEIPHOBUS: I know this is the only thing which can.
If you will bring salvation is unknown,
But you are bound to make this last attempt.
If they should kill the Lydian, folk will say:
"It was not fated, then!" If you refuse,
They all will say that you brought us destruction.
King Onomaus is coming to you now,
So that you yourself will say the word,
The single word "Agreed!"—and straightway,
Arrayed for war, the Lydians will march.

CASSANDRA: My brother, that would be threefold betrayal,
Of self, of truth and of the Lydians,
For in one word, one single word, I would
Have sent forth a whole army to its ruin.

DEIPHOBUS: Are foreigners dearer than your own land?

CASSANDRA: Why should they perish for us, though, in vain.
Hector, the god-like, could not bring salvation,
So what good is this Lydian?

DEIPHOBUS: Cassandra,
You forget that Achilles was here then,
And, more than god-like, he was goddess-born,
But now he is not here.

CASSANDRA: And just so spoke
    Penthesilea, the fair Amazon,
    Who for Troy's sake perished before her time.
DEIPHOBUS: Penthesilea! She was just a woman!
    It's not for women to bring Troy salvation.
CASSANDRA: That's right, my brother, it's not for Cassandra.
DEIPHOBUS (*angry*):
    Don't be so literal!
SLAVE WOMAN (*entering*): That foreigner
    Keeps on demanding why he's not called in.
CASSANDRA: Go, tell him to come in; and you, my brother,
    Please leave us here alone.
DEIPHOBUS: What will you say?
CASSANDRA: What the god shall ordain.
DEIPHOBUS: Well, but remember,
    If he ordains that you say "Not agreed,"
    Then you will have the name of a foul traitress,
    Now and for evermore.
CASSANDRA: Deiphobus!
DEIPHOBUS: I'll be the first to call you by that name,
    In public, on the square. Remember, then! (*Exit.*)
ONOMAUS (*enters and stops short on the threshold. Silence*):
    Greetings, Princess!
    (*Cassandra is silent.*)
    I have a high regard
    Indeed, for modesty, nevertheless
    I should be wishful to hear that word spoken,
    That one word which, indeed, belongs to me.
CASSANDRA: You are quite sure that it belongs to you?
ONOMAUS: Your father and your brother have assured me
    That word is mine.
CASSANDRA: Then from them you have heard it,
    But I do not assure you of that word;
    You have not asked it and you have not sought it,
    You simply want to take it as your right.
ONOMAUS: Forgive me, Princess, I know that young maidens
    Love pretty speeches; I, alas, am not
    Skilled in these matters. My cause is but brief;
    You have not sought my hand, I have sought yours,
    That means, quite clearly, that you took my fancy.
    And so, therefore, I want you for my wife.

CASSANDRA: However can you want me for your wife?
 For you can see I'll not be yours in spirit.
ONOMAUS: If I can have that figure and those eyes,
 Those lips, and all the proud grace of that form,
 How can the spirit run away from it?
 And therefore I shall have the spirit too.
CASSANDRA: Not more so than the spirits of your slave girls!
ONOMAUS: Do not compare yourself to slaves, Cassandra!
 For you shall be a queen, as is befitting
 To one who is my wife and Priam's daughter.
CASSANDRA: To live in slavery befits her not,
 Though as a queen.
ONOMAUS: I shall not bear you off
 In hostile arms; in freedom you shall come,
 I could have joined forces with the Achaeans,
 Brought Troy into destruction, led you off
 Into captivity, but I prefer
 To take you honourably from your father,
 Having won you by mighty deeds.
CASSANDRA: You wish,
 Then, King, to buy me?
ONOMAUS: Every hero buys,
 Even the greatest hero buys his wife
 In such a way.
CASSANDRA: That is not heroism,
 A hero never seeks for his own gain.
ONOMAUS: Heroism must have its due reward,
 Both gods and people recognize this fact.
CASSANDRA: Is glory not enough, then?
ONOMAUS: I have glory,
 Enough, Princess, and more, but still I have not
 Taken a wife, and so I shall take you.
CASSANDRA: Take me, already? I have not consented.
ONOMAUS: Princess, to tell the truth, I wished to pay you
 Due honour, by thus asking, for you are
 A priestess of the gods, a Trojan princess.
 But it is not our way in Lydia
 To ask the maid, once father gives consent.
CASSANDRA: Know, Onomaus, that such a marriage cannot
 Be happy with Cassandra.

ONOMAUS: Do not try
    To scare me, Prophetess, with prophecies!
    For I believe that fortune loves the strong
    The resolute and daring; every woman
    Ought to love them, but if she does not,
    Why, then, she must be made to love them.
CASSANDRA: King,
    You do not know me, if you speak that way.
ONOMAUS: I know enough of women!
CASSANDRA: But Cassandra
    Was not among them.
ONOMAUS: For that very reason
    I want her.
CASSANDRA: It will be the worse for you!
    I do not love you.
ONOMAUS: You will love me!
CASSANDRA: Never
    Could I love one who seeks his own advantage
    By cheating our misfortune.
ONOMAUS: Who with glory
    Has saved your country?
CASSANDRA: Not so quickly, King,
    That is still lying on the lap of Zeus.
ONOMAUS: But if it comes to pass?
CASSANDRA: Then I should give
    Honour and thanks to our defender, if
    He would refrain from seeking as reward
    Myself . . .
ONOMAUS: I see that you are wise, Princess!
    "Honour and thanks"—that is the sole reward.
    But if I were to give to a poor beggar
    Meat from my table, he would give to me
    Honour and thanks enough.
CASSANDRA: And have you seen
    How liberated folk praise their defender?
ONOMAUS: Not only once or twice. I tell you, Princess,
    It is no different to the way that vanquished
    Folk praise the conqueror. I have heard both,
    And both have equal value, for always
    The powerless will praise power. But as for wasting

One's power for such a thing—it would be madness!
I am not without sense. To risk one's neck,
To lose an army just for "thanks and honour"
Said in the Trojan manner? I can hear it
Said by our women folk at home, in Lydian,
When I lead back the army without war.

(silence)

Well then, Princess?

(He prepares to go. Cassandra is silent but seems to be
    struggling with herself. Onomaus notices this and
    lingers.)

DEIPHOBUS (enters. He sees the two motionless figures and looks at
    Cassandra penetratingly and fiercely):

Agreed sister?

CASSANDRA: Agreed!

ONOMAUS: In all sincerity?

CASSANDRA: If you are ready
To risk your neck and lose an army simply
That I should say: "Indeed, these lips are yours,
This figure and these eyes"—well then, agreed.
And if your people are prepared to leave
Their wives as widows, so that they may win
A bride to wed their King—well then, agreed.
In all sincerity I say it!

ONOMAUS: Strange
Is your sincerity, Cassandra. Well,
Enough of arguing with words. It's time
To go and win with deeds my due reward.

CASSANDRA: As are the deeds, so the reward shall be!
Farewell then, Onomaus!

ONOMAUS: Goodbye to you.

(Exit Onomaus and Deiphobus. From without is heard the
    dull lamentation of a great crowd.)

POLYXENA (enters, running):
Cassandra, tell me, what is it you've done?

CASSANDRA: Dear sister, I was forced to say the word.

POLYXENA: You have said yes? You mean it isn't true?

CASSANDRA (coldly):
Polyxena, you're acting foolishly,
You know not why it is you blame and praise.

POLYXENA: I praise the fact that you obeyed the will
    Of father, brother, and of all your kin.
CASSANDRA: That means your will as well?
POLYXENA: As for that, sister,
    Clear death is terrible.
CASSANDRA: But for salvation
    Isn't it worth mourning at least a sister?
POLYXENA: But everything will be well for you, dearest,
    For you will be Queen of rich Lydia,
    A land, they say, that has no lack of gold.
CASSANDRA: Cassandra is not envious of gold,
    A single bracelet is enough for her.
    (*She looks at Dolon's bracelet on her right arm.*)
POLYXENA (*embracing her*):
    I know well how hard it is to forget
    Your love, dear sister, but what do the dead
    Need but shorn hair and blood and sacrifices.
    You can give Dolon a whole hecatomb
    As to a god, for Lydia is richer
    By far than Troy, once you become the Queen.
CASSANDRA: Of one I love not?
POLYXENA: What can you do, sister?
    Are there so many women who can marry
    Guided by their free choice and love? It is
    A woman's lot to listen not to heart
    But to her kin. And lucky if it's kin,
    For very often a proud conqueror
    Compels a captive maid to be his wife.
    Why, when Deiphobus wed Anthea
    She was not willing, but nevertheless
    Now she is a true wife to him, a tender
    Mother to his babes.
CASSANDRA: Polyxena,
    Suppose that they betrothed you once again,
    After Achilles, to another man?
POLYXENA: Well, but . . . I know there cannot be another
    Such as Achilles, but I do not wish
    To live a maiden to the end of time.
    I'd marry him, if he were a good match.
    If not my husband, I would love my children,

          If not true love, then at least wifely duty,
          Obedience and fidelity I'd bring
          As dowry to my husband.
CASSANDRA: And suppose
          That you had nothing besides hate and curses,
          What would you have to bring your "husband" then?
POLYXENA: You terrify me when you speak this way!
          Cassandra, then admit that it is true,
          That you called down, prophesied doom for him
          And for the Lydians?
CASSANDRA: How do you know?
POLYXENA (*somewhat embarrassed*):
          My slave women were underneath the window,
          Drying the wool. They chanced to overhear
          What you were saying. But I do not know
          Who took the message to the Lydians.
          D'you hear the noise? The Lydian army rose:
          "King, we shall not go forth to meet our doom!
          Cassandra cursed us! We are going home!
          So let Troy fall if it is fated so!"
          And three whole legions have set off already.
CASSANDRA (*involuntarily*):
          Thanks to the gods!
POLYXENA: Cassandra, You are shameless!
CASSANDRA: But why should they all perish so in vain,
          For my betrothal is to be their death!
POLYXENA: Why did you say the word, then, to the King?
CASSANDRA: Don't turn the sword within the burning wound!
          It is dishonour, heavy shame upon
          My head, Polyxena, the word I gave.
          It was compulsion and deep hate that spoke
          The shameful word, it was not I. O sister!
          I hated him with such a fervent hate,
          Him and all his witless, senseless army,
          That horde of slaves. Gladly and most sincerely
          I said the word "Agreed" to their destruction.
POLYXENA: You're terrifying, past belief, Cassandra!
ANDROMACHE (*enters running*):
          Praise to the gods! The Lydians go forth,
          Go forth to war. King Onomaus proclaimed:
          "I have received Cassandra's word 'Agreed.'"

Helenus stated he saw from the birds
A lucky sign for victory and marriage;
Deiphobus proclaimed it was not true
That you had cursed the King and Lydians.
Then they grew quiet and went forth to war.

CASSANDRA: Helenus said that he saw from the birds
A lucky sign for victory and marriage?
Then he is lying!

ANDROMACHE: All the same, Cassandra,
Of your truth we have had enough and more,
Evil-presaging, evil-bringing, let us
Live now in hope, even if it is false.
Oh, I am weary with your kind of truth!
O sister, at least grant me dreams and visions!
Let me for one short day believe my little
Son, my Astyanax, at least will live,
That he will not perish at hostile hands,
But will grow strong and powerful and god-like
As was his father, my beloved Hector!
O sister, at least grant me dreams and visions!

CASSANDRA: For dreams and visions you would let the army
All be destroyed? For shame, Andromache!

ANDROMACHE: It is not shame, no; any mother will
Tell you it is not shame. What are these strangers
To me? What cause have I to weep for them?
And maybe it is true that they will save
Troy for us? Maybe it is really true?

CASSANDRA: But only "maybe?"

ANDROMACHE: That is all I need.
For hope, Cassandra dear, is always hope!

CASSANDRA: I beg you, dear sister Polyxena,
To send your slave woman to fetch Helenus.

POLYXENA: Indeed I will. (*Exit.*)

ANDROMACHE: But why Helenus?

CASSANDRA: I
Wish to ask him. I do not believe
Myself. Now you see the god's doom accomplished.
Not only others but Cassandra too
Mistrusts Cassandra. I do not know whether
All this is true or not which now I see.

ANDROMACHE: What do you see?

CASSANDRA: Enough, Andromache,
    You ask me so that you can curse me later,
    And on my head already heavy curses
    Weigh heavy like an iron diadem,
    Upon my forehead stinging words are twisted
    Like serpents on the forehead of Medusa,
    Wrathfully hissing, poisoning the mind. . . .
    Go, gather up your slave girls, let them take
    Cithera and flute, and let them join
    In subtle music, maybe they will call,
    Evoke the dreams and golden visions for
    Your eyes that have grown weary—tired with tears.
    You have a slave girl from Phoenicia
    Who is skilled as a snake charmer, maybe
    She'll lull to sleep the snake of your alarm,
    And you shall sleep and in your sleep shall come
    Nothing of evil nor of war nor death
    Nor terror nor Cassandra.
ANDROMACHE: Do not mock me!
    I still believe the Lydians will come
    With King and victory. Farewell to you. (*Exit.*)

ACT VI

    Again Cassandra's room. Cassandra and Helenus.

CASSANDRA: So, brother, you will tell me truly what
    You have seen in the omens from the birds?
    (*Looks him straight in the eyes. Helenus drops his glance.*)
HELENUS: What of such matters! Both of us are seers,
    And we know well that birds and victims' entrails,
    And blood and sacrificial smoke are only
    Adornments and a veil for naked truth
    Before the public gaze, for truth, you know,
    Is a great lady, noble and esteemed,
    She mustn't walk abroad without a dress. (*Smiles.*)
CASSANDRA: But I too am a woman, therefore I
    Can look on truth even undressed.
HELENUS: My sister,
    Tell me who ever looked on naked truth?
CASSANDRA: Myself I've looked on her, and often, too!

HELENUS: And are you quite sure that truth has not put
      The evil eye upon you?
CASSANDRA: You, Helenus,
      Have touched upon a burning sore, but I
      Will bear it bravely, for I wish sincerely
      To take advice with you. You are the wisest
      Of all my brothers, for your understanding
      Is quick and lithe like fire.
HELENUS: Or like a snake?
      Phrygian understanding, sister! We
      Trojans throughout this long siege have learned well
      To crawl around like snakes. What else to do?
      If you had seen just how Deiphobus
      Was crawling to the Lydian, you would say
      A second brother, too, was quick and lithe!
CASSANDRA: Don't talk about the litheness of a reptile,
      For me this is no wisdom, but repulsion.
      Tell me sincerely, as a brother should
      Tell a dear sister, do you really think
      (Whether from birds or simply, it's the same)
      If Troy's salvation lies in this betrothal,
      And if this Lydian will bring salvation?
HELENUS: You have put a hard question to me. Truly:
      Sometimes I thought so, sometimes I did not.
CASSANDRA: How shall I understand this?
HELENUS: Thus. At first
      I was quite certain, when I saw his army,
      Bristling with spears and numerous past counting,
      Fresh in their strength and mighty in their courage,
      That the Hellenes, who are worn out by war
      And weakened by the siege, could not stand firm
      Against a king so eager for the triumph.
      And I am certain that if victory lay
      In Helen's hands or in Polyxena's,
      Andromache's or any other woman's
      You choose—not yours—then it would be for us.
CASSANDRA: Do you then mean that all of our misfortune
      Comes from Cassandra?
HELENUS: Not the whole of it,
      But a great deal.

CASSANDRA: Brother! What are you saying?
HELENUS: You bade me speak sincerely. I am granting
          Your wishes and not mine, my dearest sister.
          But I am not reproaching you, Cassandra,
          You are not guilty of your nature. Surely
          The gods are guilty here who granted you
          To know the truth, but did not add the power
          For you to *guide* the truth. Indeed, you see it,
          Clasping your hands, or wringing them in grief,
          Powerless you stand before the doomful vision
          Of the dread truth, as you were turned to stone;
          As if Medusa cast a glance upon you,
          You can spread naught but horror among people.
          And truth from this becomes more terrible,
          And people lose the last of force and reason,
          Or in despair rush forth into disaster,
          And then you say: "I have foretold it so!"
CASSANDRA: And what would you do, then?
HELENUS: That which I do.
          I fight against the truth, in hope that I
          Can conquer it, and guide it on its way,
          Just as the helmsman guides a mighty ship.
CASSANDRA: And Moira, brother, implacable Moira?
          It is her will that steers the universe,
          And do you wish to steer her on her way?
HELENUS: Not so, Cassandra, Moira has decreed
          That there should be the world and sea and steersman,
          And ship and storm and time of quiet weather,
          And cliffs and haven, so that there should be
          Struggle and hope and victory and truth
          And also . . . untruth.
CASSANDRA: If so, in that case,
          She wishes there should be Cassandra too.
HELENUS: And that Helenus should fight with Cassandra.
          I see the truth, and I contend with it,
          So as to pull the Trojan ship away
          Clear of the shoal where you, Cassandra, have
          Run it in danger with that truth of yours.
CASSANDRA: And can you save the ship with your untruth?
HELENUS: And what is truth? And what is untruth? Lies
          Which then come true are hailed by all as truth.

For instance, once a slave told me a lie,
Saying my phial was stolen, simply meaning
He did not want to go and seek the phial.
But while this slave was idling, then indeed
The phial was stolen. So where was the truth.
In that, and where the lie? The thinnest line
Divides the lie from truth in what has passed,
But in the future there's no line at all.

CASSANDRA: But if one says what he does not believe,
Then that is a clear lie.

HELENUS: But if one says
It in good faith, but makes a small mistake
As to the facts, then is it now the truth?

CASSANDRA: And how, Helenus, do *you* then distinguished
The truth from lies?

HELENUS: I don't at all. I leave
This quite alone.

CASSANDRA: How do you prophesy?
What do you tell the people?

HELENUS: What is needful
Sister, and useful, what is honourable.

CASSANDRA: Does this mean you have never seen what will be,
Fate unescapable, implacable?
Does a voice never tell you in your heart:
"It shall be thus, thus and no other way?"

HELENUS: To tell you honestly—no, never once.

CASSANDRA: Then it is hard to understand each other.
But tell me how you can proclaim in public:
"The god revealed to me . . . I have beheld . . .
A voice mysterious spoke to me, . . ." when all
This is untrue?

HELENUS: Truth and untruth again!
Let's put these words aside, they have no meaning.
You think that it is truth gives birth to speech?
I think that it is speech gives birth to truth.
And by what name are we to call the truth
Which is born from a lie. Have you not looked
Upon this kind of generation ever?
I've seen it countless times. The word is fruitful
And gives birth more than Proto-Mother Earth.

CASSANDRA: But you yourself said: "I do what is needful,

And what is useful, what is honourable."
Why is it needful you should play the Prophet?
Is it so useful and so honourable?
HELENUS: Indeed so! If today father and brothers,
　　　　　And with them all the Trojan men and women
　　　　　Tried to beg and entreat the Lydians,
　　　　　It would all come to naught. The Lydians
　　　　　Would simply say: "The Prophetess Cassandra
　　　　　Has cursed—the war and wedding are unlucky!"
　　　　　But I came with the dignity of priesthood,
　　　　　In prophet's diadem, and with a staff
　　　　　Silvered; I held it high above my head.
　　　　　Like lightning the staff flashed before the eyes
　　　　　Of all the foreigners. I said: "Be silent
　　　　　And wait. I have let fly from out the temple
　　　　　The sacred doves." At once there died away
　　　　　All tumult and all hubbub. I proclaimed:
　　　　　"King Onomaus insulted Lord Apollo,
　　　　　By plighting troth with his own Prophetess
　　　　　Without seeking consent of him the Lord
　　　　　Of Arrows; hence the god pronounced his anger
　　　　　Through the lips of the seer Cassandra. Maybe
　　　　　We yet can turn away his wrath, by giving
　　　　　A noble hecatomb to him of white
　　　　　Oxen which never yet have felt the yoke."
　　　　　"I promise it!" shouted the Lydian King,
　　　　　And I exclaimed: "I see the doves have come
　　　　　Back home and give nourishment to their chicks!
　　　　　A lucky outcome, and a lucky marriage!"
　　　　　And with this very word I vanquished you,
　　　　　Far-seeing sister.
CASSANDRA: 　　　　　　　And for how long, brother?
HELENUS: That we shall see. Truly, out in the field,
　　　　　It is not Lydians and the Achaeans
　　　　　But you and I that fight. Helenus guides
　　　　　Courage; Cassandra, though, commands despair.
CASSANDRA: And what will happen if Cassandra conquers?
　　　　　How will Helenus justify his lie?
HELENUS: He will say publicly: "King Onomaus
　　　　　Destroyed himself, he gave to Lord Apollo

Only a promise, not a hecatomb."
And to himself he'll say: "The weapon broke,
But we shall find another. Death is always
More honourable armed than empty handed."

CASSANDRA: Why did you not go out to fight today,
Not with a staff, but with a sword and spear?

HELENUS: The sword and spear are small weapons for me,
For human souls—they are my proper tools,
The winged word is my arrow, nations set
In conflict with each other form my duel!
All these I govern; Phrygian understanding.
This diadem, this staff, they are the signs
Of power and domination above kings.
I have no equal like unto myself
Among all rulers and above all heroes.
Only you are my equal, maybe greater,
And we shall fight each other to the end.

CASSANDRA: Oh, I myself do not know if I wish
To conquer you today or not. This marriage
Is as hateful to me as is death.
I fear it as I fear the fall of Troy.

HELENUS: Indeed you have no Phrygian understanding.
Have you not heard how sometimes the gods will
Enfold their chosen ones about in cloud?
I have a secret way beneath the altar—
You shall stand there with Onomaus together,
Offering the gods the wedding sacrifice.
And from the offering dense smoke shall come,
A brimstone cloud, and when it melts—instead of
Cassandra—empty space. You understand?

CASSANDRA: It is disgrace and shame to counsel so!
Is this way out what you call "honourable?"

HELENUS: At least it's useful and it's safe, my sister.

CASSANDRA: I'd rather take my own life with the sword!

HELENUS: And that way you would anger Onomaus,
And still would break your word to him. That would be
Neither useful nor honourable, sister.
(looks at her, smiling)
No, we are not alike, yet we are equal,
If not in deeds, at least so in our thoughts.

POLYXENA (*entering*):
>King Onomaus is slain. The Lydians
>Have all been put to flight. O sorrow, sorrow!

HELENUS: Rejoice, Cassandra, victory is yours!

CASSANDRA (*in prophetic tone*):
>Not mine, but Moira's. I am but her tool.
>The quick and lithe Phrygian understanding—
>Moira has overthrown and broken it,
>Her strong right hand falls heavily and stern,
>She forges the world's weapons out of nations,
>You and I are but rivets in those weapons.
>Don't overestimate yourself, Helenus.

ANDROMACHE (*enters running and in a frenzy hurls himself at Cassandra*):
>You, fierce destruction, have destroyed us all!

CASSANDRA (*calmly pointing to Helenus*):
>Ask him why he could bring no salvation.
>We are both seers and, so it seems, are equal.
>(*She takes the distaff from her girdle and sits down to spin.*)

ACT VII

A large square with a temple in the middle on a somewhat elevated site. To the right, in the background, the palace of King Priam, in the foreground various other buildings of the Citadel of Ilium. To the left, in the foreground, the Scaean Gate. It is a bright morning, the square is bathed in sunlight. There is a large crowd of Trojans coming and going to and from the Gate, they crowd together in front of the temple, talking together, now loudly, now softly, then suddenly there is complete silence, and they wait for something, expectantly. From the royal palace comes Helenus, in white robes of a priest, wearing a silver diadem, with a white, silver-adorned staff in his hand, walking with a solemn, hieratic step.

VOICES FROM THE CROWD:
>Helenus comes! Way for the mighty seer!

HELENUS (*goes up onto the peristyle of the temple, and gives a sign with his staff, striking it three times on the marble pavement, then he begins to speak in a solemn, prophetic voice*):
>Fathers, brothers and sons! O native Troy!
>The Olympian gods took pity on our tears,
>Upon our hecatombs, on our entreaties—
>And without arms they overcame the foe.

Zeus put it in the hearts of the Hellenes
Of their own will to go away from Troy.
Go to the gate—the Achaean camp is empty,
Only a horse alone upon the site—
An offering made to the gods of Troy
By the Achaeans is this horse. Of wood
It is, not splendid, no rich prize of war,
But it is dearer far than gold or silver
To us, richer than costly stone or marble.
Gifts of accord are better far than booty
Won on the battlefield at price of blood.
The Greeks departed of their own free will
And all the gods' will, and they left this gift
Of honour and accord. Hail to the Greeks!

PEOPLE: Hail to the Greeks!

CASSANDRA (*from the temple*):
                              For blood, for death, for tears!

DEIPHOBUS (*turning to the temple door*):
          Silence, Cassandra!

HELENUS (*to the Trojans*): You, O men of Troy,
          I counsel: bring that gift into the temple
          And set it there by the Palladion.

CASSANDRA (*appearing at the door of the temple with a black staff in
          her hand and stretching it forth as if barring the entry*):
          I shall not let you in.

HELENUS (*striking down her staff with his own*):
                              Make way, Cassandra!

CASSANDRA (*again barring the way*):
          I have the power not to let you in.
          Men may not dare to venture to approach
          Pallas's statue. I am guardian
          Of the Palladion. Helenus, you
          Make way; go, watch your birds!
          (*She looks him in the eyes, he lowers his staff.*)
                                        A gift impure,
          A gift accursed!
          (*The people murmur together, evidently confused.*)

VOICE FROM THE CROWD: Away, chase her away!
          Ill-boding wretch!

ANOTHER VOICE: Quiet! She's a Princess!

FIRST VOICE: So much the worse! We have grown weary of

These prophecies of hers. We can endure them
No longer!

A THIRD VOICE: Kill the woman!
(*A young man brandishes a spear.*)

HELENUS (*making a sign with his hand*): Do not move!
Do not spill blood—this is a holy place!

DEIPHOBUS: And what shall we do, brother, with the gift?

HELENUS: We shall build a new temple for it, named
"The temple of accord." And in the meantime
The gift shall stand within the palace court.
(*to Deiphobus*)
You shall appoint a guard as its due honour.

CASSANDRA: The blind man sets the beaten to keep guard.

DEIPHOBUS: Cassandra!

HELENUS: Brother, and you, men of Troy,
Bring in the horse into the palace courtyard.
(*Deiphobus gives them the sign to move and himself goes
to the Scaean Gate.*)

VOICE FROM THE PEOPLE:
Helenus has commanded! Come, my brothers!
He is our wisdom and our seeing eye!

CASSANDRA: A single eye—and that bedimmed with film!
(*All the people move out through the Scaean Gate.*)

HELENUS: Cassandra, listen to me, why are you
Trying me with this scoffing and this jeering?

CASSANDRA: To try if at least once you'd be clear sighted.

HELENUS: Cassandra, this is folly. It is plain:
The Achaean camp's deserted; on the sea
There's not a boat, no, not the smallest speck.
Deiphobus and I have sent forth scouts,
Far and wide, the swiftest of our lads,
On horseback and on foot. They could not find
A garrison or sentinel or any
Such thing, not anywhere.

CASSANDRA: An enemy
Does not give gifts in vain.

HELENUS: But this gift is
A sign of peace. Do you not understand?

CASSANDRA: Indeed no. If upon the sea there were
A burning stick floating among the waves,
Glowing with fire, would that be a sign

Of peace between water and flame? Who would
Perceive it so?

HELENUS: Men are not elements,
There is a bound to human wrong and anger.
Many Achaean maidens have grown up
During the war, and maybe Menelaus
Will find a younger bride instead of Helen.

CASSANDRA: But he saw Helen on the Scaean Gate
Yesterday morning.

HELENUS: Well, then?

CASSANDRA: Go to her,
Helenus, in the women's bower, and there
Think over what you've said.

HELENUS (*is lost in thought. Meanwhile, from the Scaean Gate, there
appears a troop of armed Trojans. Helenus points them
out to Cassandra*):   You see those spears,
And those sharp swords? There is no need for warnings
By prophecy. There is our watchful herald.
The trumpet has a voice, and Troy has ears.

CASSANDRA: The dumb man will be watchman for the deaf!

HELENUS: Enough, Cassandra. I am deaf to you,
And likewise all your words are dumb to me.
We've talked the matter to an end. Enough.

DEIPHOBUS (*from out of the crowd of armed men, leads a captive
Greek up to Cassandra and Helenus*):
Bring him here, bring him here. Let them speak,
Let our Trojan seers decide this matter,
And say to us what we ought best to do
About this stranger. Brother, and you, Cassandra,
Listen and ponder on it. We have caught
This stranger in the field beside the horse.
Wandering as if stunned, and shedding tears,
Wringing his hands and murmuring meanwhile
Disordered words. We took him prisoner,
Seeing he was by dress and speech a Greek.
But now we are divided in our thoughts:
Some people say we ought to let him go—
He was left here because he is demented,
And therefore, surely, can do no one harm;
But others say: this is some cunning spy,
So let us kill him, then he'll do no evil.

(*While Deiphobus is speaking, people, men and women,*
are gathering, some from the field, coming in through
the Scaean Gate, and some from the houses in the
town, and forming into a crowd.)

VOICES FROM THE CROWD:
    Yes! Kill him! Kill him!

ONE VOICE: For what cause?

ANOTHER VOICE: For vengeance!

THIRD VOICE: As an example.

FOURTH VOICE: But Zeus will avenge
    Innocent blood.

DEIPHOBUS (*in a loud voice*): Be silent, men of Troy!
    Judgment is not for you. Tell us, Helenus,
    Are we to kill him or to set him free?

HELENUS: Neither of these proposals. It would be
    Useless to kill him, would bring us no honour,
    And would mean danger. Once the Achaeans learned
    A Hellene had been slain without a cause,
    Then once again they could renew the conflict
    For long years more. All the same, to set free
    An unknown stranger—that would be imprudent.
    So let him live, but let him live in chains
    And watched by a strict guard.

SINON (*the captured Greek*):   O noble King,
    Or Prophet all-foreseeing. I know not
    How I ought to address my Lord in honour. . . .
    But I can see wisdom like to a god's
    Upon your brow. All-wise one, you know well
    A Hellene's soul. I am myself from Hellas.
    Hellas, that is the cradle from all time
    Of holy freedom. A true son of Hellas
    Out of his native element cannot
    Live, or if he can, will not.

CASSANDRA: With these words
    You've earned an honourable death in Troy.

HELENUS: Why speak of death? Set him at liberty,
    Since no guilt has been found in him.

CASSANDRA: My brother,
    Say, what is guilt? Is the hyena guilty,
    That it must live on death and on corruption?

DEIPHOBUS: And do you really know this stranger's motives,
    So that you liken him to a hyena?
    For if you know, then say so openly
    That he has come resolved on our destruction.
CASSANDRA: I can know nothing, I can only see
    The bloodstained form of a hyena, hear
    The piercing and rapacious voice. . . .
    (*in a sudden ecstasy*)
                                   Alas!
    Hyenas roam on the ruins of Troy,
    Licking the blood that is still living, warm . . .
    Sniffing the corpses not yet stiff in death,
    Howling with joy. . . .
    (*Groaning, she covers her face with her hands. The people
        stand in a heavy silence, then begin to whisper among
        themselves. Sinon looks from side to side in alarm.*)
DEIPHOBUS (*takes Cassandra by the arm and shakes her. She grows
        quiet*):
                         Sister, control yourself!
    Enough of these dark, fearful words, that have
    Weighed down the people like a smoky cloud. (*loudly*)
    If you see a hyena in this stranger,
    Why, kill him then, and we shall not oppose you.
HELENUS (*offering her a sacrificial sword*):
    Here, take this sword!
CASSANDRA (*embarrassed*):   No, brother, I've no skill
    To wield the sword.
HELENUS: A priestess should be able,
    When need be, to slay any sacrifice
    With her own hand.
CASSANDRA: Is this a sacrifice?
HELENUS: It is a sacrifice to your clear vision.
CASSANDRA: But why do you not slay this sacrifice?
HELENUS: The blind has no wish to shed blood in blindness,
    So let your seeing eye clearly direct
    Your certain hand. So let a single heart
    Give the commandment to both hand and eyes.
DEIPHOBUS: Let it be so. Then at least once Cassandra
    Cannot reproach men's incredulity.
    If the Hellene is guiltless, let Cassandra

To Zeus be answerable for his blood,
And human judgment shall be silent now,
The eldest son of Priam guarantees it.
(*Helenus puts the sword into Cassandra's hand. Cassandra
silently takes the sword. At a sign from Deiphobus
they bring Sinon closer.*)
SINON (*stretching out his bound hands to Cassandra and falling on
his knees*):
O Prophetess, Oh, how should I entreat,
Unworthy I plead with your Holiness;
Strange to you are the small affairs of men,
You, goddess-like, like Moira, gaze upon
The agony of weak and mortal hearts.
Perhaps, indeed, the grief of nearest kin,
To you, as to the gods, appears as holy.
But hapless I have no kin left on earth,
An orphan, without father, without mother,
I must confess it, for you are all-knowing!
But I have someone—she is my betrothed,
She loves me dearly. . . . O, I understand
That to your ears these words are vain and empty.
But if you knew. . . . Oh, if you only knew,
How my heart's breaking from our separation,
And my soul's dying from anxiety! . . .
(*Among the Trojan women there is a movement and sighing;
some of them wipe away tears.*)
CASSANDRA (*struggling to control her own emotions*):
Stand up, O Hellene, stand, and speak more calmly.
SINON: (*stands*): Forgive me, but to speak of this more calmly
My lips have not the power. Forgive me that
They tremble . . .
(*He covers his face with his cloak, and is silent. Then he
uncovers it, and continues.*)
          O why did I, hapless man,
Not heed the words of my own Leukoté
She pleaded with me, O so fervently,
As earnestly as now I plead to you.
"O do not kill me," she cried out to me,
"Look well upon my youthful, spring-like charms!"
But I stood firm as rock and looked upon
The black ship and the darkness of the wave.

And Leukoté was crying to the sea:
"O sea, O sea, thou living separation!"
Times without number she cried out these wild
Words, poor unhappy girl, lamenting, wailing . . .
And I heard them until, at last, around me
Sounded the great surge of the dark, black waters . . .
(*He clasps his head and quietly, as if at a great distance,*
says in a whimper.)
O sea, O sea! Thou living separation!

CASSANDRA (*perturbed*):
Did they leave you on purpose?

SINON (*humbly*):   Yes, Princess!

CASSANDRA: For what cause?

SINON: O Princess, I do not know!
They left me in my sleep. When I awoke,
I was out in the field, all, all alone.
Probably mighty Diomede grew angry
With me long, long ago, because in public
I said he was a Charon without mercy,
On the occasion when he and two others
Of our men put to death a Trojan scout.

CASSANDRA: (*tense*):
When?

SINON: Long ago, O Prophetess, when still
Achilles was alive. But Diomede
Has a long memory for anger. He
Was roused that I strove to defend a captive
Taken for death by him with his own hand.
But I felt such deep pity for this Trojan.
He was so very handsome and so young,
And O so pitifully begged for mercy . . .
O sorrow! I plead now in such a way,
But there is none to intercede for me,
Not say a single word. . . . They all are silent. . . .
Death is inevitable. . . . Why prolong
These last few minutes underneath the sword?
(*Suddenly he falls on his knees and bows his head.*)
Smite with your sword then, implacable maiden!

CASSANDRA: Helenus, I am doubtful, maybe truly
This stranger's innocent. What do you say?

HELENUS: Sister, without my birds, I shall say nothing.

DEIPHOBUS: But I'm amazed to see your hesitation
　　　　　Once you were able to send a whole army
　　　　　Of men, quite innocent, forth to destruction
　　　　　With just one word, and yet you felt no pity.
　　　　　So what can this one stranger mean to you?
　　　　　Has he indeed won favour in your sight
　　　　　By a single offer of protection
　　　　　To a single Trojan, while the Lydians
　　　　　Wished to bring salvation to all Troy
　　　　　And yet it found no favour in your sight.
CASSANDRA (*with a despairing movement, raises the sword over Sinon,*
　　　　　but her hand trembles and she slowly lowers the sword
　　　　　without touching Sinon):
　　　　　You have drained the last strength away from me
　　　　　With this remembrance. The blood shed in vain
　　　　　Cries to the gods against me. A dark cloud
　　　　　Of crimson creeps upon my eyes, upon
　　　　　My mind . . . O, an impenetrable cloud! . . .
　　　　　(*The sword falls from her hands.*)
　　　　　My hand has failed, my heart is dry and sere,
　　　　　Darkness, all darkness . . .
　　　　　(*She sways, and falls into the arms of Helenus.*)
HELLENUS:　　　　　　　　　She has swooned! O Trojan
　　　　　Women, assist her!
　　　　　(*The Trojan women carry Cassandra into the temple.*)
HELENUS (*to Sinon*):　　　Hellene, you are free
　　　　　The gods are not desirous of your death.

ACT VIII

The same square. It is evening. Night is falling rapidly, a dark moonless
night, but the stars shine sharply as on cold winter nights. A guard has
been posted in the square. One sentry is near the palace gate, another near
the Scaean Gate, a third near the temple. The fourth guard walks about
on patrol, watching over the Trojan's houses. All are armed as if for war.
For a time the guards keep watch in silence. From the royal palace, sounds
of music and the noise of a gay banquet are heard.

1ST GUARD (*from the palace gate*):
　　　　　Well brothers, what a feast!
2ND GUARD (*from the Scaean Gate*): A feast indeed!
　　　　　Some drink and revel, but we have to stand
　　　　　On guard against who knows what or from whom!

3RD GUARD: Hector has gone, and with him, sense has gone.
         He would not make us waste our time this way.
         Wouldn't have made a joke of lesser men—
         He was a hero, but knew others' worth,
         While these . . .
4TH GUARD (*who is patrolling, approaches the 3rd Guard and says
              quietly*)
                         You'd better be more careful, brother,
         Cassandra's there, and she's their sister!
3RD GUARD: So!
         She and her brothers are like fire and water,
         That's their accord!
4TH GUARD: But still, they are one kin!
3RD GUARD: May Hades bear the lot of them away!
         The Trojans have grown weary of them all,
         And worst of all that bird of evil omen—
         (*He nods towards the temple.*)
         All troubles come from her!
4TH GUARD: Hush! Here comes Paris!
         (*From the royal palace approach Paris and Sinon. Paris is
            dressed in festive, colourful embroidered clothing, un-
            armed; on his head is a red Phrygian cap with a garland
            of roses round it, from beneath which his hair falls
            upon his shoulders in long curls.*)
PARIS: Well? Are you keeping guard? Deiphobus
         Sent me to make the rounds. Well, are you keeping
         A good strict watch?
1ST GUARD (*gloomily*):   Of course we're keeping watch.
PARIS: Then why are you so sad?
1ST GUARD: Small consolation
         To stand here hungrily and parching dry
         Upon a feast day.
PARIS: That is true. But still
         We shall think of a way.
CASSANDRA (*from the temple*):   Guards, keep good watch!
PARIS (*with a start*):
         What was that?
1ST GUARD: It was your sister, Cassandra,
         She keeps watch over the Palladion.
PARIS: Ah, so indeed!
         (*He shudders again, and looks around anxiously.*)
                     What a cold night it is!

1st GUARD: With mountain winds, we'll freeze without a fire.
PARIS: Well go and bring some logs of wood, and light
       A fire. (*Exeunt the nearest guards.*)
SINON: Yes, indeed, the night is cold.
       (*Paris wraps himself closer in his cloak.*)
       Your lady-wife, the golden-haired, has surely
       Kindled the hearth fire now, and has prepared
       Herself with scattered scents, so that they rise
       Like smoke from incense, like to a light dream,
       Over the snow-white forehead delicately.
       (*Paris is silent, and dreamily looks towards the royal palace.*)
       Perhaps, indeed, now, those eyes, clear as stars,
       Are filled with tears. She is all, all alone,
       Sitting and spinning, thinking her own thoughts,
       While you are either feasting or on guard.
PARIS (*quietly, as if to himself, not looking at Sinon*):
       What is the sense in it? Should I leave all
       Of this? . . . Well, what would happen? (*He prepares to go.*)
CASSANDRA (*appearing at the door*):   Paris, wait!
       Where are you going?
PARIS (*embarrassed*):   I? For a warmer cloak!
       The night is cold.
CASSANDRA: Did you say cold? My brother,
       It is in vain that you fear cold so much,
       The cold will not destroy you.
PARIS: Ah, Cassandra,
       When will you cease this chatter about death,
       About misfortune, about vain destruction?
       It is all over now, the war and sorrow.
       It's time to rest.
CASSANDRA: How quickly has misfortune
       Finished for you. Come hither, Paris, and
       Look over there.
       (*Paris makes a sign at Sinon to go off by himself, and goes
          to Cassandra, who points out to him the moonlit valley.
          Exit Sinon.*)
CASSANDRA: What is that in the field?
PARIS: There? It's a grave mound!
CASSANDRA: You've forgotten whose?
       (*Paris is silent and drops his eyes.*)
CASSANDRA: Under it lies our Hector, Trojan glory.

PARIS: But he fell long ago . . .
CASSANDRA: And you remained!
      That signifies: Be joyful and rejoice,
      People of Troy?
PARIS: Sister, never before
      Have you hurt me so deeply with your words.
CASSANDRA: Because never before have I beheld you
      As now I see you. These your roses have
      Pierced me to the heart with their sharp thorns
      And drained its blood.
PARIS: Cassandra!
CASSANDRA: Ah, enough!
      Go, go to her, O hateful one, go to
      The bewitching beautiful Medusa,
      And turn to stone, falling down there before her
      Upon your knees—so is our glory fallen.
PARIS: How has it "fallen?" Victory is ours.
CASSANDRA: You call this victory? Why, all our glory
      And all our honour perished long ago.
      And only stolen Helen has remained,
      And, too, that senseless lump of wood. Indeed,
      A famous victory!
PARIS: Listen, my sister,
      If you have kept me standing here for this,
      For me to take such words from you, then I
      Do not agree to it. (He turns to go.)
CASSANDRA: Indeed, then, go!
      Let people never say that all in vain
      Perished the Trojan strength and glory. Let
      Paris become drunk with that love of his,
      So that for him we all must walk in mourning,
      Let him make his heart glad with happiness,
      For which we have paid in eternal sorrow!
      This was indeed the glorious aim of the
      War of destruction. Thus complete your great
      Victory there at Helen's side in the
      Sumptuous women's bower.
      (Paris, who was about to go, has stopped at Cassandra's
         first words, and now stands in indecision.)
CASSANDRA: Where is your sword?
PARIS: Why should I need a sword?

CASSANDRA: You think you are
    Armed enough then with your red cap, your fine
    Embroidered chiton, roses and dark eyes?
    They are enough to gain your victory?
PARIS (*blushing*):
    And for your victory, say, what is lacking?
    I might ask too: Cassandra, where's your sword?
    For you have held it in your hand today,
    Did you not win honour and glory with it?
    Prophetess, you are silent, you lack words!
CASSANDRA (*as if depressed*):
    Forgive me, brother . . . it is true . . . well . . . go. . . .
PARIS (*with childish joy, forgetting his anger*):
    Yes, I shall go. . . . I'll not be long, of course. . . .
    No, do not think. . . . (*He is already on his way.*)
                   I'm going for my cloak,
    For it is cold . . . I'll be back very soon. . . .
    (*The further he goes, the faster he walks. Soon he disappears
        through the gate of the royal palace. Cassandra goes
        into the temple, and closes behind her the veil of the
        temple door. The sound of a flute is heard, the
        twanging of a cithara and singing. Soon Sinon with a
        flautist and citharist, who are carrying a big amphora
        of wine between them, enter. Sinon is carrying a basket
        of fruit and has a phial at his belt. He is garlanded with
        flowers, and has more garlands hung over his arms.
        From the opposite side the guards enter carrying logs
        of wood and pieces of meat; they make a fire in front
        of the temple and start to roast the meat. The musicians
        put down the amphora, setting it carefully in the sand,
        and prepare to play.*)
SINON (*sings. The flautist and citharist play*):

        In the Asphodelian meadows,
        In the deep Elysian valleys,
        Wander, robed in robes of glory,
        Shades of our departed heroes,
        Why, O why are they so sad?

CHORUS OF GUARDS:

        For in Asphodelian meadows,
        In the deep Elysian valleys,
        Blossoms never bloom.

(*During the singing, the third guard himself unties the phial from Sinon's belt and starts drinking, then gives it to the others.*)

SINON (*sings*):

> There by Styx's waters murky,
> There by Lethe sad and gloomy,
> Wander, crowned with crowns of laurel,
> Shadows of our "unforgotten,"
> Why, O why, are they so sad?

CHORUS:

> For in Styx's waters murky,
> There in Lethe sad and gloomy,
> Water flows, not wine!

SINON (*sings*):

> There in Hades' mighty palace,
> Where Persephone is thronéd,
> Rise up in eternal glory
> Shadows of our great defenders,
> Why, O why, are they so sad?

CHORUS:

> For in Hades' mighty palace,
> Where Persephone is thronéd,
> Songs are never heard.

1ST GUARD (*sings in a rough voice and out of tune*):

> On the banks of the Cocytus,
> Roam the heroes ever gloomy,
> Smoke from sacrifice comes curling,
> Blood from hecatombs is pouring,
> So why are they grieving yet?

(*shouts*)
Where's the antistrophe!

CITHARIST: I do not want to!

1ST GUARD (*continues singing alone*):

> For there is no meat or bacon,
> No plump steaks are there for eating,
> Only smoke and blood!

5TH GUARD: It's out of tune.

1ST GUARD: So what, the sense is good!

SINON: Sit down, my brothers, quickly, by the fire,
> And praise the gods that we still walk the earth,
> That there is wine, and song and flowers enough.

1ST GUARD: And still good meat enough!
    (*He busies himself with the roasting.*)
SINON (*distributes garlands to everyone, and himself puts the garland
    on the head of the 1st Guard, who is doing the roasting*):
                      Pour me some too!
    (*They pour some wine for him and he drinks. To the 2nd
    Guard.*)
    Why don't you drink? Is it not to your liking?
2ND GUARD: (*indecisively*):
    There is no water . .
3RD GUARD: What's the need of water?
    Tonight we'll drink our wine unmixed. Let's dance!
2ND GUARD: But unmixed wine goes straight into the head!
3RD GUARD: What does it matter! Well, don't drink at all!
    Go, guard the gate, as you were ordered to!
2ND GUARD: What a wise fellow!
3RD GUARD: Then keep quiet and drink
    What you are given.
    (*The 2nd Guard drinks. They fill the phial again, and
    pass it from hand to hand.*)
3RD GUARD: One phial is no good!
    It's most annoying waiting for one's turn.
4TH GUARD: (*laughs*):
    Then go and ask Cassandra for the loan
    Of offering cups. She's in the temple there.
CASSANDRA (*from the temple*):
    Guards, keep good watch!
1ST GUARD: You see, she answered you!
    Princess, just wait until the meat is roasted,
    Then we shall give you some! (*They all laugh.*)
3RD GUARD: I've an idea.
    (*He takes off his helmet, pours wine into it, and drinks.*)
    Isn't this a good phial?
    (*The others follow his example and do the same.*)
1ST GUARD: That's very clever
    And no mistake! Here's the roast! Eat, good friends!
    (*He takes a piece of meat from the spear and divides it
    among them with his sword.*)
2ND GUARD (*eats*): It's rawish, never mind! It's good and hot!
SINON: Here, take a peppercorn to flavour it!
2ND GUARD: Then it will be too hot!

3RD GUARD: The wine will quench it—
It's not a small amphora!
4TH GUARD: When it's finished,
We'll fetch another.
(*They eat the meat, cutting it up with their swords; they eat the fruit and drink wine from their helmets. Gradually, the wine begins to make them quite noticeably tipsy. The musicians meanwhile go on playing.*)
2ND GUARD: You should sing some more.
3RD GUARD: And you?
2ND GUARD: I can't alone, I'll follow you.
(*Sinon plays the flute for a while, then hands it to the flautist who continues playing; the citharist takes up the melody and the others join in the song.*)

> By the river, the vineyard is a-growing,
> Ah, the vineyard is a-growing!
> If fair Leukoté comes down to the river,
> Then embrace her, my curly headed friend!

1ST GUARD: Eh, that's a dull one!
CITHARIST: Which one would you like?
1ST GUARD: (*sings without music in a clumsy recitative*):

> Watch your wife, or watch her not,
> You won't stop her! Vain's your labour!
> Though you're an Olympian god,
> Like old crook-leg, old Hephaistos!

(*He sways, staggers and falls. He mutters once or twice, reminiscently "Like old crook-leg, old Hephaistos . . . old Hephaestus. . . ." then he becomes silent and sleeps.*)
2ND GUARD: Now that's a jolly song indeed!
3RD GUARD: Goodnight!
(*They go on drinking. The flautist and citharist go on playing, without singing. Gradually all except the musicians are overcome by the wine, lie down round the fire and sleep. Sinon also pretends to sleep.*)
FLAUTIST (*stops playing*):
They're all asleep! Now what are we to do!
CITHARIST: Let us sleep, too!
FLAUTIST: No, let's go to the feast!
(*The two of them drink up the rest of the wine and go into the royal palace. It is quiet on the stage for some time;*

everyone is asleep, only from the distance is heard
music and singing and sounds of revelry.)

CASSANDRA (*from the temple*):

Guards, keep good watch!

(*Complete silence. The sounds die away. Sinon slowly gets*
up and looks about him cautiously.)

CASSANDRA (*from the temple*):   Keep a good watch! Keep guard!

(*Sinon jumps up, runs to the royal palace, and vanishes*
through the Gate.)

CASSANDRA (*at the door of the temple*):

Do not sleep, watchmen! (*She notices the sleeping guards.*)
                 Guards, alarm, alarm!

(*Cassandra bends over the guards and tries to rouse them;*
some of them move and mutter something incompre-
hensible, but none of them has the power to wake up.)

CASSANDRA (*goes to the royal palace, calling*):

Hey! Is there anyone alive there? Trojans!

(*Sinon comes out from the palace gate towards her, and with*
him armed Greeks: Menelaus, Agamemnon, Odysseus,
Ajax and Diomedes. They cross their spears and bar
the way to Cassandra.

AJAX: Stop, girl! Who are you?

ODYSSEUS: Why, it is the mad,

Senseless Cassandra? Don't you recognize her?

CASSANDRA (*tries to throw herself on their spears*):

Trojans! Treachery! Treachery! Hurry, Trojans!

AGAMEMNON: Seize her, and stop her mouth with a strong gag!

(*Cassandra swiftly turns, and escapes into the temple, where*
she falls before the Palladion, tightly embracing the
statue.)

CASSANDRA: Don't touch me! I claim temple sanctuary!

AJAX: Indeed!

DIOMEDES: What matter, you're our prisoner!

(*Diomedes seizes Cassandra by the hand which holds the*
staff. Ajax seizes her by her hair. She tries to grasp the
pedestal of the Palladion with her free hand, but the
statue sways and falls, together with the pedestal. The
soldiers drag Cassandra from the temple, tie her hands
with their sword straps without taking away her staff,
then bind her to a column in the temple portico, at the

top of the steps. Meanwhile Menelaus and Odysseus
open the Scaean Gate, while Diomedes returns to the
temple and carries off the Palladion.)

DIOMEDES (*shouts*): Ours! The Palladion is ours! Come, heroes!

(*The Achaean army charges in through the open Gate.*)

CASSANDRA (*calls, gathering all her strength*):
Awaken, Troy! Your death approaches you!

(*Alarm lights are lit in the palace and other buildings. The*
Greek army quickly fills the entire square, and spreads
in various directions through the streets of Troy. Soon
a great clamour is heard in the city. Unarmed Trojans
in festive clothing run across the square; after them in
close pursuit, come Greek soldiers, taking some prisoner
and killing others. Soon a great fire springs up. Grad-
ually the fugitives and their pursuers become fewer
and fewer, and more and more frequently there appear
victorious Hellenes, who drive before them with their
spears, like a flock of sheep, captive Trojans, men and
women, bound with ropes. Some of them are brought
into the temple. Others are taken out through the
Scaean Gate, and others are made to sit down in the
square. Then they fall face down on the ground, and
lament. The captive women of Priam's family are put
and told to sit in the portico of the temple, near
Cassandra. When the commotion has died down a
little, Andromache, Polyxena and several other women
find themselves near Cassandra.)

ANDROMACHE (*lamenting*):
My dearest child! My only, only son!
They have killed him! Dashed him against a stone!

POLYXENA: O bitter sorrow! Father! Dearest Mother!
Your daughter now will be a concubine!

OTHER WOMEN FROM THE ROYAL FAMILY:
Now we are doomed to die as slave women,
As slave women, far in a foreign land!

ANDROMACHE (*to Cassandra*):
Why silent? Why not prophesy our death?
Now death will be our only consolation!

CASSANDRA (*with a terrible calm, with a voice as of the dead*):
Here are those who'll find other consolation!

ANDROMACHE: A curse upon you!
CASSANDRA (*as before*):   Yes, a curse on me,
          Because I now behold the worst of all,
          Trojan women captives and yet living!
          They walk around the loom, share victors' beds,
          They nourish children for the Hellenes' joy. . . .
          A curse upon the eyes which see such things!
ANDROMACHE: A curse upon the lips which speak such things!
CASSANDRA: A curse upon me! I cannot be silent!
          (*Fettered members of the Trojan royal family, including
              Helenus are led into the temple.*)
HELENUS (*as he passes Cassandra*):
          Rejoice, Cassandra, victory is yours!
CASSANDRA: No, it is yours. You've killed me with this word.
          My reason's broken. Yours will travel far,
          With it you'll gain the victory over victors,
          But mine will be extinguished with this fire.
HELEN (*runs across the square. Menelaus pursues her with a sword*):
          Rescue me, brother Hellenes! Rescue me!
          For what cause does he seek to punish me?
          I was brought treacherously and by force
          To Troy, I lived here an unhappy captive,
          Weeping each day for my own native land.
          (*The Achaeans irresolutely step aside before her, but they
              do not thrust her aside when she catches hold of one
              of them and tries to hide behind his shield.*)
MENELAUS: Here is the blood of Paris on this sword,
          It's craving for your blood as well!
CASSANDRA: O, Paris!
POLYXENA: Dear brother!
ANDROMACHE: Poor unhappy lad!
HELEN (*surrounded by young soldiers, suddenly proud*):
                                   O man!
          Do you really wish to punish me?
          Have you spilled this sea of blood in order
          To shame my honour and yours, publicly?
          And so the Queen of Sparta has awaited
          Such an honour? Who will then believe
          In Spartan women's virtue, when the King
          Has glorified his wife as treacherous?
          (*to the soldiers*)

Spartans, do you also agree to this?

SPARTAN SOLDIERS (*surrounding Helen*):

She's innocent! A goddess among women!

Vainly, O King, you seek your wife's dishonour!

MENELAUS (*to Helen, kindly*):

Forgive me—I'm hot-tempered, as you know!

HELEN (*smiles and extends her hand*):

I see, my King, you haven't changed at all.

(*Menelaus extends his hand to Helen. She takes him by
the hand and leads him through the Achaean ranks
and out by the Scaean Gate into the field; all step
aside before her with a murmur of admiration.*)

ANDROMACHE: She is a queen again, and we are slaves!

O gods, where is your justice?

CASSANDRA: Ha ha ha!

ONE TROJAN WOMAN (*to another*):

Cassandra laughed. . . . Oh, it is terrible!

I've never heard her laugh in all my life.

CASSANDRA (*in a trance, watching as the tongues of flame play about
the palace buildings*):

Bring here, bring here these glowing flowers of fire,

The pomegranates bloom! It's wedding time!

(*Off stage is heard the voice of an old woman, it laments,
wailing terribly, as if howling!*)

POLYXENA (*listens in terror*):

It is our mother!

CASSANDRA: It's the wedding song!

Our mother sends her daughters to their bridal!

Cassandra never told the truth at all!

There is no ruin! It is life! All life!

(*The voice of the old woman resounds more strongly.
Suddenly it is lost in the crash of the falling buildings.
The glare of the fire floods the stage.*)

Robert Bruce, King of Scotland

(Dedicated to my uncle, M. Drahomaniv)

PROLOGUE

We shall recall the days far back and wonder,
We shall recall that unforgotten story
Of a far-distant, freedom-loving country,
Of Scotland in past ages, famed in glory.

An old tale, like a fable, for within it
There is bias, true, there are illusions,
But like a lovely star, truth ever glimmers,
Pours forth its golden rays in broad profusion.

Piercing the clouds, the truth will shine upon us,
In thought we'll fly, into the distance soaring,
We shall look upon the martial conflict,
And plunge in memory into ancient glory.

I

'Tis now five hundred years ago,
When through free Scotland riding
King Edward went, on war intent,
The English monarch mighty.

He summoned all his knights to him,
All proud and noble lordships,
In order the free Scottish folk
To bring within his wardship.

Throughout all Scotland sped the cry,
Re-echoed without ending,
"Brothers, to arms! Behold, there comes
King Edward, war intending!

Hey, brother dear, is our bright store
Of weapons, maybe, waning,
Or are there, in the Scottish land
No warriors remaining?"

The knighthood comes, the land resounds,
The hostile ranks clash, dauntless,
Great, indeed, will be that day
The revelry of slaughter!

The bright spears clash, the bright swords
    slash,
And helmets brightly flashing,
The raven horses neigh, the hosts
Shouts fierce with martial passion.

They fight a day, they fight for two,
The third—O lamentation!
The Scots cry: "Woe, King Edward now
Defeats the Scottish nation!"

The English army strikes and slays,
The English swords are shining;
The Scottish swords all fall away,
The Scottish knighthood dwining.

King Edward now drew rein; at once
Resound the trumpets mighty,
Above the host the banners rise—
Not coloured—gleaming whitely!

All silent stood, and each man dipped
His spear in confirmation;
The herald shouts: "King Edward now
Entreats the Scottish nation

To give back peace unto the land,
Turn from all evil missions,
And without war to come to terms
In brotherly tradition."

Thus says our King: "Whoever to
Our terms turns his opinion;
He over his estates and folk
In peace shall hold dominion.

The simple folk must pay to us
Tithes and a tax of money,
But each knight shall a free lord be
In his forefathers' country.

Each knight shall be obliged to ride
Forth with the King, campaigning,
And for this service he shall win
Favour and noble payment."

Down came the banners, all the lords
Of Scotland cried together:

"Enough! Now long may Edward live!
Free Scotland's King forever!"

The Scottish knighthood yielded then;
But one was left remaining,
Armed and ready, a young knight—
And Robert Bruce they named him.

Straight looked he Edward in the face
As if forked lightning throwing,
His iron gauntlet drew he off,
And hurled it at the foeman.

Then straight he spurred his raven horse,
Away the steed sped swiftly;
Into the mountains like a dart,
Among the dark glens hidden.

II

Robert rode wide over Scotland's fair land,
A national rebellion inciting,
Through the whole country his heralds he sent,
The folk to a council inviting.

But when in a broad glen, among mountains
    steep,
A mighty assembly had gathered,
Robert went forth to the people and said:
"Scots! Here is treachery savage!

We have no knighthood, we have no strong lords,
In England's cause they endeavour,
But still in the land dwell the bold Scottish folk,
They will not wear fetters forever.

Straightway, therefore, let us arise, one and all,
In brotherly action combining,
Let us beat ploughshares to swords. . . . Who will
    plough
When the field without freedom is dwining?"

Then all the folk roared, like the waves of the sea:
"We shall go forth, our strength to recover,
Or else our own heads, bold and daring and free,
We shall lay on our own field forever!"

And there in the broad glen, among mountains
    steep,
The country folk camped for the night time,
And all through the night mighty fires were
    ablaze,
Each man forged a sword gleaming brightly.

Next morning the army was ready for war,
And he who'd no weapon to flourish
Did not lack sickle, nor hatchet, nor scythe,
Nor, in his heart, valiant courage.

No banners bright gleaming this army did bear,
No armour flashed lordly with argent,
No slogan nor word of vociferous power
Adorned simple country folk's targes.

In the whole host, one device, one alone,
"For freedom and native land cherished!"
Though none bore these words in display on his
    shield,
But deep in his heart, till he perished.

And thus they went forward, advanced on the
    lords,
Robert led them to war in swift sally:
But not one bold knight in addition to him
Did the Scots have in their rally.

The knighthood of Scotland had all broken faith,
In the army of England they mingled;
They went to defend, with sword and with
    shield,
The Crown and Dominion of England.

Untimely the hour when the Scottish folk drew
Bright weapons in manly endeavour;
In that first battle, they were overcome,
Many laid down their heads there forever.

They met for a second time—ah, heavy fate,
Again was the Scottish host shattered;
They clashed for a third time—the field all round
With the slain of fair Scotland was scattered.

Strong was the might of the powerful lords,
And wise were the leaders to guide them,
Neither into the mountains nor into the glens
Careful lords would not let the Scots drive them.

Six times the wide meadows, six times the broad glens
With spilt blood were drenched and repleted,
Six times rang through Scotland the echoing cry:
"The Scots, ah, the Scots are defeated!"

They would not their banners, they would not
     their swords
At Edward's feet lay and surrender,
But in defence of their freedom and land
The folk no more strength had to tender.

Some fallen in death, some were scattered afar,
Departing to sow their own furrow.
Without fame, without army, bold Robert
     remained,
What now must he do in his sorrow?

Should he, like the Scottish lords, go forth, depart
To Edward his sword to surrender,
Or should he remain in his poor native land,
And wait for the last shame to rend her.

No, better by far not to see nor to hear
How the sad country will perish. . . .
"Farewell, O thou land of my birth! Ah, forgive
Thy son whom cruel fate never cherished.

If only I might once again see thee free,
But this was not given nor granted . . .
Now, on far distant shores, on a holy campaign,
My life I shall lay down, undaunted!"

So Robert spoke forth, and he journeyed away
To a poor Irish shore turning,
He thought that to Scotland, that poor hapless
     land,
He would never more be returning.

In Ireland a ship was expected, that sailed
Bold knights unto Palestine bearing,
And on it would Robert together with them
Depart, to that distant land faring.

Together with knight brave and valiant, he wished
To go on a holy crusade there.
That he might on a blesséd campaign, with the
    years
And the strength that remained, give some aid
    there

III

On the desolate shore of the ocean,
One cottage stands near to the foam,
And in that poor fisherman's cottage
A knight sits in armour, alone.

It is Robert. He looks at the window,
Seeking whether those ships loom in sight,
Which out to the Holy Land carry
The valiant Crusaders to fight.

No, naught to be seen on the ocean,
No sails glimmer white in the sound,
Freely the wild sea is dancing,
The waves with loud music resound.

But to Robert it all appears gloomy
Out on that wild joyful sea,
As he recalls his own country
His mournful heart throbs gloomily.

And Robert stepped back from the window,
Lay down on the bench on his back,
Glancing up at the ceiling; a spider
Was spinning a web in a crack.

And Robert's eye caught, of a sudden,
The work that the spider thus wrought,
The knight saw how, little by little,
The thread came in view, thin and taut,

How, when she had spun it, the spider
Swung through the air on that thread,
To the wall wishing to join it,
The web thus, extended, to spread.

But each time she swung, the thread breaking,
The spider fell down the floor,
But straightway again started climbing,
Spinning a new thread once more.

And thuswise six times fell the spider,
And six times she climbed, till at last,
The seventh time, she was victorious,
And the thread to the wall was made fast.

Straightway Robert sprang to his feet, grasped
His sword to his hand in grip sure,
And cried: "Can it be that a knight has
Than a spider less will to endure?"

IV

Ah, not a falcon to the glen
From mountain heights descending,
But to his native land young Robert
Swiftly homeward wending.

Through the land on raven steed
He sped and never dallied,
A final time the Scottish folk
To battle line he rallied:

"All men, to arms! Lives yet your bold
Renown? And for our freedom
We would of old lay down our lives.
Where now is our allegiance?

Who still has not surrendered freedom,
Let him to the fighting!
Who honour still recalls and fame—
To arms! Now who's behind me?"

Scotland will rise! The Scottish soul
Has not burned out forever,
A seventh time as at the first
The folk will throng together.

King Edward nowise did expect
A Scottish insurrection.
Now all his knighthood was dispersed
For rest and for refection.

Of all his army there was but
A small part left assembled.
And safe that English war band sat,
And laughingly they revelled.

Always the warriors discuss
What spoils of war and booty
The King of Scotland will collect
In taxes and in duty.

Among the English warriors
The Scottish lords were mingling,
The King had given back their rights
And their lordly Dominion.

Tomorrow each of them will go
To his estate returning,
Why then are they sitting so,
Filled with mournful yearning.

Because their soul gnaws them within
With shame and bitter grieving,
It seems that everything around
Cried out: "Ah, treason, treason!"

The English knights sing merrily,
Their songs re-echo loudly,
And cheerfully upon their spears
They bear their pennants proudly.

The country folk stole down upon
The host from mountain cover,
Appeared as if from underground,
And into battle drove them.

All resounded and re-echoed
Like a tempest swirling,
Robert at the enemy
Like thunderbolt flew hurling.

Ah, fierce the fight, the final fight,
Blest he who conquers rightly!
The English in dismay cry out:
"Ah, save us, God almighty!"

To them the King sent reinforcements
Speeding from the border,
They meet the Scottish cheer: "To us
Is victory awarded!"

The reinforcements came in strength—
Alas, but all too tardy!

The Scots pursue their foe; they clamour,
Pressing on them hardly:

"No more shall ye have power to seize
Another's freedom, rend her!
Now if your lives be dear to ye—
Lay down your arms, surrender!"

The Scottish folk against the mountain
Caught the English, hemmed them,
There is no help, no help—they lay
Their arms down and surrender.

Then from the host stepped Robert forth
And spake this proclamation:
"Thus now the Scottish folk dictate
Terms to the English nation:

Our land from days of yore was free,
So shall it be forever!
Ye see now how our folk defend
Their rights with bold endeavour.

In England Edward can collect
Tithes and his tax of money!
But each Scot shall a free lord be
In his forefather's country.

To our folk 'tis of small account,
Favour and noble payment,
They'll not go seeking from the King
A knighthood by campaigning.

Now all your weapons I'll impound
As pledges, as conditions,
And I shall send you home again
In brotherly tradition.

Go, tell to Edward how ye heard
The words that here were said ye.
If he does not agree to peace—
To fight once more we're ready!"

The English silently withdrew
Without their arms or banners,
Back home into their native land
They went in downcast manner.

And looking back as they went down
Dejected to the valley,
Robert they saw upon the slopes
Among the peasants' rally.

A mighty crowd of people thronged
The verdant mountain hiding,
And Robert stood above them all,
The flags before him lying.

The bright swords they had ta'en in war
All lying on the ground there,
The Scottish banners and bright swords
They raised up high around him.

Robert, it seemed, addressed them, tried
To save himself, defending;
Then drew off his bright helmet, bowed,
Unto the people bending.

The English heard how all the throng
Of peasants roared together:
"Glory! Laud! Long may Robert live!
Free Scotland's king forever!"

V

Thus Robert became king in Scotland,
For his true might and renown,
In Edinburgh's glorious city,
Before all, he accepted the crown.

The magnificent ritual ended,
From the church to the square he came out.
"Glory to Robert! Long live he!
Our King evermore!" they all shout.

When sudden the shouting grew silent,
The folk seemed expectant; a small
Group stepped out from the assembly,
Chosen to represent all.

And from the small group one stepped forward,
Turned to the King, bowing low,
He looked round about at the people,
Then read out a speech that ran so:

"Through God and the choice of the people,
We greet thee as King in this hour,
And gladly as subjects entrust we
Ourselves to thy mercy and power.

While the freedom thou dost of thy people
And their independence defend,
Forever shall we pay thee honour,
And love thee as our truest friend.

Thou shalt call us to war, we will gather,
Under thy banner we'll throng,
We are ready with sword and with buckler
Both thee and our land to serve long.

But should thou not remember the honour
And liberty due to thy folk,
Or wish the rich lands of another
To subjugate under the yoke,

Then we shall not follow behind thee
To seize on another's rich hoard,
The land of our birth is not narrow,
What need we to wander abroad!

And if thou amidst lordly comforts
Shalt sell to the lords thine own folk,
To fight for the laws which are ours, we
Are able to wield a strong stroke.

And if thou shouldst yield to the English
Crown thine own Kingdom, be sure
That in that self-same hour of dishonour
Thine own rule shall cease to endure.

We have crowned thee as King and our ruler,
We'll uncrown thee again easily,
And if thou shouldst rise up against us,
Then we shall rise up against thee.

God grant we be joyful forever
That we chose thee as King to command,
May there blossom in thy reign and prosper
Free will in the fair Scottish land!"

"God grant it!" cried Robert in answer,
"I shall know well the task I go to,
God grant that we live out our lives in
Agreement sincere, order true!"

VI

Sincere agreement, order true prevailed there,
Robert did not break the word he spoke,
It did not fall nor scatter on the breezes,
That honourable agreement of the folk.

And neighbours on the border wondered greatly
At the Scottish will, and thus they spoke:
"While still the sun is shining in the heavens
The Scottish people will not bear the yoke!"

It did not burn out, was not lost forever,
The freedom spirit in the Scottish nation,
And the free Scottish land to firm agreement
Even with former foes gave confirmation.

And when in time the Scots and English nations
In a joint Dominion were united,
The English learned how in the Scots to cherish
Honour and liberty and glory rightly.

For this praise Robert Bruce who once defended
His native land and did to freedom guide her;
With boldness and with firmness in endeavour
He drew a lesson from a little spider.

And for himself he won great fame and glory
That will fade away nor perish ever,
Living on in song and tale, proclaiming
All its story to the world forever.

Seven Strings

A CYCLE
(Dedicated to Uncle Mykhailo)

I   DOH
(Hymn. Grave)

DOlorous mother, Ukraina, fortune neglected,
    To thee a string is tuned firstly,
And that string with a quiet solemnity this will re-echo,
    And song from the heart will flow, bursting.

Across the wide world the song will fly forth, ever-speeding,
    And with it a hope, well-beloved,
Speeding will fly, through the world among human-kind seeking
    Where fortune still hides undiscovered.

And maybe my song all alone will meet out on its roaming
    In the wide world, with bird songs melodious,
And that resonant flock will take wing thither, hastening, coming
    By pathways afar, brambled over.

Beyond the blue sea, beyond the great hills they'll speed flying,
    To a field open, unbounded,
Into spaces of heaven they'll soar, higher-higher,
    Where fortune, maybe, they'll encounter.

And thither, maybe, to our own native home, she will come then,
    That fortune desired, long-expected,
To thee, Ukraina, my own and dearly beloved,
    My mother by fortune neglected.

II   RE
(Song Brioco)

RAging the storm bowls, lamenting,
What's a storm—I do not fear it,
Though I meet with misadventure,
Yet I dread not revere it.
Hey, you storm-clouds, grimly-glaring,
Spells against you I'm preparing,
See, a magic sword I'm drawing,
I shall arm my songs for warring.

All your little raindrops early
Shall be changed to little pearlets,
Then shall fail and break your brightly
Flashing fires of silver lightning.
I'll set misadventure drifting
On this water flowing swiftly,
All my sleep I'll scatter spreading
With free songs in the dark meadow.
Raging the storm howls, lamenting,
What's a storm—I do not fear it,
Though I meet with misadventure,
Yet I dread not nor revere it.

III MI
(Lullaby. Arpeggio)

MEek the moon shiningly,
Quiet rays beguilingly
   Pours on us, shines,
Sleep then, my tiny one,
   Late grows the time.

Now you sleep happily,
What sorrows drab can be
   You do not know;
You'll learn too rapidly
   Heartache and woe.

The hour goes wearily!
The minute—drearily!
   Woe does not sleep. . . .
Lullaby, dearest, to
   Live is to weep.

Shameful detestably
To yield to destiny!
   Your hour will come,
With fate your fight shall be—
   Sleep will be done. . . .

Meek the moon shiningly
Quiet rays beguilingly
   Pours on us, shines,
Sleep then, my tiny one,
   While there is time.

IV   FAH
(*Sonnet*)

FAntasy, thou art the magic force
Which built a world in spaces empty, brinkless,
Poured feeling in the star rays that, unthinking,
Waken the dead from sleep's eternal course.

Life into chilly billows thou dost force!
Where thou art, fantasy, is joy and springtime.
To thee, bright fantasy, our greetings bringing,
We raise our bent brows once more heavenwards.

Fantasy, thou goddess light of plumage,
Opening to us a world of gold illusion,
Thou with a rainbow dost to earth unite it!

Terrestrial and mysterious dost unite,
If the human soul knew not thy brightness,
Life would be sad and gloomy as black as night.

V   SOL
(*Rondeau*)

SO Lovely in springtime there streams
The nightingale's song in green spinneys,
But I cannot hear the sweet singing,
And the spring flowers where fragrances team,
Not for me in the woodland are springing—
I see not this heaven of springtime;
Those songs and the blossoms' bright gleam
I recall, like some tale, wonder bringing,
          In dreams! . . .

Songs that echo, resounding free themes,
In our own land I long to hear ringing—
On all sides sorrow's grieving voice keens!
On my land, shall in thee fly forth winging
Free songs, only thus, as it seems,
          In dreams?

VI   LAH
(*Nocturno*)

LArgessed with moonlight, mild nights of springtime,
Where have you fled from us, whither?

Nightingale music, like silver bells ringing,
Are you silent and vanished forever?

O no, still not time, for we have not yet sounded
All the wonders of night, heavy-laden,
For still there resound, as of old there resounded
The wonderful spring songs of maidens.

Still the light phantom high over us hovers,
The springtime's azure-blue dreaming,
While in the heart still unfolds in full blossom
The flower of hope, golden and gleaming.

Into the land of mysterious night time
On fantasy's plumes thoughts go winging,
There with rays playing, so lovely are shining
The fair tranquil eyes of the springtime. . . .

There the bright stars and there tranquil blossoms
In wondrous speech are united,
There the green boughs whisper, quietly tossing,
There hymns of love echo widely.

And the blossoms and stars and the boughs greenly verdant
Speak together, in words where love flowers,
Of the forces of springtime, world-wide and eternal
Of the magic of spring, strong in power.

VII SI
(Settina)

SEE, seven strings I pluck, string after string,
    May my strings echo, resounding,
    May my songs fly, swiftly bounding,
Through my dear land may they fly on swift wing.
    And maybe they'll find flying onward,
    A kobza, tuned loud to the concord
Of the strings, to my songs' quiet soft murmuring.

And that kobza shall play, maybe, stronger and freer,
    Than my own quiet-sounding strings,
    And its notes, bold as they ring,
May find in the world a more sensitive ear;
    Though that kobza be heard far around,
    Yet never its music shall sound
More true than my own quiet strings, nor sincere.

Shorter Poems

CONTRA SPEM SPERO

Thoughts, away, you heavy clouds of autumn!
For now springtime comes, agleam with gold!
Shall thus in grief and wailing for ill fortune
All the tale of my young years be told?

No, I want to smile through tears and weeping,
Sing my songs where evil holds its sway,
Hopeless, a steadfast hope forever keeping,
I want to live! You, thoughts of grief, away!

On poor, sad, fallow land, unused to tilling,
I'll sow blossoms, brilliant in hue,
I'll sow blossoms where the frost lies, chilling,[1]
I'll pour bitter tears on them as dew.

And those burning tears shall melt, dissolving
All that mighty crust of ice away,
Maybe blossoms will come up, unfolding
Singing springtime for me, too, some day.

Up the flinty, steep and craggy mountain
A weighty ponderous boulder I shall raise,
And bearing this dread burden, a resounding
Song I'll sing, a song of joyous praise.

In the long dark ever-viewless night time
Not one instant shall I close my eyes,
I'll seek ever for the star to guide me,
She that reigns bright mistress of dark skies.

Yes, I'll smile, indeed, through tears and weeping,
Sing my songs where evil holds its sway,
Hopeless, a steadfast hope forever keeping,
I shall live! You thoughts of grief—away!

---

[1]Line 11 is ambiguous. If "morozi" is taken to be the prepositional case not of
"moroz," but of "morih," the line should be translated:
'I'll sow blossoms, on the greensward spilling,"

UNTITLED

And thou, like Israel once fought great battles,
O my Ukraine. For God Himself had placed
A force of sightless destiny, unblessed,
Contending with thee. He encompassed thee
With nations that, like lions in the desert,
Roared in their raging, eager for thy blood.
He sent on thee such darkness that within it
A brother could not know his true-born brother
And in the dark appeared one, undefended,
Some spirit of the time, willing the doom
"Death to Ukraine!"

                Then there appeared on high
The right hand of Bohdan, the hostile nations
Scattered and fled like jackals slinking craven,
Brother once more knew brother and joined with him;
The spirit spoke, "Bohdan, thou art victorious,
And now, indeed, is thine the Promised Land
From end to end." A convenant of friendship
Was made, resounding, 'twixt him and the spirit
There in the gold-domed town.

                    And straightway the spirit
Betrayed him.

         Darkness, terror, brothers' parting,
Captivity of Egypt came again
Not in a foreign land, but our own country.
But afterwards—once more the Red Sea parted,
Flowing asunder, in two halves divided,
And once more came together, flooding, drowning
Whom? Woe, alas! The new-made Pharaoh came
Living from out the waves of the Red Sea—

But with his horse the Cossack drowned forever.
Rejoice and sing, base daughter of the foeman,
Beat on the drum, and whirl in dance ecstatic
For horse and rider in the sea have perished!
To thee remained an heirloom as adornment,
For thou wilt wear our Ukraina's jewels
Making a festal day to greet her conquest.

And thus for us the Exodus from Egypt
Like to the Deluge. The Red Sea raged fiercely
And then grew quiet, dried up, left remaining
A tract of joyless desert in its wake,
And through this desert the new Israel
Began to wander through its Promised Land,
Like some poor flock that cannot find a haven,
And with the flock the shepherds wandered too.
By night they walked in shade, by day in fire,
But when appeared to them a spirit mighty
That blazed, a fiery pillar in the dark,
And went by day like a cloud of dread whiteness
They were not scattered by untrodden pathways,
Nor fell as captives to the enemy.

How long, O Lord, how long that we must wander
How long that we must roam with yearning seeking
For our own country in our native land?
What sins have we committed 'gainst the Spirit,
That He His mighty Testament has broken,
That Testament, taken in the war of freedom?

Well then, complete this treachery, and finish,
And strike us, scatter us all the world over,
Then maybe sorrow for our native country
Will teach us, rightly, where and how to seek.
Then father to his son will teach the story
About his silver dreaming for the distance,
And say "Behold the land of thine own people!
Struggle and strive for the land of thy fathers
For else we are all doomed to perish, exiled
Far among stranger-peoples in dishonour."

And maybe a new Testament will be granted
The Spirit write new Tables of Commandments.

But as for now How are we to go seeking
The land of our own people? Who has smitten
Our heart's Commandments, Spirit's Testament?
When shall this great Captivity find ending
That holds us prisoners in the Promised Land?
How long this Egypt in our native country?
O when shall perish this new Babylon?

EPILOGUE

He who dwelt not among tempests
Cannot strength's true valour savour
Cannot realize how sweet to
Man are struggle, toil and labour.
He who dwelt not among tempests
Cannot know the grief of weakness,
Cannot realize the torments,
Of compelled inaction's meekness.
How I envy them who know not
Any resting or reposing
Till exhaustion past man's bearing
For a moment overthrows them.
Day and night they watch as sentries,
Long the toil, short respite coming,
Day and night they are at labour
Until hands and spines ache numbly.
Then it seems to them that surely
No worse torment comes to people . . .
Fighters, if you could but know it,
What it is when hands are feeble!
What it is to lie, unmoving,
Like one shipwrecked by fate's dangers,
To surrender to the mercy
And the strength and will of strangers;
What remains for such a creature?
But to think, to muse, to ponder . . .
Then accept these thoughts, you fighters,
Nothing more have I to offer.

www.ingramcontent.com/pod-product-compliance
Ingram Content Group UK Ltd.
Pitfield, Milton Keynes, MK11 3LW, UK
UKHW050114250425
457848UK00007B/112